D1606142

OBJECT RELATIONS GROUP PSYCHOTHERAPY

*The Group as an Object,
a Tool,
and a Training Base*

OBJECT RELATIONS GROUP PSYCHOTHERAPY

The Group as an Object,
a Tool,
and a Training Base

RAMON GANZARAIN, M.D.

INTERNATIONAL UNIVERSITIES PRESS
Madison, Connecticut

Library of Congress Cataloging-in-Publication Data

Ganzarain, Ramon C.
  Object relations group psychotherapy: the group as an object, a tool,
and a training base / Ramon Ganzarain.
    p.   cm.
  Consists mostly of articles previously published in various journals.
  Bibliography: p.
  Includes indexes.
  ISBN 0-8236-3725-5
  1. Group psychotherapy.   2. Object relations (Psychoanalysis)
I. Title.
  [DNLM: 1. Object Attachment—collected works. 2. Psycho-
therapy, Group—collected works.   WM 430 G2115o]
RC488.G24   1989
616.89′152—dc20
DNLM/DLC
for Library of Congress   89-2240
                                                                  CIP
Manufactured in the United States of America

With gratitude
   To my wife, Matilde, and to
   our children, Ramon,
   Mirentxu, and Alejandro,
   for their patient encouragement.

   To my teachers,
      collaborators,
      patients, and
      students
   for their contagious search.

CONTENTS

ACKNOWLEDGMENTS

Many persons were helpful, instrumental, or enthusiastic supporters of the work described in this book, across almost four decades. I can express my gratitude to only a few of them here.

First, I wish to acknowledge my teacher, Dr. Ignacio Matte-Blanco, who taught me psychoanalysis and psychiatry. When he was head of the Department of Psychiatry at the University of Chile, he made it possible to experiment with using group psychotherapy in the psychiatric training of medical students. Drs. Hernan Alessandri and Amador Neghme, successive deans of the School of Medicine of the University of Chile, sponsored the use of group methods with faculty members to train them in the methodology of education. They sought the help of the Pan-American Health Organization, a branch of the World Health Organization, for practicing and spreading the use of this method in medical education. Wilfred Bion influenced my thinking in a significant way, although our personal contact was brief. Leland P. Bradford, President of the National Training Laboratories for Group Development distinguished me with his friendship and helped me to significantly learn and practice the "training-group" techniques. Drs. Otto Kernberg and Herman Van der Waals invited me first to visit the Menninger Foundation in Topeka, Kansas, and later to work there, thus making it possible for me to learn, practice, and teach psychoanalysis and group psychotherapy in that internationally renowned psychiatric center. Alice Brand, Chief Librarian of the Menninger Foundation, helped me to reach the literature on the subject. Dr. Margaret Emery, Mrs. Virginia Eicholtz, and Mary Ann Clifft helped me with editing. Several typists have been efficient and patient in helping me put this book together: Mrs. Mary McLin, Ms. Aleta Pennington, and Ms. Jeannine Riddle.

Finally, I owe a special debt to my multiple coworkers who actually worked or wrote with me, across more than thirty years: Bonnie Buchele, Ph.D.; Edward Bridge, M.D.; Hernan Davanzo, M.D.; Esther Burstein Drobny, Ph.D.; Ornella Flores, M.S.W.; Guillermo Gil, M.D.; Mrs. Ketty Grass, M.S.W.; and many others too numerous to list. I am also grateful to all my colleagues in the Group Psychotherapy Service of the Menninger Foundation, for their support, constructive criticism, and help in discussing or polishing some chapters.

PREFACE

All but six of this book's chapters have been published previously in various journals. Colleagues teaching group psychotherapy have expressed the wish to have them available as a unit.

These articles cover a period of three decades, and consist of reports of my experiences as a group psychotherapist with psychiatric outpatients, psychiatry and psychology students, faculty members of medical schools, psychiatric residents, group psychotherapists, and some specific patient populations.

Another source of my views on group psychotherapy derive from my experiences as a patient, in 1951, within a group formed by Chilean candidates, in analysis with the same training analyst; and as a participant in the National Training Laboratories' 1961 internship program in Bethel, Maine. I observed, behind a one-way screen, some groups at the Tavistock Clinic in London, and I was briefly supervised by Bion. I attended in 1971 a conference on leadership and authority at Leicester University, England, sponsored by the Tavistock and A. K. Rice institutes.

Besides writing articles on groups, I prepared edited videotapes, from closed outpatient groups, for teaching and scientific presentations during the American Group

Psychotherapy Association's annual conferences as well as
at the International Congresses on Group Psychotherapy,
held in Copenhagen (1981) and in Zagreb (1986). The use
of such videotapes was central in the seminar on group
psychotherapy I taught for Menninger Foundation staff
members, between 1973 and 1987. Ninety mental health
professionals attended it during those fifteen years. Some
have become distinguished group psychotherapists. Several state or regional American Group Psychotherapy
societies have invited me to conduct seminars, presentations, or workshops. I have also offered seminars on
analytic group psychotherapy in Japan, Spain, and Chile.

This book is organized into three sections:

   I. the group as an object, a theoretical segment;
  II. the group as a tool, a technical section; and
 III. the group as a training base, an educational
      section.

I hope group psychotherapists and beginners will find
stimulating ideas, interesting experiences, and useful
guidelines in these pages, where I examine some psychoanalytic theories about group psychotherapy, with enough
flexibility to adapt them to different purposes.

SECTION I

THEORY: THE GROUP AS AN OBJECT

INTRODUCTION

> *Did you know we are all the object of another's imagination?*
> —*The Old Gringo,* Carlos Fuentes
> (1986, p. 143)

The group can be conceptualized either as a real, "objective," scientific topic having its own reality and dynamics or as a mental object of "subjective" members' cathexis and fantasies. Actually, the group-as-an-entity is often represented by emotionally laden mental images manifested in the patients' dreams, fantasies, or responses to group meetings. Therefore, the group therapist may sometimes focus attention on the interactions taking place, within each member's mind, between the self and the group-as-an-entity. At other times, the treaters may explore instead the exchanges between the self and internal representations of other persons. On both occasions, the therapist applies object relations theory to group psychotherapy.

This section starts with a discussion about object relations group psychotherapy, followed by a comparative study of Bion's concepts about groups, stressing how his development of Kleinian ideas (such as projective identification and schizoparanoid anxieties) helped us to better understand primitive group phenomena. Theories on object relations are compared with those on general sys-

3

tems, and a combination of both is discussed, as clinically useful to conceptualize significant group interactions. The notion of the "bad mother" group is then reviewed in order to focus on a paranoidlike view of the group as an object. A chapter on the psychoticlike anxieties and primitive defenses against them illustrates some clinical material to make these general concepts more relevant.

1

OBJECT RELATIONS
GROUP PSYCHOTHERAPY

RAMON GANZARAIN, M.D.

Object relations theory is basically a clinical theory, in spite
of a terminology that sometimes seems highly abstract or
"metapsychological," especially when describing patients'
fantasies regarding various mental representations of objects and the interactions with or among them. I have
enhanced the clinical usefulness of this theory, in the
practice of group analytic psychotherapy, both in my
writings (see chapter 3) and in various communications.
However, there is no systematic, coherently integrated
object relations theory.

The concept of object changed as the split in psychoanalysis became evident (Balint, 1949), contrasting a the-

The author is grateful for permission to quote from the following:
Greenberg, J., and Mitchell, S. (1983), *Object Relations in Psychoanalytic
Theory*. Cambridge, Massachusetts: Harvard University Press. La-
planche, J., and Pontalis, J. B. (1973), *The Language of Psychoanalysis*.
New York: W. W. Norton, pp. 179, 280.

ory, based on a "one-body psychology," with a technique focused on communications within a "person-to-person" relationship (Laplanche and Pontalis, 1973).

The concept of object has three different meanings:

1. In *correlation with the subject* who knows or perceives, the philosophical studies about how we know, or "epistemology." Consider that an object is what presents permanent qualities recognizable by all subjects, irrespective of individual wishes and opinions.

2. In *correlation with instinct*, the object is the thing that the instinct seeks for its satisfaction, to reach its aim. It may be a person or a part object, real or fantasied.

3. In *correlation with affects*, mainly love or hate, each object has a relationship with the self or whole person. The group can be considered as an object within all the above contexts.

As a topic of knowledge, the group has been studied regarding its dynamics, from the viewpoint of leadership, norms, different roles, communication, and so on; in reference to variations in size or position vis-à-vis a broader system, and also as a sociometric network (Moreno, 1951) and matrix (Foulkes, 1975).

In correlation with instinctual aims, the group has often been described as an oral object, providing emotional nurturance or feedback by supporting members' self-esteem and their sense of identity. In correlation with affects, the group can be described as a good mother surrogate or as a hateful, bad one.

"The unfamiliar reader may be misled by the term 'object,' which is to be taken in a special psychoanalytic sense, as in the expressions: 'Object-choice' and 'object-love.'" A person is described there as an object, insofar as that individual is "the object of someone's passions"; . . . there is nothing pejorative in this—no particular implication that the person concerned is 'in any sense' not a subject" (Laplanche and Pontalis, 1973, p. 278).

Seeking to analyze the concept of instinct, Freud (1905) distinguished between the instinctual source, object, and aim. As regards the object, Freud often underscored its "contingency"—a term connoting two complementary ideas:

1. The object is relatively interchangeable, since it has no conditions imposed upon it, other than to procure satisfaction. For instance, at the oral stage, every object is treated according to the possibility of incorporating it.

2. On the other hand, "the *object may become so specific*, during the subject's history, that only a precise object—or a substitute endowed with the essential traits of the original—is capable of procuring satisfaction. In this sense, the object's characteristics are highly particularized" (Laplanche and Pontalis, 1973, p. 179).

We may thus understand how it is possible for Freud to assert both that the object is "what is the most variable about an instinct," and also that "the finding of an object is in fact a refinding of it" (1973, p. 180), as if life were a constant search for the same original object.

The present-day concept of object relations represents a shift in emphasis. The source of the instinct, as organic substrate, is now definitely assigned a secondary role. Consequently, the aim is considered less as the sexual satisfaction of a particular erotogenic zone: The very concept of aim tends to fade and give way to that of relationship. In the case of the oral object relationship, for example, what now becomes the center of interest are the various guises of incorporation.

The term *object relations* is thus a designation for the subject's mode of relating to the world—as an entire outcome of a particular personality organization, of partially fantasied apprehensions of objects, and of specific types of defenses. Types of object relationships can be described by reference to points in the psychosexual development (e.g., an "oral" object relationship) or to specific psychopathology (e.g., a "melancholic" object relationship) (Laplanche and Pontalis, 1973).

The term *stage* (as in the expression "psychosexual developmental stage") is tending to be replaced by *object relationship*. The advantage of this change is that "it helps clarify the fact that several types of object relationships may be combined, or may alternate, in the same subject. By contrast, to talk of the coexistence of different stages, amounts to a contradiction in terms" (Laplanche and Pontalis, 1973, p. 280), since "stages" only can occur in a time sequence.

"Relationship" should be understood as an interrelationship, "involving not only the way the subject constitutes his objects, but also the way these objects can shape the subject's actions" (Laplanche and Pontalis, 1973, p. 280).

Melanie Klein's approach lends even more weight to this idea: The *objects* (projected, introjected) actually *act upon the subject*—they persecute or reassure him or her.

"Inasmuch as the notion of object-relationship places the accent on the relational aspects of the subject's life, there is a danger of its leading someone to look upon the real relations with others—or "interpersonal relations"—as the chief determining (mental) factor" (Laplanche and Pontalis, 1973, p. 280). This is, however, a confusion, since the object relationships must be studied essentially in terms of fantasy, not of real relation, but focused, instead, on the mental, fantasied exchanges between the self and the objects, or among various internal objects. The group-as-an-entity can become, as I said earlier, an internalized object, with distinct fantasied maternal functions such as providing "mirroring" or feedback.

While object relationships are central to the current clinical practice of psychoanalysis, their theoretical role still remains controversial. Greenberg and Mitchell, in their landmark book (1983), remark that "the patient in analysis is talking *to* someone: The communication is shaped by the individual's understanding of and relation with the person the patient is talking to" (p. 9). However, "the people about whom the patient is talking do not necessarily behave in a way that another observer of these same persons would confirm" (Greenberg and Mitchell, 1983, p. 9). "The concept of transference suggests that the object of the patient's experience is at best an amended version of the actual other person involved. People react to and interact with not only an actual other, but also an *internal other,* a psychic representation of a person, which in itself has the power to influence both the individual's affective stages and his overt behavioral reactions" (Greenberg and Mitchell, p. 10).

> The existence of these mental representations of others, sharing as they do some of the characteristics of "real" people, as well as some of their capacity to trigger behavioral responses, yet being demonstrably "different," raises critical conceptual problems. . . . Such images go under various names in the literature: "Internal objects," "introjects," and the constituents of a "representational world." . . . They may be understood as loose anticipatory images of what is to be expected from people in the "real world"; as becoming closely entwined with the individual's experience of who *he/she* is; as persecutors . . . or as a source of internal security, invoked in times of stress and isolation. They constitute a residue—within the mind—of relationships with important people in the individual's life. Crucial exchanges with others leave their mark;

they are "internalized" [Greenberg and Mitchell, 1983, p. 11].

Object relations theory presents us with the confounding observation that people live simultaneously in an external and an internal world, and that the relationship between the two ranges from the most fluid intermingling to the most rigid separation. Thus, the term *object relations* designates theories concerned with exploring the relationship between real, external people, and internal images and residues of relations with them, as well as the possible significance of these residues for psychic functioning. These considerations, on the other hand, extend and deepen Sigmund Freud's views about the complexity of psychic reality—or the realm of mental fantasy—its differences and relations with the objective, external reality.

In accordance with the subjective experience of patients, their exchanges with objects have all the experiential reality of transactions in the external world. However, although in the patient's experience "internal objects" are actually felt to exist, these are certainly not entities or homunculi within the mind.

OBJECT RELATIONS IN GROUPS

Groups tend to regress to primitive levels of mental functioning. Bion (1961) compared the initial anxiety upon entering a group with the first experiences of the infant at the mother's breast. Intense psychoticlike anxieties shake the normal infant's incipient ego at this stage, as they do the member who starts in a group, making both first fear for the annihilation of their own self (schizoparanoid anxieties) and later on for the destruction of their loved objects, carried on by their possibly surmounting hostility (depressive fears).

The group as an object is often seen as a caring, maternal one, or as a nurturant mental surrogate of mother's breast. But, since objects are also easily interchangeable, affects are displaced from the group-as-a-whole, to the therapist or to any groupmate. Object relations group psychotherapy examines these various displacements of affects, as they are directed sometimes to the group or to the therapist, now to one particular group member, and soon to another one.

The whole group or some groupmates can also become "transitional objects," à la Winnicott, or a "self-object," à la Kohut, that provides safety and/or nurturance to the members. Group patients sometimes experience their therapeutic group as a "bad" mother that despises, devalues, and demeans them, by means of overdemanding criticisms or a relentless perfectionism (see chapter 4).

When a patient is "lost for the group" because of termination, death, or expulsion, the member "gone forever" is often introjected within the minds of the remaining groupmates. The member's disappearance leads to his or her being mentally "brought back" by the groupmates, then identified with the lost member (see chapter 5 for some clinical illustrations of the vicissitudes of identifications within psychotherapeutic groups).

Specific contributions of object relations group psychotherapy can be summarized as follows:

1. A central focus on the relations between the self and the object whereby the anxieties about losing the self or the loved objects is placed within the conceptual frame of the psychoticlike primitive fears, related emotions, and early defense mechanisms.

2. An understanding of the crucial interactions that occur at the boundaries between self and object, where the

opposing contrast between "internal"/"external" helps to define several related, unstable distinctions such as fantasy/reality or self/object. However, besides the constant efforts to create and enhance the above distinctions and boundaries, through different levels of splitting, there are also ongoing identification processes (mediated both by introjection and projection) which blur such boundaries, sometimes creating confusions: What is real/fantastic, or external/internal, or object/self?

3. There is a conceptual kinship between the psychoanalytic object relations and the psychosocial role theories that become clearer when relating the analytic idea of identification with the psychosocial notion of role. The concept of role perhaps also brings object relations theory closer to psychodrama.

The concept of role describes the mental meeting point between parts of an individual's identity, or self, and the group expectations and needs, the point where both converge and coincide (see chapter 11 for a better understanding of what follows). The help-rejecting complainer described in chapter 11 acted out the group's anger at the therapist. She was a victim of abandonment, angrily claiming her right to receive care and attention. Her core self identity met the group's needs and expectations, which were to have someone expressing the members' anger at the therapist for "abandoning" them, placing them all together in a group instead of continuing with "private " meetings. That help-rejecting complainer's core identity and the group's wishes to violently criticize the therapist coincided and overlapped so she then became the "spokesperson" for the group's anger. There was a *concordant* identification between the help-rejecting complainer patient and her groupmates.

Racker (1960) used the psychological ability to put one's self in someone else's place to describe the "concordant" countertransference reactions, based on a mental identification between the psychotherapist and the patient. Concordant countertransference reactions are based on an introjective identification. By contrast, Racker considered the "complementary" countertransference reactions, as based on an interaction between reciprocal, opposed, but complementary roles, one of which can be assumed by the patient, while the therapist is cast in the opposite one. Complementary countertransference reactions are based on projective identification. We used this conceptual model to study "Countertransference When Incest Is the Problem" (see chapter 7).

Complementary, opposite but reciprocal roles can be psychosocial expressions of the mental split within a person's self, whereby being, for instance, a masochistic victim alternates with being a sadistic abuser, exercising mastery and dominion. My masochistic patient, the help-rejecting complainer, displayed her suffering as a way of sadistically attacking her helpers; she then shifted from acting as a victim to behaving like "an abuser," implying that she might herself abandon the group, searching for better help, just as her parents had left her home (see chapter 7 for an elaboration of the frequent splits in incest victims between a part of them identified with the aggressor and most of their selves cast as victims).

Jacobson's (1971) study on depersonalization, based on her observations in a Nazi concentration camp, on how victims identify themselves with their torturers and afterwards feel "depersonalized," alienated from their real selves, focused on a split in these persons' selves into two opposing, conflicting parts. The roles of victim-torturer expressed a masochistic-sadistic split; that is, antagonistic parts within these individuals' selves. The psychosocial concept of "conflict of roles" includes a reference to a mental "conflict of identifications" within the self.

Heimann (1952) described "unassimilated" introjects within the person's self. The boundaries between self and object are there represented within a person's mind when "choosing" whether to accept an introject as an "assimilated" part of the self, or to keep it "unassimilated," alien to the real self.

Groups may include in their exchanges frequent references to persons who are not present in the room but only in the members' minds: Somebody's spouse may become transiently a "satellite" member, absorbing the group's attention (see chapter 8) or the entire group may address itself to an "invisible group," such as the one Blay Neto (1986) described, which was made up of relatives, bosses, dates, and friends "brought to" the group meetings, by the intensity of the member's affects.

A group patient's self can be modified through an identification with someone else—the therapist or a groupmate or a lost love object. Introjection as a defense mechanism may re-create, bring back, to that patient's mind vivid images of an object, which may induce a transformation of that patient's self, making the patient imitate or become identified with such object.

Other patients' selves may change by eliminating unwanted split parts of their selves into external "containers," which, through projective identification, become like the initially rejected parts of the patient's self eliminated as unwanted. A groupmate may then become a "spokesperson" or a "scapegoat," unconsciously impersonating the above split parts, "dumped" on him (Horwitz, 1983). Sometimes another group, an "outgroup," is cast as the container of "all the evil" of which a particular group wants to rid itself.

The boundary permeability allows for changes within the self leading to changes, sometimes to improvement or emotional growth. Thus, the object relations theory offers concepts and approaches that provide an understanding of how group psychotherapy induces change.

Role-playing in a psychodramatic situation lends itself to a patient asking: "Who am I, really? Is this a genuine part of me?" Often playful participation in a dramatic "game" brings out performances where spectators and actors alike may wonder: Was that behavior part of the role portrayed or is that the actor's "real" self? Psychodrama can thus help to explore issues related to the false self and the obstacles in expressing the real one.

The real self may be underdeveloped because of conflictual needs to deny and to block it, or to split it as a parasitic subself. The real self may also be buried underneath repressions, or evacuated out through projections. Psychodramatic techniques, such as "alter ego" or "role-reversals," can be related, on the one hand, to the exploration of the unconscious (somehow related to free association), while, on the other hand, they can be conceptualized as the psychodramatist offering himself to become a "container," or a "transference screen," where the "split parts" are projected as on a screen. The role reversal technique lends itself to bringing out into the open parts of the self so far kept as alien by ongoing projections.

The entire group or some groupmates can become "self objects"—à la Kohut—for a given patient, whose self may blossom, through absorbing the positive "mirroring" offered to him by the group as a self object, validating the individual's aspirations, ideals, and efforts, or developing an expanded view of the self now "seen through somebody else's eyes" (see chapter 11). In groups, the self can obtain a sense of belonging and of being valued. Idealized, mirroring, and partnering selfobjects are available (Bacal, 1985). Introjective and projective group processes make self/object boundaries permeable and fluctuating. In groups, object relations are often experienced as identifications, introjective (for instance, all members with the group leader), or projective (for instance, a "spokes-person").

Since Kohut's self psychology also pays attention to the interactions between self and objects, it is another object relations theory, different from M. Klein's. Self psychology has legitimized the self's need for selfobjects across every person's life. Such needs are, according to Kohut, above possible reproaches; they are not seen as selfish, grandiose, ruthless, or self-centered. The person's need to engage in selfobject relationships has been declared "not guilty!" There are basic differences between Kohut's self psychology and Melanie Klein's object relations theories. Kohut developed the view of the *tragic* man, while Klein elaborated on Freud's *guilty* image of man. Klein's concern for the object emphasizes as the maturational ideal outgrowing the boundary confusion between self and selfobjects, so that a clear-cut distinction is achieved, and the differences between self and object are fully acknowledged. Self psychology stretches instead throughout life the human need to sustain confusion between self and object, to avoid full awareness of their differences, because realizing the existence of differences may become a narcissistic injury, provoking tension and envy.

We do not have to choose between these two theoretical formulations. Some analysts attempt to integrate both (Grotstein, 1983); however, they are difficult to combine. For instance, guilt's centrality in the depressive position and envy within the schizoparanoid position are basic concepts in Klein's theory, while self psychology attempts to do away with both guilt and envy. However, Kohut could not succeed in eliminating guilt and envy, nor did he achieve his goals of legitimizing the self's needs and blurring boundaries/differences between self and objects.

Kohut empathizes with the tragic human condition, but ignores the emotional reality of guilt and envy within us.

What follows is only speculative, yet I wish to explore these possibilities: Could it be that Kohut's view of mankind as "tragic" was an honest but questionable belief of an analyst who put himself in the role of victim? As a matter of fact, Kohut (1968, p. 103) criticized the emotional abuse perpetrated by a training analyst who offered a crown and a scepter to a candidate as a confrontation, sarcastically mocking the narcissistic need to be seen as a king. Kohut's (1979) paper on "The Analyses of Mr. Z." compared the first "Freudian" treatment with the second, along Kohutian lines; both analyses were done by Kohut himself. What the second discovered was Mr. Z.'s fearful submission to a psychotic, brutal, sadistic mother who had abused poor Mr. Z. What Kohut offered then was his empathy in attempting to compensate for Mr. Z.'s deficit in good mothering.

Narcissistic disturbances "are indications of an inner prison" because individuals who suffer from them "are compelled to fulfill the introjected mother's expectations" (p. 45). When these individuals were children, their mothers found in them "someone at their disposal who [could] be used [and] controlled and [was] completely centered on them" (p. 35). What is missing in this relationship "is the framework within which the child could experience his emotions. Instead [the child] clearly develops something the mother needs" (p. 34). The narcissistic mother entraps her child by making the offspring feel indispensable for mother's happiness, hence enslaving the child as mother's favorite, dominating through admiration, to the point of inducing the loss of the child's self. Miller (1981) derived the following thoughts from "interviews with candidates for the psychoanalytic profession": An emotionally insecure mother depends on her child for her narcissistic equilibrium. The child responds intuitively by taking the assigned role, which secures mother's "love." These children's ability to reassure their mothers transforms them into "mothers (confidantes, comforters, advisors, supporters) of their own mother"; later on, some "eventually choose the psychoanalytic profession" (pp. 8–9).

"A child may learn very early what he is not allowed to feel, lest he run the risk of losing his mother's love" (Miller, 1981, p. 46). Likewise, the psychoanalyst may learn early, while in training, what not to feel lest some maternal psychoanalytic institution may ostracize or disaffiliate him. Unfortunately psychoanalytic education may have the undesirable potential to abuse trainees, attempting to use and to control them (they are so eager to be accepted!) for some analytic authorities' self-centered needs, or occasionally questionable ideals.

Since pathology of the self is frequent among psychoanalysts, Kohut's self psychology appeared to have relevant immediate, direct application to training analyses. Finell (1985) wrote:

> Psychoanalytic work can be extremely gratifying to the analyst's narcissism, leaving little incentive to resolve it personally or in one's patients. Politics and other extra-analytic situations can become the repository of split-off hostile and devaluing feelings while the personal analyst remains idealized. . . . The problem is a difficult one, particularly when the transference involves symbiotic features and mutual gratification. Working through narcissism should be central in the analyst's personal analysis in order to foster high levels of ego integration, self-development, and analytic ability [p. 443].

Roth (1982) studied a typology of borderline patients, describing as type 3 the false self personalities. This category includes patients who join our professional ranks. As I have quoted elsewhere (see chapter 9) they are able to make psychologically accurate mechanical remarks about themselves or others, a defensive maneuver that "serves to deflect attention from themselves and inhibits the sharing of their own infantile anxieties." Battegay (1983) recommends analytic self-experience groups for the training of psychotherapists since the experience in these groups is an opportunity for "colleagues who have passed through an individual analytic experience to make acquaintance with different sides of their personality than those seen in the dyadic psychotherapeutic situation. For example, it is more possible in a group to recognize narcissistic disturbances than in individual analysis" (p. 209). (See also chapter 9.)

Even if Kohut did not intend to specifically defend analysts' legitimate narcissistic needs, he appeared to some as an idealized selfobject and their eloquent spokesman. The analytic candidates who may feel "emotionally battered" welcome Kohut's empathy for the "tragic" human condition, including theirs during training: indoctrinated in the "party line" official ideology, "controlled" in their incipient practice, railroaded (or "convoyed") in their progression, torn between their postgraduate educational status and their regression on the couch, their creativity often discouraged. Kohut appeared as a spokesman who defended their needs.

Kohut implicitly, but clearly, addressed himself to the person's narcissistic suffering. He appeared, like Neruda (1966), to invite the "oppressed":

Give me your hand out of the depths
Sown by your sorrows
. . . light up the whips

glued to your wounds. . . .
Come quickly to my veins and to my mouth.
Speak through my speech, and through my blood
[p. 67, 71].

If so, Kohut became a twin soul, empathically "tuning in" with the victim's view of our tragic condition.

However, Kohut ignored certain aspects of the human mind, namely, the existence of brutal, sadistic, violent destructiveness, the universal potential to be like Hitler or Charles Manson (Rush, 1982). Self psychology's "claim to fame" seems to have been earned by denial of patients' hostility and of their own partial responsibility in shaping their destiny. Denial and splitting of significant parts offer an impoverished, passive view of the self, with little room for proactive initiative. Aggression is not acknowledged as a significant elemental force in the patients' own mind but only addressed to in the analysands' parents and treaters. Some analysts question how effective is a therapeutic approach based upon denial and splitting. Kohut's integrated self may still be truncated after therapy, because of excluding important parts of the personality. By contrast, M. Klein's integration of the self aims at reducing splitting and achieving full use of the patients' total personality endowment.

Psychoanalytic theories express, among many issues, their authors' dreams, their personal attempts to fulfill our curative wishes. The treater's own ailment leads us to search how to make reparation to our damaged internal objects. Object relations theories (including self psychology) also are, in part, analysts' dreams of fulfilling hopes to be cured of their ailment (Main, 1957). In these pages, I shall share some of my dreams, including those I thought were occasionally coming true!

Although the preceding paragraph is correct, it is also true that I patiently gathered data to substantiate my theoretical formulations and the belief that some group patients were helped: Using videotapes, observer recorders, dictating notes on each session's issues, having supervision, following up some patients, and mainly "having been there," when emotionally significant events happened in group sessions, including members' observable changes, all provided a mixture of objective and highly subjective evidence, supporting my conviction that object relations group psychotherapy is conceivable and sometimes effective.

2

A COMPARATIVE STUDY OF BION'S CONCEPTS ABOUT GROUPS

RAMON GANZARAIN, M.D.

Paradox becomes Bion; he abandoned his studies on groups, but the professionals working in this field keep him as a leader. Bion, who had a "strong BaF [Basic Assumption of Fight/Flight] valency"—to use Bion's own terminology (Trist, 1985)—was accordingly cast as the leader in battles waged by different groups. Since he certainly did not back away from many struggles, in war or in peace, why did he then wish to leave the embattled area of groups?

When Bion supervised me, in 1961, I asked him: "Why did you stop working with groups?" He replied: "Well, Paula Heimann and Melanie did not like analysts working with groups!" Upon listening to himself, he quickly reacted, with a chuckle, "Well, that sounded pretty childish!" and then he added: "I guess I had already made my contribution to that area. Hence, I moved on, to explore another topic, namely psychotic thought."

23

Trist (1985) recalls a 1949 conference, where a dispute was going on regarding Bion's ideas on groups and Lewin's field theory. Trist quotes Bion asking himself then: "Why does it always have to be me who has to bear the brunt? . . . I have been in the front line unrelieved for ten years. I don't want to stay there another ten years" (p. 4).

The field of groups includes group dynamics, a chapter in social psychology, and group psychotherapy, a treatment modality in psychological medicine. Bion contributed to both areas, and his ideas on groups have different relations with three theories: Melanie Klein's psychoanalysis; Lewin's field theory and general systems theory (GST). Bion applied Klein's concepts of psychotic anxieties and early defense mechanisms to groups. His notions integrated Klein's theories with his own views about groups. Bion's ideas compete with Lewin's (1952) theoretical formulations (derived from the Gestalt school of psychology) to explain groups better. He tangentially touched upon von Bertalanffy's (1968) GST in a potentially complementary relationship to the ideas of living systems.

First, I shall briefly review Bion's theory in groups, and how scientists have responded to it across four decades, and then I shall take a glimpse into the future, discussing some dilemmas facing us.

GROUP DYNAMICS

Margaret Rioch (1970) brilliantly described the work of Wilfred Bion on groups as follows:

Bion's central thought is that in every group, two groups are present: The "Work-Group" and the "Basic

Assumptions Group" . . . two aspects or two different ways of behaving.

The Work-Group has to do with the real task of the
group, takes cognizance of its purpose, and defines its
task. The structure of the group is there to further the
attainment of the task. Members cooperate. The Work-
Group tests its conclusions in a scientific spirit. It is
conscious of the passage of time and of the processes of
learning and development [p. 58].

"A large part of Bion's theory has to do with why
groups do not behave in the sensible way described, as
characteristic of the Work-Group" (p. 58). The work is
only one style of group functioning. The other aspect Bion
called "The Basic Assumption Group." He singled out
three basic assumptions: of dependency, of fight/flight,
and of pairing. All basic assumption groups have "characteristics in common." Basic assumption life is not oriented
toward reality, but inwards toward fantasy. Basic assumptions are anonymous. They are not formulated by any one
member in the group.

No one wants to own them. There is a kind of
conspiracy of anonymity. . . . The Basic Assumptions
seem to be the disowned part of the individuals, and
individuals seem to fear the Basic Assumptions. Since
[they are] anonymous, the Basic Assumptions can
function quite ruthlessly, which is why they are
feared. . . . Basic Assumptions represent an interfer-
ence with the work task. However, the Basic Assumption's energy can be harnessed to serve the group's
task, can be used in the service of the task. Hence the
same man or the same group which has filled the world
with horror at its capacity for evil can also amaze by its
capacity for good [p. 58].

Bion's contribution to group dynamics was welcomed and acclaimed by social scientists. The clash between Bion's and Lewin's concepts increased the attention devoted to Bion, but also limited the focus on them, as if he were *only a "group dynamicist,"* not a group psychotherapist also. The more his ideas were accepted in the area of group dynamics, the more they could indirectly be pushed outside the field of group psychotherapy, creating a confusion about where his concepts belonged.

A gradual idealization of Bion had taken place. He was transformed into a guru, a personification of his own concept of the mystic. Once, when he was invited as a small-group consultant to an A. K. Rice Institute Group Relations Conference, he was so dismayed with the idealization of him going on, that he mocked it, asking those who kept quoting him: "Who is this fellow Bion?"

As part of the residency programs in psychiatry, many schools include experiential learning of group dynamics which includes Bion's contributions. Walter Reed General Hospital in Washington, DC, and the Karl Menninger School of Psychiatry in Topeka are two examples.

Bion's concepts on group dynamics are now seen as complete, well-rounded, packaged ideas, ready to be applied flexibly, outside the context of these laboratories or group conferences, to many fields of human endeavor: education, mental health, administration, industry, community life, and so on.

No doubt, Bion has made a major contribution to the area of group dynamics; his writings have almost become a bible in the field. His theory is widely used after four decades, a rare exception among many theories proposed in the social sciences! However, this simplified acceptance of his ideas and their applications to human groups seem to be carrying Bion's theory away from the more complex field of group psychotherapy, limiting its application only to group dynamics.

GROUP PSYCHOTHERAPY

Bion treated groups only from 1947 to 1949. He did not write systematically on group psychotherapy proper; he produced no books on the subject; even his papers on group psychotherapy constitute an "incomplete" piece of work. He had no direct followers. Ezriel (1952) soon formulated his own concepts about interpretation in group psychotherapy, modifying and expanding on Bion's formulations.

Kleinian Theories Applied to Group Psychotherapy

Bion applied Kleinian analytic concepts to group psychotherapy, and presented condensed theoretical formulations: group regression to early stages of mental functioning, whereby psychotic anxieties and early defenses are reactivated; namely, projective identification and splitting.

He gave some hints about technique, however. For example, he made an original contribution to countertransference, studying its relation to projective identification (Meltzer, 1978). He defined the criteria for identifying the experience of being the object of a projective identification; namely, "a temporary loss of insight during an emotional experience, whose quality seems unquestionably justified, followed by insight and the feeling of having been dominated by someone else's fantasy" (Bion, 1961, p.148).

Another valuable contribution is contained in his criteria for the timing of interpretations: "I judge the occasion to be ripe for an interpretation when the inter-

pretation would seem both obvious and unobserved"
(1961, p. 143). If an interpretation has become obvious, it
will likely be immediately acceptable as evident; if it has
gone unobserved, it is the therapist's primary task to
formulate the interpretation. Notice, by the way, that
Bion's implicit advice is to first "wait and see," if group
members observe the obvious. Bion only intervenes, "en
faut de mieux," when and if the group members fail to
observe the obvious. However, some group therapists
criticize Bion's technique for his *apparent* monopolization
of therapeutic functions in the group (Yalom, 1975).

   Bion also concluded that "verbal exchange is a function
of the work group. The more the group corresponds with
a basic assumptions group, the less it makes any rational
use of verbal communication" (p. 185). He quoted Melanie
Klein's 1930 discussion of the breakdown of the capacity
for symbol formation as relevant to the group state where
communications are nonverbal "in terms of short interjections, long silences, sighs of boredom, movements of
discomfort. The group appears to be capable of enduring
almost endless periods of such conversation, or none at all.
There are protests, but endurance of this monotony
appears to be a lesser evil than action to end it" (Bion,
1961, p. 185). Bion elaborated on how group regression
induces a breakdown of the capacity to symbolize and to
communicate verbally. By contrast, verbal communication
is a function of the work group. I wish to underscore two
important implications: the need to work through the
depressive anxieties in order to achieve meaningful verbal
communications and the potential for "acting" (out and/or
in) unconscious mental contents without verbally acknowledging the meaning of such actions, thus preventing
immediate insight about them. This latter point is further
elaborated in a chapter in this volume on acting out
(Ganzarain and Buchele, 1988).

In "Group Dynamics: A Review," Bion (1952) brings together the group mentality and the individual mentality, the preoedipal and oedipal unconscious contents. He adds the *sphinx* as "one component of the oedipal myth of which little has been said" (Bion, 1961, p. 162; Meltzer, 1978). Some suspect that Bion's personality lent itself to casting him in the sphinx's role. But he insists that what he observes in groups is not the consequence of his presence in the group—some kind of artifact linked merely to his personality—but is a response "inevitable, where the group includes *anyone* (emphasis added) with a 'questioning' attitude. This approach stirs up the very primitive fantasies about the contents of the mother's body and mobilizes defenses typical of the paranoid–schizoid position. Consequently, the pairing group is seen as closely linked to the primal scene, perceived at a primitive level" (Meltzer, 1978, p. 15).

A Clinical Illustration

Here is a description of a situation of "pairing" in the ninth session of an outpatient psychotherapy group, composed of four women and four men. Rose was absent for the first time. During the first half of the meeting, Judith, the youngest and most attractive female, spoke about her sexual difficulties, vaginismus and frigidity, which had made her first two years of marriage almost impossible to endure. The group discussed her situation, asked pertinent questions, and suggested possible additional treatments. I will now focus in detail on the second half of this meeting. Roland shared that he was having an extramarital affair, because his sexual needs were not satisfied with his wife. He proceeded to describe a Don Juan–like sexual life, adding his feelings of guilt for having to lie to his wife, but also his unwillingness to change his sexual behavior.

Male members responded with criticism: "You're a philanderer! You are insecure about your masculinity and therefore trying to show off, bragging about your harem," and so on. Judith responded with worried curiosity inquiring, "If you are not pleased with your wife, why do you stay married then?" For her, Roland's infidelity was exactly what she feared the most regarding her own husband, that is to say, that he would walk out on her because of her sexual dysfunctions.

Secretly, however, Roland had picked up this moment to talk about his promiscuous sexual life as a response to Judith's sharing her sexual difficulties. It was as if he were saying to her, "Do you need a sexual 'expert'? Let me introduce myself; I can help you." He had, as a matter-of-fact, preceded his statements about his sexual performances by recommending to Judith a bibliography of works on how to enjoy sex, obviously presenting himself personally to her as an alleged sexual expert. There was an attempt on his part to pair with Judith.

Cathy started asking Roland for more details of his sexual adventures and in the process she revealed that she was also having an affair behind her spouse's back. Cathy elaborated on her emotional conflicts, feeling guilty and trying to push men away from her by becoming overweight, while on the other hand starving for the emotional gratification of sexual intimacy. She stated, "I do it 'not for the sex but for the love,' or my problem is with love not sex"; she looked for intimacy to counteract her depression and loneliness; she did not want to put on her husband all the many "rotten things" that she felt she contained. There were further group criticisms for those stepping out on their spouses. However, the group gradually moved to try to understand Roland and Cathy: What was the psychological explanation of their extramarital affairs? By now Roland and Cathy had become another "pair," united by their unfaithfulness and by the group's current attention to their sexual lives.

Maybe they wanted to get back at their spouses because they were angry at them? Most certainly they were afraid of losing the spouses! Daniel, whose wife had threatened to divorce him, was sure that was their case. Another member concurred. Judith thought they did it because of sexual frustration! The older male member took a grandfatherly role, advising them to "stop hurting themselves." Daniel insisted: "I am afraid she'll be gone any day." Suddenly this brought up an ah-ha experience to Cathy's mind; she burst into tears and said, "That's it. I'm afraid I'll lose him . . . as I lost my father! That's it!" She then proceeded to tell the group about her father's suicide. He killed himself when he was forty-two. He had been an alcoholic since adolescence but had gone to AA meetings and successfully achieved sobriety. His two sober months were interrupted by a relapse into drinking. He killed himself after this relapse. Group members gradually shared their feelings that loved persons could also abruptly leave them. They asked for details about the suicide and the life of Cathy's father. Roland said, "There is a curious parallelism: 'My father was a control-oholic' who couldn't relax, couldn't enjoy life, and was always tense. He saw me doing 'meditation-type' exercises and learning to relax myself; he wanted to learn them. I taught him, but he couldn't stand what he discovered within himself. He lost his mind and killed himself shortly after." Some members exclaimed, "Oh my God!" The group's "grandpa" then started reflecting about his vulnerability; he reported how he could manage his professional activities without feeling anxiously weak, but in his personal family life he felt tremendously vulnerable, particularly in his relations with his wife. He wanted to explore and understand how one can become so vulnerable. He point-edly addressed this question to the therapist.

This question marked a significant change in the style of interacting with the therapist during this session. In the second half of this session, the intensity of the inter-changes among members did not leave any opening for the therapist to intervene; in addition, once he tried to say something and nobody paid attention. He was literally silenced by the frantic rhythm of exchanges among mem-bers. When "grandpa" asked about his vulnerability, the therapist was in a dilemma. There were only three more minutes left to end the session, but very important mate-rial had come up; the group was now sending him messages that they wanted him to say something, maybe to prove to them that he was still with them in spite of their having ignored him. He decided to intervene, saying that becoming involved in the group was making them vulner-able to the fear of losing or missing each other and that perhaps that was why they had not inquired about Rose's absence. He also reminded the group that upon convening the previous meeting, Roland had shared the information that psychiatrists are the professionals with the highest rate of suicide. Some members spontaneously interrupted, saying "The group will be gone too! Or you may be gone!" Judith was then crying. The therapist briefly added: "There is a fear of the responsibility of harming someone, maybe Rose, the missing member? Or perhaps driving me to become suicidal." A brief silence followed. Roland said, "When you [the therapist] were talking, I had the impulse to stand up and start giving a hug to everyone in the room." Cathy responded immediately with loud laughter, and said, "Oh yeah!" Judith was still crying.

The therapist's comments brought first a brief mo-ment of reflectiveness, with Judith crying and others acknowledging their fears that the group or the therapist might be gone forever. But shortly after, the group's hypomanic defenses were reinforced, and there was again a brief plan to "become physically intimate," by hugging. Significantly, it was Roland who proposed it and Cathy who immediately endorsed it. In other words, the two "acting outers" had briefly "acted in" their defensive styles in dealing with depression. The group had previously indulged in pseudointimacy through "talking about sex," as if the topic would bring them closer, without having to pay attention to their fears of hurting each other. Significantly the subject of the meeting's second half was "casual sex," perhaps used to fill in the void of depression and to forget anxiety. Anxiety was, however, significantly present, with unconscious worries about the group's survival. It was as if members were feeling: "If one patient starts missing a session, will this mean that Rose will later on drop out and then others may do the same, or have we hurt Rose, the missing member? Or the other way around: if I get more involved here, would I be hurt here? I risk losing persons that I may need here." The group's anxiety about its survival was defended against by the pairing basic assumption, expressed as a hope that members could help each other to overcome the fears of love being hurtful. Similar expectations about the omnipotent "cure-it-all" magic quality of love had also inspired Roland's and Cathy's acting out.

During most of the session, the therapist was perceived as a threat. His treatment could make them face the truth about themselves, as the AA meetings and the impossibility of remaining sober had killed Cathy's father, or as the truth discovered during meditation exercises had pushed Roland's father into madness and suicide. The therapist had become in their minds like the sphinx: a silent witness whose knowledge had killing powers. He was, off and on, perceived then unconsciously as the persecutor that group members had to eliminate because of his "knowing too much!" In other moments, they projected into him their vulnerability, their potentials for suicidal depression, and were fighting with a sense of guilt for wishing to lethally harm him.

The group's request for the therapist's intervention probably was an attempt to restore him, by innuendo, and thus relieve the patients' fears of him, by listening to his comments and implicitly realizing that he was intact, "all right." In addition, his references to their most intense anxieties soothed them, albeit briefly, making them feel understood.

Group Psychotherapy Goals

Bion also describes important intermediary goals of psychoanalytic group psychotherapy. He sums up that "groups would, in Freud's view, approximate to neurotic patterns of behavior, whereas in my view they would approximate to patterns of psychotic behavior" (Bion, 1961, p. 181). He adds: "I very much doubt if any real therapy could result unless these *psychotic patterns* were *laid bare* with no matter what group. In some groups their existence is early discernible; in others, work has to be done before they become manifest" (emphasis added).

Bion writes (1961):

Each Basic Assumption contains features that corre-spond so closely with extremely primitive part-objects that sooner or later psychotic anxiety, appertaining to these primitive relationships, is released. . . . The Basic Assumptions phenomena appear . . . as defen-sive reactions to psychotic anxiety, not so much at variance with Freud's view, as supplementary to them" [p. 189].

Bion's theoretical works in group psychotherapy describe the central goal of working through the primitive group defenses (or "Basic Assumptions") against the common psychotic anxieties, reactivated in the transference relationships in the group. He does not present, however, a detailed account on how to reach this goal.

When adults regress in groups, they search for analogous experiences upon which to establish a relationship with a group as an entity, thus getting in touch with preambivalent "good" and "bad" objects as well as with part objects of their earlier internal world (Eisold, 1985).

Some British analysts, including R. Gosling and P. Turquet, followed Bion's model both in group psychotherapy and when consulting in group dynamics at group relations conferences.* But they did not organize systematic training in, or the private practice of, group psychotherapy as Foulkes and others later on did at the London Institute of Group Analysis. Bion's work has not been widely accepted by the group psychotherapists in the United States. A factor that might have dampened their enthusiasm is Bion's use of Kleinian concepts to present his theories. Kleinian concepts, terminology, and clinical experiences are often difficult to convey to analysts trained within the Freudian ideological orientation to psychoanalysis.

The confusion between group dynamics and group psychotherapy made it more difficult to take Bion's ap-

---

*Group relations conferences, offered by the A. K. Rice Institute, are experiential workshops where students learn about group behavior as it happens by participating in small and large groups and in intergroup exercises. Such conferences are usually held for a week or two at college campuses or in isolated resorts; they offer opportunities to learn about "group dynamics" and leadership, but not about group psychotherapy.

proach to group psychotherapy seriously. There are legends about "people becoming psychotic" at the group relations conferences. Hence, it may seem reassuring to view the use of Bion's approach as limited only to such group relations conferences; madness can be "contained." Thus, Bion's program to deal with the group patient's psychotic anxieties may be regarded as not being that attractive after all! His method has also been criticized as inflicting too great a narcissistic injury on individual group members (Gustafson and Cooper, 1979).

Confusion, splitting, and projection seem altogether different responses to madness, attempting to delete or to encapsulate it perhaps within group relations conferences as if group madness did not have anything to do with human everyday group life, at home or at work.

"The strict use of Bion's approach has never in fact been widely adopted by analytical psychotherapists, not even in the Tavistock Clinic," writes Sutherland (1985). His conceptual framework regarding groups, however, formed the basis for the "group-centered," "integralists," or "holistic" approach to group psychotherapy. His technique of focusing on the group-as-a-whole can also be described as "psychotherapy *of* the group" or "*by* the group." This approach attempts to go beyond the application of individual psychotherapy to the group setting, integrating individual with group psychodynamics. Some authors searched to develop a distinct form of psychotherapy that operates through the group processes (Whitaker and Lieberman, 1964).

Other Theories of Group Psychotherapy

Two different group analytic psychotherapy modalities are "the interpersonal" (focused on the interactions between and among persons in the group) and the "intrapersonal" (or psychotherapy of the individuals in the group). Practitioners of these last two approaches object to the integralists' focus saying that "the group phenomena are, at best, irrelevant for therapy, and at worst antitherapeutic. Moreover, the group dimensions studied by social scientists seem superficial, for they have not dealt with the unconscious" (Parloff, 1968).

Lewin's Field Theory in Group Psychotherapy

Lewin's (1952) ideas influenced group psychotherapy approaches differently from those of Bion. The Sullivan school of interpersonal psychiatry applied Lewin's field theory to psychopathology and to psychotherapy. Sullivan's (1953) ideas inspired the "interpersonal" (or interactional approach) to group psychotherapy, represented, for instance, in the United States by I. Yalom and J. Frank. However, Yalom (1975) also uses group-centered, mass interventions, but only when the primary group task is being avoided by the members' flight.

Field theory also provided Foulkes (1948) and Foulkes and Anthony (1957) and Foulkes's London followers with their notions about group dynamics. Foulkes's differences with Bion were compounded by his rejection of Melanie Klein's psychoanalytic theories, following instead Anna Freud's ideas regarding early emotional development.

A summary of Lewin's field theory seems useful here. Lewin tried to elevate the scientific methodology for research in social psychology to a level comparable to that of mathematics and physics. He moved from the empirical and intuitive to the abstract and formal. He insisted that the determinants of human behavior can be presented in rigorous mathematical terms. He borrowed from physics terms such as "field," which evokes a "magnetic field"; or "dynamics," to imply group "forces"; or "feedback."

Lewin's fundamental construct is that of "field." He conceived all behavior as a change of some state of a field, in a given unit of time $(dx)/(dt)$. In individual psychology, the field is the "life space" of the individual. Groups also have a "life space." It is the task of the scientist to develop constructs and techniques of observation and measurement adequate to characterize the properties of any given "life space," at any given time, and to state the laws governing changes of these properties.

It is a basic assertion of field theory (inspired by Koestler's Gestalt psychology) that the various parts of a given life space are to some degree interdependent (like foreground and background in visual perception). A set of interdependent facts can only be adequately handled conceptually, with the mathematical notion of space and the dynamic ideas of tension and force. For Lewin contemporaneity was essential. At a given time, the determinants are the properties of the field present at the same time.

Lewin did not consider the subjective phenomena of human psychology, such as fantasies or dreams. His emphasis on the contemporaneity of properties within a field as the only relevant causes to explain the effects on such field promoted an ahistorical view of psychology, focused only on the here-and-now. He treated the time dimension in a way that seems to deny the importance of early emotional development. When proposing a nonsubjective and ahistorical psychology, the field theory seems opposed to matters essential in psychoanalysis. Field theory tends to confuse the real relations to others with the fantasized interrelationships between a person and his internalized objects, whereby "the subject constitutes his object" (i.e., by projection), while also "these objects shape the subject's actions," actually "acting upon the subject, persecuting, reassuring him, etc." (Laplanche and Pontalis, 1973, p. 280). These essentially subjective exchanges cannot be grasped by the analysis of objective external situations or field forces interacting among real persons.

Interpersonalists ignore group forces as antitherapeutic. Hence, they underexplore the negative transferences, mainly the ones to the group as an entity or as a whole. Consequently, they limit the range of their psychotherapeutic interventions, leaving the psychotic anxieties out of their scrutiny. They barely considered the regressive pull exerted by groups upon individuals or the anxieties experienced by the group members' regressed egos, in response to their heightened aggression. A central core of psychopathology is therefore systematically ignored.

Foulkes and his followers (Pines, 1985) likewise do not pay central attention to deep regressions, to group negative transference, or to the psychotic group anxieties.

General Systems Theory and Group Psychotherapy

General Systems Theory (GST) is a method of analysis that lists the essential components of a system and describes their reciprocal influence within such totality. Since GST is an abstract formulation applicable to many topics, "only a skeleton, it needs to be filled with specific descriptions of the concrete subject matter that is being studied. Therefore, to apply GST in group psychotherapy, we have to fill the general schemata with specific group theories, such as, for instance, the psychoanalytic views on object relations within groups." (See chapter 3.)

The different psychoanalytic approaches to group therapy can be consistently coordinated around a combination of general systems and object relations theories, without contradiction among their intra-, interpersonal, or holistic focuses, while also keeping open a wide spectrum of options to the psychotherapist's interventions. A combination of general systems and object relations theories can become the "metatheory" that integrates the various analytic concepts about groups.

General systems theory concepts can help us to better understand the interplays between individual and group mental processes. For example, isomorphism (the basic structural similarity among subsystems, and between them and a global system which encompasses them) can enrich the comparison between ego and group regarding their shared fluctuations between the opposite states of integration and fragmentation. A split, noncohesive schizoid ego state is comparable to a similarly unintegrated group period, while the well-integrated ego states reached after working through the depressive position are comparable to cohesive therapeutic work-group times, focused on the therapeutic task of insight, integration, and reparation.

General systems theory emphasizes "how boundaries are constantly crossed, from the inside and the outside of the living systems, in a dynamic, holistic interaction." Hence, it "adds a new understanding of how groups and self boundaries are extended—through projection and introjection beyond the more obvious ones of space and time," or how the here-and-now blends with the then-and-there.

Group phenomena such as "scapegoating," "spokesperson," or "satellite group members" can be better grasped as mixtures of group and individual psychologies by the members' common use of projective identification and splitting. Such defenses dispose of the mental parts, rejected by the group, through "dumping" them on certain specific members. These individuals' own proclivity to fit with, and to contribute to, these group phenomena provides a clearer, more integrated view of them.

The Future: Beyond Bion?

Progress in research about groups has been "hampered by one-sightedness" (Scheidlinger, 1982); reaching flexible new conceptual integrations should be our theoretical goal.

Some dilemmas about priorities in our work with groups have produced rigid solutions. What should prevail?

1. The individual or the group?
2. Fantasy, or the real psychosocial group phenomena?
3. The resolution of the members' schizoparanoid anxieties, or working through their depressive concerns?

The individual versus the group can be overstated as a dilemma, ignoring that "there is a continuous interplay between individual and group psychological processes" (Scheidlinger, 1982, p. 52). I examined such interplay in the section on GST. Bion's binocular vision of man's individual and group psychologies speaks clearly to that point.

Whether to pay attention primarily to psychic reality, to the world of fantasy, or to the external social reality of the group environment is another dilemma prone to one-sighted solutions. Research on the process of perception (Ganzarain, 1960b) can be of special interest here: "Each group member could perceive each other member and the therapist on a continuum—from the way they are—'in reality'—to the most 'fantasized distortions'. . . . Similarly the group-as-a-whole could be perceived on many levels from reality . . . to the deepest symbolic ideations. Perhaps the group entity could also be perceived in fantasy as the pre-oedipal mother or . . . as the mother's breast" (Scheidlinger, 1982, p. 56).

Bion did not study in detail the transference to the group-as-an-entity. "The Mother-Group" concept (Scheidlinger, 1974) or Foulkes's matrix describe preoedipal "good" maternal group functions which foster trust. The group does have a social reality that sometimes provides an emotional support and is perceived as maternal. However, other regressive perceptions may focus on the group's high, cold demands on its members, making it a serious, callous threat, a "bad mother" group (Durkin, 1964; Glatzer, 1969). (See also chapter 4.)

Although Bion was interested in studying schizophrenic thinking, unlike Fairbairn (1952), he did not claim priority of the schizoid phenomena over the depressive ones. Bion kept instead the Kleinian view about their reciprocal influence and the constant fluctuations throughout life—between both "positions." Schermer (1985) applied, however, Bion's last notions on schizophrenic thought, attempting to solve the group's paranoid-schizoid fixation and to go "beyond Bion." His strategy was to deal first "with schizophrenic-like defenses," which led him to criticize Slater (1966) for focusing instead on depressive group anxieties, "offering a maternal holding." He wondered whether Slater was dealing with "an ideal group composed of college students or psychiatric residents"(!) and questioned how the group "displayed such upward mobility, whereas the Tavistock-type groups seemed to drone on endlessly" (p. 145). Schermer's group experiences seems to be mainly in group relations conferences, with nontherapeutic groups that lasted two weeks.

The complex fluctuations between schizoparanoid and depressive anxieties will be examined here. Schizoparanoid anxieties are closely intertwined with depressive anxieties. Difficulties in tolerating depression induce regression to the schizoparanoid position. Hence, the solution of a schizoid fixation may paradoxically lie in slowly overcoming the defenses against the depressive anxieties, since those defenses, again and again, bring the group back to the schizoparanoid modality of mental functioning. When guilt, the depressive anxiety, induces unbearable self-reproaches, to regress to a schizoparanoid stance offers the relief of perceiving instead someone else as carrying the burden of guilt. The focus of anxiety also shifts from concerns regarding loved objects' well-being, to fears for the victimization of the self. Splitting, projection, and denial are the pathogenic defense mechanisms against depressive anxieties. The first two frequently combine their effects to produce schizoidlike mental disintegration. Omnipotent denial can either contribute to such regression or promote a flight into a maniclike state. The resolution of depressive anxieties is, by contrast, a progressive, upward emotional development based upon effective reparation of the damaged loved objects, achieving a realistic integration of love and hate of them, as well as of their good and bad features. Guilt is then overcome by acknowledging how love mitigates the hate for the objects while both effects coexist.

Psychotherapists have been concerned with strategies to help patients overcome these defenses and their psychopathological consequences. Some advise respecting, rather than challenging, the needs of these patients' egos to defend themselves. For example, Rosenfeld (1979) observes that if projection is interpreted while the patient is intensely paranoid, it will lead to a tug-of-war and to a therapeutic impasse; he recommends avoiding interpreting projection—"shoving back" the patient's projected bad contents—and waiting instead until the patient's observing ego regains his reality assessment. Meissner (1982) uses the same rationale for prescribing detailed techniques on how to treat paranoid patients, specifying, for instance,

the advantages in repeatedly asking the patient questions
to obtain more details of the alleged persecutory situations, so as to offer the patient renewed opportunities to
reassess them, while the psychotherapist provides emotional support. Epstein (1979) offers similar considerations
to respect the use of splitting as a defense.

Other psychotherapists have proceeded differently
when treating psychotic anxieties: Some tried to interpret
defenses soon after they were observable. Theoretically
clearer concepts plus trying different therapeutic approaches have resulted in the current understanding of
how best to handle the defenses against psychotic anxieties. The Kleinian analysts, for instance, were first over-
active, premature interpreters of projection, but later on
recommended, like Rosenfeld, not shoving back, through
interpretations, the patient's projected bad contents. Bion
likewise compared the analyst's "capacity to contain"
(1962) the patient's psychotic anxieties with the mother's
ability to intuitively take care of her infant's mental distress. He acknowledged projective identification as the
mental vehicle for such unconscious communication, promoting empathy. A "metabolization" of anxieties occurs in
the caretakers, thus offering living models to infants or
patients on how to cope with those anxieties. Followers of
the Kleinian psychoanalytic school may inadvertently apply the early strategies when dealing with psychotic anxieties, without realizing the advances in technique that
advise how to avoid premature interpretations, so as to
allow the patient's ego to regain its capacity for reality
assessment, whether in groups or in individual psychotherapy.

Schermer's (1985) observation that "the Tavistock-type
groups seem to drone on endlessly," without upward
mobility, may be his description of a group "learning
impasse," similar to Rosenfeld's observations of therapeu-

tic impasse when interpreting projection to paranoid individual patients. The primary task of the Tavistock-type
groups is not therapeutic, but "to study group behavior as
it happens." It is, therefore, easy not to respect the group
members' ego needs to protect themselves against psychotic anxieties, and to actively interpret instead projection and splitting, attempting to take away these defenses
when they are needed. The paradoxical result could be an
increase in the group's schizoparanoid anxieties, while
trying to resolve them.

My group work with average, ordinary outpatients
helped them during years of treatment to achieve some
working through of their depressive anxieties. When
manic or schizoid defenses become operative, guilt and
dependency are denied, split, or projected; these defenses
have to be understood to help the patients to experience
relief from the unconscious, denied guilt. This relief can
help the patients to relax their defensive stance and to
move instead from intrapsychic fragmentation to personal
integration. Therapeutic groups can then display "appropriate dependency," leading to assimilation of the help
offered, integrating it to foster the members' further
emotional growth. The dependency basic assumption is
then put to the sophisticated use of the therapeutic task,
insofar as the group members adaptively benefit from the
group's and the therapist's interventions, to understand
themselves better. The resultant individual's integration
increases group cohesiveness: Each group member then
works harder to reach the common therapeutic goals. The
patients tolerate their guilt over their oral-sadistic impulses, accepting their hostile greedy parts. The patients
develop thus a sense of psychic reality, acknowledging
both dependency and ambivalence toward their objects.
They also modify their belief in the omnipotence of
destructive and loving impulses. They discover and prac-

tice instead actual ways of affecting reality through hard-working reparation, accomplished by means of effective therapeutic interchanges. (See chapters 5 and 16.)

To sum up, Bion made a major contribution to group dynamics and applied Kleinian analytic concepts to group psychotherapy. He described groups' situations comparable to a regression to early stages of mental functioning where psychotic anxieties and defenses against them are reactualized. But innumerable other aspects need to be added to develop a systematic group-as-a-whole psychotherapy; like America some years after the arrival of Columbus, its future is still wide open.

Bion left us the most valuable legacy in his relentless questioning of experiences with different topics. He often quoted M. Blanchot's sentence: "The answer is the misfortune of the question" ("La reponse est la malheur de la question").

3

GENERAL SYSTEMS AND OBJECT RELATIONS THEORY: THEIR USEFULNESS IN GROUP PSYCHOTHERAPY

RAMON GANZARAIN, M.D.

General systems concepts have been related to psychoanalytic notions, mainly to ego psychological ones. Systems' basic ideas can also be relevant to the psychoanalytic object relations theory, and I have found that the integration of both theories in my group therapy practice has enriched my understanding of psychotherapeutic phenomena.

I shall examine the "boundary subsystem" as it relates from the object relations viewpoint to the schizoparanoid and the depressive positions. How boundaries are crossed by introjection and projection will also be reviewed. I plan to illustrate the clinical usefulness of such a synthesis for group psychotherapy.

This chapter was first published in *International Journal of Group Psychotherapy* (1977), 27:441–456, and it is reprinted with permission.

The "decider subsystem" will be briefly discussed in order to describe how, in object relations theory, some of the psychoanalytic ideas about the ego are modified.

THE DECIDER SUBSYSTEM

Karl Menninger proposed a personality theory in general systems terms (Menninger, 1963). He reviewed mainly the psychoanalytic theories of the ego and the instincts, emphasizing the Freudian defense mechanisms and the ego's role as the central executive or "decider" concerned with the governance of the organism.

The decider subsystem has been characterized as the "executive subsystem which receives information inputs from all other subsystems and transmits to them information outputs that control the entire system" (Miller, 1971, p.341). The deciding process at all levels has four stages: discovery of purposes or goals, analysis, synthesis, and implementation. Complex living systems are organized into multiple echelons, from lowest to highest, with decisions being made by decider components at one echelon while another type of decision making is made at another echelon.

The psychoanalytic school of ego psychology limits the type of decision-making ego processes almost exclusively to the automatic regulation of defense mechanisms. The ego appears as determined by the unconscious con ents and has only a passive stance vis-à-vis its internal conflicts. The concept of the ego is limited to being in control of when to discharge the instincts after assessing the external reality.

Freud's work devoted particular attention to "two main elements": "instincts" (conceptualized as the "id") and "object relations" (centering on relations with parents and conceptualized as "oedipal" conflicts). The basic problems posed by "instincts" were those of gratification and control, which led to the concept of the ego as a control apparatus. This aspect of Freud's work was carried to the utmost limits of its possible development by Hartmann (1965) in his detailed analysis of ego apparatuses and techniques, developing into his theory of the "autonomous system-ego" and the "conflict-free area." In Hartmann's theory the superego declined markedly in importance. "The superego, however, is just that part of Freud's theory which is most bound up with the "object-relational" element and which was the main point of departure for Melanie Klein's work. Here, in the superego, are enshrined the child's earliest "whole-object" relationships with mother and father, by identification and introjection" (Guntrip, 1967, p. 220).

Out of Klein's deductions certain new facts emerged. The Oedipus complex and the superego seemed to be in evidence at an earlier age than one would have expected.

It was out of this line of investigation that Melanie Klein's theories of "internal objects" and the "inner world" emerged, and she struck out a genuinely new line of development which laid the foundations for, and necessitated the emergence of, the broadly "object-relational" type of theory. Klein's internal objects theory necessitated a fresh development of ego theory along different lines from that pursued by Hartmann. The works of Fairbairn (1954) and Winnicott (1965) are deeply rooted in that of Klein, even though they are not "Kleinians" [Guntrip, 1967, p.220].

Klein's work became the major turning point in one of the modern developments of psychoanalysis because she "forced to the forefront of inquiry the whole problem of 'ego growth in object-relations'" (Guntrip, 1967, p.220).

Transference becomes more dynamic and therefore more "personally" oriented. "We are not dealing with ego apparatuses mastering id-drives, but with an infantile ego relating to good and bad, part and whole, parental objects, a potential "person" relating to other "persons," with a constant interplay of projection and introjection between them. The whole of this must be worked through in the transference relation to the analyst" (Guntrip, 1967, p.220).

Hanna Segal (1967) says that "the factor that Kleinian analysis is most concerned with is integration. This involves a full differentiation between the self and the object, a lessening of projective and introjective identifications, a reduction of splitting, enabling the patient to have full use of his total personality endowment" (p.211). Here again, integration cannot take place in a vacuum but occurs insofar as the analysis is a "facilitating environment," to use Winnicott's (1965) term.

Hartmann (1965) defines the ego as "an organ of adaptation." "If we define adaptation in terms of the human being and his environment mutually adapting to each other, we are far beyond biology. . . . The concept of the environment has now changed. It no longer means nature in general. . . . The part of the human environment that is most significant is the society of his fellow beings" (Guntrip, 1971, p.104).

In studying human life, adaptation is replaced by a higher concept, that of a *meaningful relationship* in terms of values. Adaptation, strictly speaking, can only express one side fitting in. Personal relations involve mutual self-fulfillment in the communication and shared experience of two or more people. Personal meaningful relations are a matter of caring and concern.

What do these notions of object relations add to the ego function as a decider subsystem? They emphasize the active role of the ego in its dealings with the objects. It is remarkable that both general systems and object relation theories agree in emphasizing an active ego-person (von Bertalanffy, 1966). The working through of guilt within the depressive position promotes the capacity for loving and developing concern for the well-being of the objects. These attitudes are the prerequisites for developing a responsibility vis-à-vis the objects.

Two basic levels of decider sub-subsystems interact: an older, more primitive one and a newer, more sophisticated sub-subsystem of decision making.

Within the self the archaic decider sub-subsystem continues past interactions between internalized objects, as perceived back then, and old, childish self-representations charged with affects appropriate to the childhood situation. The quality of such affects is affected by the infiltration of primitive anxiety. Within the self the more sophisticated decider sub-subsystem is formed by a self-representation willing and able to try new behaviors (having relatively clear purposes about how to change and where to aim), and renewed perceptions of old objects which are benign, fostering the decision to change and supporting growth.

Reciprocal influences between these two levels of decider sub-subsystems allow a double (or multiple) vision of the same phenomena. It can be compared to the picture one gets of one's hometown if one looks at it with the attitude of a tourist. Old memories are rechecked and corrected by fresh views of familiar objects and places.

The new decider sub-subsystems will gradually define other purposes for action and new options to achieve them.

Within the psychotherapeutic group system the old level of decision making tends to be determined by the patients' previous maladaptive behavior. The therapist's task is to help the patients develop newer, more refined levels of the decider sub-subsystems beyond the patients' old childish anxieties. The therapist will help the patients and the group to redefine their goals in therapy. This redefinition will clarify the designs of strategies to achieve such goals.

The development of trust in one's own capacity to love is one of the essential developmental achievements, one of the main outcomes of the working through of the depressive position. Guilt, the essential depressive anxiety, is overcome by developing the capacity to make reparation or, in other words, to love the objects beyond and above hating them. The predominance of love over hate is reassuring. Such trust is a prerequisite for the exercise of one's own responsibility in dealing with the objects. If the individual acknowledges his capacity to care for the objects, then the ego accepts the fact that it has choices regarding how to treat its objects. This view of the ego functions pictures the self in an active stance during its dealings with the objects and being in a limited but clear way the master of its own destiny.[1] Integration is one of the crucial effects of the working through of the depressive position. It allows the combination of part objects into images of "whole" objects. The "oral-mother" is integrated with the "genital-mother"; in other words, the mother who provides "oral" care is perceived as a whole object with her own needs, including her own ties with father. Integration of the self takes place simultaneously by integrating the good and the bad aspects of the self or, in other words, the love and the hate for the objects. No part of the self

---

[1]The existential viewpoint in psychotherapy has also emphasized the exercise of the individual's own responsibility and the sad reality of death as the unavoidable destiny.

will be avoided or excluded as "bad," but everyone can be included and accepted as part of the self[2] (Ganzarain, 1972).

THE BOUNDARY SUBSYSTEM

"This subsystem, at the perimeter of a system, holds together the components that make up the system, protects them from environmental stresses, and excludes or permits entry to various sorts of matter-energy and information" (Miller, 1975, p.77–78). The functions of the boundary subsystem are therefore: (1) holding together the components; (2) protecting them from the environment; and (3) controlling the permeability through permitting entry or excluding information and matter-energy exchanges.

In object relations terms, protecting the components that make up the system from environmental stresses can be connected with the early paranoid anxieties that the human infant must undergo. The outer, external world appears during the "schizoparanoid position" as the site of very threatening contents.

The psychological defense mechanism of projection is used by the self to get rid of contents perceived as undesirable, as "poisoning" the system. The intense primitive hostility with unbearable sadistic contents (connected with the hypothetical death instinct) is perceived by the infant as threatening him with his own destruction; therefore, he needs to deflect such contents through projection. The infant then perceives the environment as dangerous and destructive, while being reassured of his own survival by having extruded his own destructiveness (Heimann, 1952).

---

[2]The Gestalt school of psychotherapy has also as a major strategic goal the integration of previously excluded parts of the self.

The threat of being unable to hold together some components of the system and experiencing a decisive impoverishment of the system are dangers connected with the possibility of splitting the self and thus losing parts of the system, which may later be extruded into the external environment. Those are the schizoid anxieties of impoverishment of the self, based upon the defensive mechanisms of splitting.

On the other hand, the attempt to hold together the components that make up the system expresses some of the anxieties with which the infant is confronted when turned inward to his internal world. Holding the "internalized good object," and keeping such an image internalized and protected, are crucial steps in the psychological development of the infant. These are the anxieties of the "depressive position"; namely, that the good internalized object may be destroyed by the rage and the destructive discharges experienced by the infant, leading eventually to a complete disorganization of the infantile internal world. The depressive anxieties lead to the development of the capacity for concern for the object.

The working through of the depressive position can be described as a very elaborate psychic effort to adapt the self to the realities of the internal world as well as those of the external world. It implies an exploration of the limits between the self and the objects, with a painful acknowledgment of the limitations in the ability of the self to experience love. To experience love means to receive and to give. The development of the capacity for concern depends on the ability of the mother to accept the infant's love, which allows the baby's reparatory activities to take place and be exercised (Winnicott, 1965).

Introjection and projection mediate the crossing of the boundaries of this system of the self and influence the exchanges between the self and the objects.

Introjection and projection are also mediators in the processing of information, insofar as they mediate efforts to gather information about the objects, the self, and their interactions. From the point of view of information gathering, the end result is usually quite inaccurate. Insofar as introjection and projection are strongly colored by wishes and fears, the images introjected or projected are distorted images of the self and the objects. Only after an intensive working through of the depressive anxieties has taken place may the introjected or projected images become more real. The object's resiliency and its capacity to accept and endure hate, without being destroyed, contributes significantly to enhance the ego reality assessment of both the internal and the external worlds. The object's capacity to allow for the repair of the damaging effects of such hate is essential to the growth of the ability to assess reality. Aggression and how to deal with it is what ultimately "makes things real" (Winnicott, 1965).

Perhaps the essential functioning of the boundary-processing subsystem is the control of its permeability, the fact that the boundary excludes or permits entry into the system to various sorts of matter-energy and information exchanges.

In the psychological realm this control of the boundary's permeability is not always in the power of a well-planned and rationally operating "decider." Instead of that, early anxieties of a paranoid and depressive nature determine the automatic functioning of defense mechanisms, such as splitting, introjection, and projection. These mechanisms are triggered into action without the higher level of functioning in the decision process that would allow for distinguishing the complexities of the deciding process. Anxieties connected with holding together the components that make up the system or with threats perceived as being "out there" in the environment may trigger these primitive defense mechanisms.

Both introjection and projection may lead to fantasies of identification between the self and some objects. Introjection may lead sometimes to the "melancholiclike" identification in which the shadow of the object hides the self; that is to say, the self is perceived as having the characteristics of the object.

Projection may lead to attributing to the objects (which become the "containers" of what is projected) those elements that are perceived as undesirable, as poisonous to the system of the self. The object that now contains the projected parts is perceived as being controlled by the self—at its mercy— through the domination which the self imposes upon the object. There remains, however, a vague potential and intermittent awareness that such an object is like or represents the self. What was projected can be reintrojected. These are the characteristics of the so-called projective identification.

The psychological functioning of the group can be characterized as a system insofar as it is a "whole" consisting of dynamically interacting "components." Introjection and projection are frequently used. Both lead to identifications. Identifications form the glue that cements the components of the group. Freud emphasized the crucial role of identification in the psychology of groups. Bion (1961) stressed the importance of projective identification in groups. We are familiar with the concepts of "scapegoat" and "spokesman" in our therapeutic groups, as operating examples of the wider use of projective identification. Boundaries between and among members become highly permeable in a therapeutic group. Each patient has a script about the role of objects which were important in his or her past and is ready to cast different members of the group in those preestablished roles. Each patient will manipulate the others to fit into those preexisting patterns which he expects to actualize in the group.

On the other hand, the self-image of each one of the patients is gradually expanded so that it now includes a new element of identity, that of being a member of a particular group. Boundaries are formed around the therapeutic group, with an increased need to hold together with the other members of that group. Group cohesiveness has developed.

There are boundaries between the group and the outgroup. These boundaries can be crossed by different psychological phenomena occurring between the ingroup and the outgroup.

There are advantages in adding the outgroup as a fourth "target" of transference in group psychotherapy. Three targets are generally described; namely, the therapist, the other members, and the group as a whole. The outgroup can also be utilized as a screen for transferences, through displacement, projection, splitting, and other unconscious mechanisms. The fact of conceptualizing the outgroup as another transference target may clarify matters considerably.

The outgroup as a transference target may take many forms; frequently, it leads to projection in terms of the "we/they" paranoid lines of splitting, visualizing the outgroup as a container of all the primitive, undesirable, unacceptable impulses and characteristics. Through history all cultures have developed the idea of the barbarian (or alien) in different ways, but essentially as a negative caricature of the outgroup. In today's medical, scientific, and educational institutions, "they" can be represented by the members of an opposite school of thought, the family of hospitalized patients, or the parents of the students. These examples of outgroups are also distorted through projection and are perceived as being endowed with the most primitive and threatening qualities.

During "intergroup exercises," modeled after the Washington School–Tavistock design of conferences on groups, it is frequently possible to observe the outgroup as a target of negative transferences, along splitting lines of "us and them," with projection to the outgroup of all the ingroup's own "badness."

The outgroup can sometimes be perceived as a "holding container," which is like a good mother or like an idealized and demanding one. I had an opportunity of watching the outgroup phenomena in this context when some patients moved as a group from a community clinic to the Menninger Foundation, a private psychiatric clinic. These patients perceived the private clinic as a demanding, idealized mother who would threaten them with exorbitant demands, while the first service appeared as the already known, familiar, and less demanding institution. The idealization of the Menninger Clinic was, however, gradually toned down to the point of allowing a more realistic appraisal, with an element of feeling quite positive and proud of having become "Menninger patients," somehow special in Topeka. In other words, the institutional outgroup became like a holding, good mother.

More could be written about the outgroup as another group transference target, but it is mentioned here only in passing, and I shall now return to the main topic.

Interactions across the boundary between the ingroup and the outgroup occur frequently between a psychotherapy group and the marital couples formed by its members. I would like to illustrate some of these concepts with a clinical example taken from the third session of a group of married outpatients. This group was formed by four new patients, recently admitted, and four "old-timers," members of a private group. One of the old-timers had attended only one session of the "old" group. He stopped attending then because his wife forbade him to go on participating. But he made a promise to himself that within a year he would apply for another group. He kept his promise. During the third session this patient, Jack, said that he was again having doubts about whether he would be able to continue attending because his wife was again raising objections, threatening him with divorce if he kept coming.

When Jack first applied for group psychotherapy, he had just learned that his wife was having an affair with another man. He was feeling rejected, jealous, and anxious. His wife apparently felt that Jack's participation in the group was some revenge for her extramarital affair, and she also viewed psychiatric help as an experience which could be addictive, without offering any warranty of effective help, since she had a sister who had been in psychiatric treatment for years without any definite improvement. The sister had developed an extreme dependency upon her therapists and expected them to take care of her problems rather than following her own initiative.

Jack himself was an infantile personality. He was also extremely anxious. He was the youngest child of a family of four. Jack's mother, a widow, lived by herself with her two younger children on a farm in the Kansas countryside. Jack's immediately older brother was mentally retarded. Around the age of eight, Jack experienced the sudden loss of his retarded brother when his mother abruptly decided to remove this child from the household and place him in a home for mentally retarded persons. Jack did not dare to ask about the decision. He was left with fantasies that his mother had kicked his brother out of the home because of the brother's "badness." Jack lived in an excessively dependent and anxious relationship with his mother, whom he needed and feared intensely. His mother kept him isolated from other children; his older siblings were gone. Because he was extremely dependent upon his mother, he did not dare to challenge her because of his fear of being kicked out of the household like his retarded brother. He was fearful of repeating with the group psychotherapists the same relationship he had with his mother. He was afraid of entering any emotionally meaningful relationship and of being abused because of his extreme insecurity and over-dependent style of relating. He unconsciously sided with his wife's hesitancy to accept his entering group psycho-therapy, and let her speak for him in voicing his own fears and doubts, while he presented himself as deeply inter-ested and determined to participate. This matter was discussed in the session I am reporting. He went on in a long-winded explanation about his relationship with his wife, his fear of losing her, and his need to get help that would foster his psychological growth. In so doing, he was more and more referring to the there-and-then of the marital relationship and apparently misusing the group's time. Some of the members began raising the question: "Why are we discussing Jack's wife? Since she is not a member of the group, why should he be talking about her?"

Before raising this question directly, the group had diagnosed that Jack was under his wife's thumb and that she was afraid of the changes that group psychotherapy might bring about in Jack's personality that would help him to resist her domination.

Significant psychological exchanges were happening on the boundary between two systems: the psychothera-peutic group and Jack's marital couple. Since Jack's wife was not a member of the group, it appeared nonsensical to guess about her motivation and how to influence her. But, on the other hand, Jack's wife had become the "container," through projection, of two fears shared by all the group members: (1) the fear of becoming "hooked" like addicts on the therapeutic relationship and (2) the fear of change. Just as they sensed the wife's fear of change, so also was each member fearful of the possible risks involved if they themselves were to change under the influence of the psychotherapeutic group.

I interpreted the projection of these group contents onto an "outsider." The rationale of my interpretation was based upon: (1) the concept of an interaction on the boundary between two systems, the psychotherapeutic group and the marital couple; and (2) the diagnosis of projection. The group had permitted the information about the exchanges between Jack and his wife to enter the group but had attempted to keep this information outside the group system. There was opposition to accepting it as something really belonging within the group system. Although the group was dealing with it, they handled it as if it were a matter foreign to the group. This was the result of the work of projection. The therapist's efforts consisted of helping the group to realize what they were doing, promoting their awareness of why they had been utilizing the information about Jack's wife as if it were something in some way alien to them, yet, in antoher way, pertaining to them.

The group also seemed to be performing another boundary function by attempting to encourage Jack to stay. The group was really concerned about the possible attrition of the group; hence, any member who mentioned the possibility of dropping out elicited special efforts to keep that member within the group. From that point of view, Jack's potential threat of quitting the group increased the activities designed to hold Jack as a group member. As for the unconscious meaning of Jack's behavior, it could be observed that Jack was doing to the group what his wife had done to him; he was threatening the group with the possibility of losing him just as his wife had threatened him with the possibility of losing her to another man.

Because of my conviction that all these things were unconsciously going on, I let the group go deeper into discussing the situation of Jack's wife. I interpreted later only the multiple meanings for the group of Jack's interactions with his wife. From a general systems point of view, Jack's interactions with his wife became like an extension of the group system through projection. It can also be said that through Jack's introjection of his wife's attitudes, she was figuratively present through Jack.

In general, through these several complex ways, the boundaries of the psychotherapy group are extended to the different personages that surround each member outside the group. The implications of this statement can be extended from the spouse to parents, siblings, bosses, workmates, and others. Introjection and projection blur the current space boundaries of the group almost in the same way that the timelessness of the unconscious blurs the time boundaries of the group; thus, we may witness an alive reproduction of the patterns of interaction between any of the members and his or her objects, both of the members' current or past lives.

The question of what to include within the group and what to leave out of the group's attention is illustrated by this clinical example. Jack's wife ended up being the container of several elements of the psychic life of the group members, and she became like a satellite member of the group. She contained some of Jack's basic fears of the group, together with the comparable fears of other members. Initially, this was evident only to the therapist, but the moment arrived for the therapist to interpret the use of the projection. This interpretation brought back to the group system the contents that were being expelled and excluded from the group. The group reaction was of some initial resistance, but gradually they began working with it and seeing the many elements that had been projected onto Jack's wife.

The role of the group psychotherapist has been described as fundamentally keeping the boundary controls oriented toward the primary task, namely, therapy. He performs this function by preventing the exclusion of contents that are being avoided or by actively bringing different exchanges into the group system. Certain contents are avoided through pushing them outside the group boundaries; for instance, outside the time limits of the sessions or out of awareness. The therapist must prevent the exclusion of those contents in order to achieve his therapeutic task. The therapist decided to increase the system's boundary permeability both within Jack's self and in the group. He accomplished it by interpreting the projection onto Jack's wife of what was going on in both systems.

By helping both Jack and the group to realize the archaic nature of the operating decider sub-subsystem (based upon childish anxieties vis-à-vis old introjects of "badmother"), the therapist opened up new possibilities. Now the *new* decider sub-subsystems could analyze their situation with a different approach. Jack began conceiving of a new, more assertive self-presentation and thought of possible interactions between himself and his wife, with himself being stronger and less fearful. Jack stayed in the group, faced the risk of a divorce, and, indeed, got divorced later on.

The therapist, with his concerned understanding, made the group boundary permeable to further analysis of the situation. The patients could now realize they were not really threatened by entering new personal relationships within the group or by planning to change. Several

of the group norms which therapists promote at the
beginning of the life of the group, and most of their
comments later on, are geared to preventing the exclusion
of contents being avoided.

DISCUSSION AND SUMMARY

What does general systems theory add to group psychotherapy, beyond what may appear as the mere translation of well-known terms into the new words? Skeptical
critics might say that it only adds a new and complicated
terminology.

The same question could be rephrased specifically
around the clinical vignette presented here. Was the
"boundary" concept really necessary in order to focus on
that clinical problem? Would it not have been enough to
use projection and introjection to understand such a
situation? What, if anything, did the boundary concept
add?

General systems theory is a method of analysis and
description of phenomena. It is like a "checklist" of the
essential variables, with a description of their reciprocal
influence within a totality. General systems theory makes it
possible to operate with multiple factors or variables and
with the complexity of their interrelationships in a way
which is probably not offered by any other method of
analysis. The understanding of the clinical problem presented is enriched by the systems' emphasis on how
boundaries are constantly crossed, both from inside and
outside the system, in an intense, dynamic, holistic interaction. General systems theory added a clearer understanding of how group and self boundaries are extended
beyond the apparent ones of time and space through
projection and introjection. The description of a transfer-

ence toward an outgroup is a generalizable idea which seems to come naturally from the systems approach.

The systems analysis clarified that Jack was a component of two systems: the therapy group and his marital couple. He was at the boundary between both systems, with a part of himself in each one. He tried to control those boundaries so that he and the group could expel some unacceptable contents, dumping them onto his wife.

The group decider "old" sub-subsystem—under the influence of paranoid anxieties—was closing its boundaries so that the expulsion of such "bad" contents could be made definitive.

The therapist acted as a "new" and higher decider sub-subsystem, making the group boundaries permeable to the "recycling" of such contents by dealing with them as a new input rather than a finalized output. A vicious cycle was thus overcome and a "virtuous" cycle begun.

But the systems viewpoint needs to be supplemented with other more specific perspectives because it is too abstract. Only a skeleton, it needs to be filled with specific descriptions of the concrete subject matter that is being studied. Therefore, in order to apply general systems to group analytic psychotherapy, we have to fill the general schemata with specific theories, such as the psychoanalytic views on object relations and groups.

What is the object relations' contribution to an understanding of group psychotherapeutic phenomena? Description of the so-called psychotic anxieties focuses on conflicts with aggression, perceived as a threat to the self (as in the schizoparanoid anxiety) or to the loved object (as in the depressive anxiety). Object relations emphasize the primitive defenses, mainly introjection and projection with the resulting identifications. The importance of identification in groups was emphasized early by psychoanalysts as a distinctive psychological characteristic of groups.

The object relations' viewpoint presents a theory of psychotherapeutic improvement emphasizing the need to overcome guilt through repairing the damaged love object in order to develop the capacity for concern. Such capacity requires the integration of love and hate, and allows the active ego-person to exercise its responsibility in dealing with its objects.

The emphasis on an active ego-person responsible for the objects' well-being along with achieving its own full development is a point of coincidence between general systems and object-relations theories.

Many human beings are only half alive. They move toward the grave like a shattered fragment of unfulfilled existence. As Thornton Wilder wrote in *The Bridge of San Luis Rey:* "There is the land of the living and the land of the dead and the bridge is love, the only survival, the only meaning."

4

THE "BAD MOTHER" GROUP

RAMON GANZARAIN, M.D.

The group becomes a maternal object for its members. Most descriptions of groups' maternal qualities emphasize the "good mother" functions (Scheidlinger, 1974; Hearst, 1981), but the "bad mother" group features and not fully discussed or clinically applied to the practice of analytic group psychotherapy. This is a study about the "bad mother" group phenomena by focusing on the mental defenses against threatening maternal images and on the clinical contexts which often elicit anxieties related to them.

To idealize our mothers is a human need, protected by omnipotent denial and splitting. When we sometimes "see through" these defenses, we experience considerable anxiety and discomfort. Consequently, there are powerful resistances to observe and reflect on the "bad mother" images. Maternal bad aspects—sometimes derived from real limitations, psychoses, or perversions—are denied, while splitting of ideal attributes promotes popular "all-good" maternal images: as the caring "mother institutions"—church or country—or the goddesslike religious maternal images.

Likewise, we defensively use splitting and projection, denying the "bad" aspects of "our" group, projecting them far away. *Groups* use yet another *defensive* unconscious *maneuver*: to *promote confusion about "Who is bad?"* whereby the "badness" is displaced from the group, as a maternal surrogate, to either the leader, or to some scapegoated member, or sometimes to another group. There is consequently a tendency to limit the frustration with, anger at, and hatred of the "negative" group attributes, by considering them as exclusively belonging either to the leader, to an accused member, or to another group or subgroup, instead of accepting that the unpleasant qualities belong to "our group" and to every member as well.

The "bad mother" group is perceived as: (1) overdemanding—it imposes group values on the individual, "leaving no freedom to be one's self" (Bion, 1961). (2) Devouring—it threatens its member with the "loss of individuality" (Freud, 1921), taking away member's credits and possessions. (3) Lacking in reciprocity—just as mother does not need her infant in order to survive biologically, while the infant requires maternal care to survive, so can the group survive socially without any given member, while members need their reference, as group members, to define themselves. Each group member may then feel "the group can do without me." Most groups do survive after losing any one member, in spite of the fact that the group "will not be the same" without any of its members. (4) Intrusive: The group inquires with hostile curiosity about secret, private affairs, attempting to influence them and ruthlessly make them public.

Groups can promote fanaticism—the "us and them" paranoid attitude—in any ideology. As in religion or politics, "heretics" are violently condemned. There are groups that demand their members' lives, ask them to die for the group to which they belong. An extreme example of such a group's demands was the mass suicide of the Jonestown, Guyana, community, which asked its members to prove their loyalty to collective values by killing themselves. Through history, young men have been drafted to go to various wars; some perceived then their countries as overdemanding mothers expecting them to die in fights of questionable moral or political value. However, the defiance of maternal possessiveness, under those circumstances, can be experienced as very threatening, evoking retaliation fears.

LITERATURE REVIEW

The mother group concept appeared relatively late in the literature, because early psychoanalysis placed emphasis on the paternal leader, as central in group psychology (Freud, 1921). Now, "the authoritarian . . . father seems almost gone. The new tyranny is that of the mother who like the Goddess Kali presents a dual face: The source of love and life and the rival for love and life . . ." (Hearst, 1981, p. 25).

Melanie Klein (1952) wrote that "a relation to objects, primarily the mother (her breast) is present, from birth onwards." She added, "There are very few people in the infant's life, but he feels them to be a multitude of objects because they appear to him in different aspects. . . ." We can therefore understand various aspects of the parents being revived in the patients' transference during psychotherapy.

Scheidlinger described (1964) group members' identification with the group-as-a-whole representing "a wish to restore an earlier state of unconflicted well-being in the child's exclusive union with mother, to counteract the

(1964): "The group serves in loco maternis. The leader represents . . . father."

Money-Kyrle (1950) distinguished three kinds of members' unconscious perceptions of their group: (1) As "good parents"; (2) like a "good father," who becomes mother's defender; and (3) like persecutory "bad" parents (p. 326–327). For Foulkes (1964) "the group . . . frequently, possibly universally, represents the 'image of the mother,' hence the term 'matrix'" (p. 289). Grotjahn (1972) also asserted that "as a general rule, the group is a truly good and strong mother." Durkin (1964) postulated two separate group maternal transference manifestations: (1) "The group conjures up the harsh, preoedipal image reactivating the individual's fear of her" (p. 80); and (2) "the therapist, in turn, is perceived in the image of the good all-giving omnipotent mother" (p. 175).

Slater (1966) wrote: "Mother-group is perceived as . . . a source of succorance and comfort, even a refuge. At other times, this mother image is a frightening one involving primitive fantasies of being swallowed and enveloped" (p. 189).

Gibbard and Hartman (1973) asserted that group members' "affective response to the group-as-a-mother is profoundly ambivalent. The positive side of the ambivalence is the 'Utopian fantasy,' which offers some assurance that the . . . destructive aspects of the group-as-a-mother will be held in check. The essence of the Utopian fantasy is that the good can be split off from the bad, and this separation can be maintained" (p. 127).

Scheidlinger in 1974 enhanced the defensive "good" elements of the mother group concept. He briefly touched upon the "bad mother" group characteristics.

For Bar-Levav (1977): "The splitting of the transference between the therapist and the group-as-a-whole, both of whom represent different, rapidly interchanging aspects of the mother . . . proves most useful" (p. 460). He described three major fears felt by patients when dealing with "bad mother" group images: (1) of erupting rage; (2) of being swallowed or engulfed, damaged, or mutilated; and (3) of starvation and abandonment. He overemphasized anger and catharsis, while overlooking sadness and working through, missing effective reparation as a means to solve the hopelessness and the fear of abandonment.

For Hearst (1981) the group functions as good mother through: (1) life-giving (a group member becomes someone, "belongs" only within the context of the group's existence); (2) confirming (being worthy for the narcissistic group self); (3) sustaining (within the group setting); and (4) accepting (everything can be expressed in and will be received by the group).

Hearst commented that the good and the bad aspects of the mother are often in the group at one and the same time, "split between the therapists and the group" (p. 25). She compared the role of the group with that of the therapist, stating that both:

> [H]ave to be available, and bear witness as long and as often as it is required. This may seem an impossible task, a council of perfection, since one's limitations as a group analyst become obvious (particularly when holding the patient's projective identifications). Fortunately, there resides the group wisdom and strength, often when these are temporarily absent in the therapist. . . . Such is the potential of the analytic group—sensitive, respectful, accepting of genuine experience: A very good mother indeed [p. 31].

Schindler (1981) discussed Hearst's ideas, commenting that to her the group offers unconditional acceptance,

wisdom, and strength, statements that seem "too optimistic
and even questionable though desirable" (p. 133).

"BAD" MOTHER-GROUP TRANSFERENCES

The "bad mother" group images appear more clearly
when oral and sadomasochistic conflicts prevail over genital group fantasies. The needs for nurturance and approval make members more vulnerable to the group's
power to provide or to withhold what individuals need. By
contrast, when genital concerns predominate, the "bad
mother" group images are displaced into primal scene
fantasies, more or less disguised, ranging from highly
symbolical references—for instance, to variations on the
myth of the sphinx (Bion, 1961)—to concrete genital
transferential references involving the therapists.

Certain group situations typically stimulate badmother fantasies by increasing the members' emotional
needs, reinforcing their anxieties and defensiveness, or
often eliciting "flashbacks" of actual traumatic experiences. Members feel threatened, angry, resentful. Understanding such situations may help us to handle them more
effectively in psychotherapeutic terms. The "bad" mother-
group transferences activated by anxieties related to oral
sadomasochistic and genital conflicts will be systematically
reviewed.

The psychotherapeutic situation includes a process
and a setting; generally the latter is constant and the
former is variable. Although the framework or setting is
objectively established in a contract, the patients gradually
build up many subjective, unconscious fantasies related to
such setting. As the "container" of the psychotherapeutic
process, the setting is where the early mother-infant
symbiotic relationship is repeated, transferred to, and
silently lodged within the typical, usual "mutism" of the

setting, according to Bleger (1967). Hence there is a transference psychosis unnoticed and immobilized as a symbiosis within the setting's immutability. But when the framework's constants are modified, the setting becomes process, and the schizoparanoid anxieties become noticeable up front, connected with "bad mother" images, no longer kept latent underneath the symbiotic silent idealization of the setting.

Oral Conflicts

These conflicts promote fears of being "smothered" or abandoned by the group. Patients may experience being in a group as "damaging" because they feel overprotected. Since their mothers offered them "understanding and support," they had no incentive to get away from the family, into the "cold world" and stand on their own feet. These patients experience a psychotherapy group as paralyzing them because it appears to postpone indefinitely their ability to take care of themselves. They therefore perceive the group help as threatening to "spoil" them.

Therapists' absences

When the therapists miss group meetings, they are seen as unavailable or abandoning parental surrogates; the group's "badness" is then often denied or confused with the therapist's. Some members (or the group itself) are meanwhile perceived as ideally reliable and helpful. These reactions further confuse the distinction between the therapists' and the group's "badness."

1. *Unexpected absence.* I once asked my secretary to call the members of an advanced group announcing with two days' notice the cancellation of the coming session. However, Laura forgot the cancellation and showed up at the group meeting time, to find no one there. She described

her reaction as an intense confusion, "feeling completely at a loss," in almost a derealization experience. She felt dizzy and needed to make a special effort to "pull herself together" to drive back home. In the parking place, she did not recognize another group member's car in the lot. He had come to watch videotapes of their group sessions, but she could not see his car. Laura felt the group's absence as a dramatic repetition of her experience of coming home to realize that mother had abandoned her and her sister, simply leaving behind a farewell note and an empty home, probably, Laura thought, because she had offended her mother. (See chapter 10.)

During the following session, the whole group responded with anxiety and anger. After Laura remembered that my secretary had called about the cancellation, she said: "I know, doctor, that your secretary does all your work!" Upon realizing what she just said, she burst out laughing. The patients then elaborated their anger at the therapist's power to cancel group meetings. For Laura, my cancelling a session turned the entire group into a bad mother: She believed "everybody missed because of being mad" at her, since she left the previous session furious with the group. Memories of her fight with her mother, preceding her abandoning Laura, came painfully back. Laura entertained the fantasy of the absent group resentfully deciding, after her fury with them, "to teach Laura a lesson" by not showing up when she needed the group the most. Such fantasies were intertwined with painful flashbacks, reexperiencing her surprise upon realizing mother had abandoned her. Fear, pain, and anger were so intense that Laura briefly went through a dissociative state of "derealization." The condensation of paranoid fantasies and painful memories, connected past experiences with current views of revengeful, unreliable mother images, personified in the past by Laura's mother, and presently reexperienced in the way she felt treated by the group.

2. *Reactions before an announced absence.* A week before my coming absence, Rose went into an orgy of self-destructiveness. She started a fire in her stove while preparing breakfast, followed by two driving incidents (in one instance she went through a red light and shortly after, rear-ended a car ahead of her). She purposefully went into a supermarket, located a security guard, and shoplifted some merchandise under his nose, provoking him to follow her while she went by the cashier without paying. Rose reported she had recovered her gun and was keeping it under her pillow, just in case. When confronted with the inappropriateness of describing her self-destructive behavior with laughter, excitement, and plea-sure at making everyone concerned about her, Rose conceded that her self-destructive behavior was related to the therapist's upcoming absence. She was attempting to force him to stay in town to take care of her since she was "becoming insane." Likewise, Rose expected her group-mates to break the rule they had adopted about not getting together outside the group sessions to give her extra support during my absence. Other members claimed that I was not taking this patient's disturbed behavior seriously enough and that we should do something extraordinary to protect her. I interpreted the group was using her as a spokesperson to tell the group and me that we were not taking seriously the group members' distress and anxiety; that I should be more responsible and possibly stay in town, or they should agree to meet and support each other while I was gone.

This interpretation led each member to complain specifically about the lack of seriousness in response to his or her needs from the group and from me. Rose's previ-ous hypomanic, triumphant mood, while aggressively parading a string of self-destructive actions, changed then to her crying, anticipating missing the group and me, experiencing the loss of both, since we would be skipping two sessions, resulting in a ten-day break before we all saw each other again. The coming unavailability of both the group and the therapist triggered Rose's attempts to force everyone to take care of her as her way to avoid experiencing loss and depression.

When Rose's groupmates finally volunteered to "check how she was doing" during my absence, she paradoxically rejected their help. Moreover, she despised these volunteers, because they took too concretely her request for attention without realizing that she felt humiliated because she appeared overdependent and weak. The help offered seemed to cast Rose rigidly in the role of an emotionally handicapped person, unable to take care of herself. Primarily she needed, however, to prove that she was resourceful and strong. So, when soon after other group members also asked for special help, Rose criticized them for being whining, weak, and dependent. She did not want to appear as they then looked to her. Rose was not a meek, submissive, passive, crazy woman like her mother. Rose was striving to be self-sufficient and therefore rejected her groupmates' help as overprotective and crippling.

In this session, there were two contradictory, conflicting maternal images alternatively occupying the center of the group's attention: the infantile introject of the needy, fragile mother attempting to extract care for her, and the overprotective, potentially crippling, smothering mother figure, ready to take over her growing children's self-caring functions. Two contradictory "bad mother" images were then reactivated alternately in this group: the overdemanding and the smothering "bad mother" group aspects.

3. *Reactions during the therapist's absence.* These reactions

vary according to whether there is no group meeting during the therapist's absence, or whether the group meets in an alternate session or with the remaining cotherapist.

The practice of alternate sessions, or meetings with the remaining cotherapist, may provide the impression that these procedures "keep the group going, as usual." Such a view denies the possibility of the group missing the absent therapist. That tendency is compounded by the absent therapist's concurrent need, out of guilt, to also deny the importance of his or her absence. This collusion between helper and patients often leads to underexploration of the group's reactions to the therapist's absence. There is a concomitant tendency to idealize the group as "always available" to provide patients with what they need, unlike the unreliable therapists.

The arrival of new patients

The arrival of new patients can be compared to the birth of a new baby in a family, stimulating the siblings' ambivalence. Likewise, it often enhances regression out of fear of losing the mother group's attention, since the newcomer will get most of it. Some old-timers overidentify themselves with the newcomer's anxiety and tend to overprotect him or her, while others attempt to scare the newcomer, telling horror stories about the group's past. Some reassure the newcomer about how good it can be, while others discredit the group.

Old-timers also take an opportunity to evaluate the therapist's choice of newcomers and intensely approve or disapprove of it as a way of expressing their prevailing emotions toward the therapist; however, the timing chosen to add new patients is almost always not agreeable and resented because it *takes away the group's attention* from other members' more pressing needs.

Sadomasochistic Conflicts

Such reactions are based on fantasies about the group acting as a sadistic superego dictating norms, demands, and expecting specific responses. Members feel threatened, as stated above, with loss of individual identity, since they seem to be asked to become instead "standard" products as members of a particular group. What is perceived as the group's "consensus" becomes a rigid punitive law.

Patients may fear the group as an abusive mother who would brainwash them, imposing her values. For instance, George was afraid that the group would impose "Freudian values" upon him, "corrupting his Christian ethics." Being in analytic group psychotherapy could become a "brainwash" for him. He gradually discovered that he distorted group comments. He "whipped himself" with sadistic distortions of what the group "told" him. He realized he had been projecting his demanding attitude about himself, assuming the group would raise exaggerated demands of compliance with "Freudian values."

Maria shared with George the mistrust of their group. She was a battered wife who managed to choose boyfriends who physically abused her. She had a knack of provoking people to attack her; therefore, she also became the group's scapegoat. She collected injustices and later on tried to induce guilt and sympathy for her suffering. She slowly realized that she had been using this same pattern with her parents, to extract their love, especially to get her mother's attention. Mother was a professional woman who was emotionally unavailable to Maria. In order to get mother's attention Maria had to parade her sufferings; so she devoted herself to collecting miseries. She engaged in all sorts of self-destructive behaviors: abusing drugs, alcohol, dropping out of school, belonging to vicious gangs, choosing men she could provoke to hurt her seriously. After finally getting a divorce, she wore the "battered wife" label. She then went back to her parents' home. But they "forced" her to get some psychiatric treatment as a precondition to accepting her back home. The group became for Maria her parents' ally or an instrument to punish her. She tried to establish a tug-of-war, questioning "the group's values," as if they were "too straight," overrestrictive, and narrowminded. Maria, in her maternal transference to the group, engaged in defiant acting-out behavior repeating the same struggles she had had at home.

Group members also fear having to "confess" their shadowy, guilty deeds or fantasies and dread facing "punishment" from the group, after exposing themselves to being criticized or laughed at by groupmates. Some expressions of internalized sadistic superego struggles are sometimes dramatized in dreams. For instance, a group patient who suffered from confused sexual identity, dreamt that she was on trial in an American Indian court, where the juror read the final verdict stating "that all the half-breed defendants should be killed." Her associations were to herself as a sexual "half-breed" who would be condemned to death by her psychotherapy group not accepting her as a member.

The projection of a sadistic internalized maternal superego to the group as a whole, to the therapists, or other group members provides opportunities for mutative therapeutic exchanges, whereby the harshness of the superego can be modified. New definitions of the self— vis-à-vis internalized or projected bad mothers—become possible then, while the self learns and practices how to stand up to the internalized, overcritical, bad mother–like superego. These proactive movements on the part of the patients' selves produce more significant therapeutic outcomes than "supportive" comments—from therapists or groupmates.

A year-and-a-half after the beginning of a group that met twice a week for seventy-five minutes, Jill changed, during a session, from starting to complain that she was getting no support or positive feedback from the group, to dismissing, later on, her submissive need to comply with, and to placate, a demanding internalized mother. After expecting more positive feedback from the group, Jill slowly developed a conviction: "There is something good about me," so that she did not need as much support from the group as she had before. She was then able to express her wish to "get rid of mother." Jill went through an "exorcism" of the "bad mother." She first realized that she could be "vicious and demeaning like my mother." Later on, she became aware that she put herself "under excessive demands," concluding: "I am as sadistic as my mother and I don't want to be like that! There are other aspects of myself which are loving, caring, loose, tolerant!"

In the process of realizing her identification with her sadistic mother, Jill transiently transferred to the group itself her "bad mother" images, fighting then against the group's alleged sadism. Jill stood up and fought its over-demandingness, while redefining her real self beyond her imprisonment by "bad mother" images. Jack concurred with her, redefining their group's purpose as a "growth group, not a support group." He had overcome both his fears of a domineering mother and a similar wife, and decided to get a divorce. He had chronic difficulties as the family's younger child. Most of his many siblings had left home during his growing years. Only his two-year older brother was available, but he was sent to a home for retarded children. Daniel did not fully realize, then, the problems of mental retardation and had instead believed that his brother was "kicked out" because of being "bad."

Therefore, he grew up in fear that he would be the next to be punished, were he not to please mother. (See chapter 3.)

The whole group celebrated their "good riddance" of "bad" mother. Each member commented on her or his mother's attempts to control them, declaring they "would no longer put up with such hostility." Furthermore, they realized their own participation in such sadomasochistic interactions by eagerly depending upon their mothers for support and reassurance; they planned to change their stance.

Sexual Conflicts

When a cotherapist couple announced that both would be absent, the group members responded with expressions of unconscious primal scene fantasies ranging from curiosity about whether they would be together, to wondering what they would be doing, to entertaining regressive fantasies assuming both would attend an office party and the members would hear the therapists' loud drunken voices, while they "had fun." The patients soon shifted to express their sensitivity about the differences between therapists and members, contrasting professional individuals with blue-collar, relatively less educated persons, thus displaying their envy and low self-images. They soon moved to criticizing authorities' abuses of power, while the common individual has to put up with them. When both therapists returned, the members tried to "turn the tables," attempting to stimulate the therapists' curiosity about alleged group secrets. "Bad mother" images did not appear then as focused on the group-as-an-entity, but centered instead on the cotherapist couple, perceived as parents in intercourse and as members of an upper class.

After my female cotherapist was absent for two consecutive sessions from a male group of intrafamilial sex offenders, the meeting started with a member saying: "Finally I discovered why Sue has been out of town. She has been gone some time, trying to keep a secret, but I got some information about why she was gone." The patient was unaware of any coincidence with the female therapist's recent "secret" absence. He was concretely referring to a letter he received stating that "Sue had been out of town hiding a pregnancy and delivering a baby." He gave this letter to the female therapist as if expecting her response. When we commented on the group's curiosity regarding the female therapist's absence, the group shifted to talk about women's privileges at work, "simply because they are women." Women had gone up the ladder of their companies' hierarchies, they said, using sex to achieve their success. Intense anger at women's alleged privileges became paramount: A woman can ruin a man's life by accusing him of law-breaking sexual actions she provoked! Women at work get easily promoted! The "bad mother" images were then centered on the negative transference to the female group therapist.

Later on, they explored their unconscious rivalry with an envy of mother's sex-related power. The group of male intrafamilial sex offenders examined their "phallic-mother" transferences, exploring the relationship between these transferences and their own degraded self-images as overdependent, powerless "wimps." Inverted oedipal rivalry and confusion of gender identity became psychotherapeutic topics, also related to "bad mother" group images as cold, unavailable, and powerful.

The group itself can represent the parental couple in sadistic intercourse by excluding each member from the group's secrets, which simultaneously arouse the members' curiosity, like the sphinx (Bion, 1961). Such raw primal scene fantasies are anxiously defended against because they are experienced as threatening the group's destruction. They call therefore for powerful defenses against them. The destructiveness of love's sadistic components needs then to be denied by proclaiming the alleged omnipotence of Eros, thus creating an emotional atmosphere of hope—characteristic of the "pairing" basic assumption—regarding the future survival of the group. In the meantime, the "bad mother" group's sexual images are kept in the distant background, replaced by fantasies about ideally good effects to be expected within the group from the love between members of a couple. Concrete images expressing sexually/sadistic-related transference to the group-as-a-whole do not appear then at the center of the group's stage; they rather exit silently.

I elaborated this point in chapter 2, where I described a session with two topics: "Love hurts" (illustrated by a member's vaginismus) and "intimacy makes you vulnerable," which triggered fears that closeness could cause the disintegration of the group because of damaging effects. Members defensively develop then an atmosphere of pseudointimacy by talking about sex and exploring implicitly possible heterosexual couples within the group.

DISCUSSION

A few notes on idealization are called for. Idealization is a defense against persecutory anxiety, a necessary way out of the schizoparanoid position. Idealization makes it possible to develop the initial core of the good internal object. Idealization brings up a mastery over envy, since, without overcoming envy, idealization would not last. Finally, because of all the above reasons, idealization does not always have to be erased with interpretations.

A clear concept on idealization may prevent taking wrong, extreme positions in dealing with it, such as emphasizing the need to allow patients to unfold their idealizing transference up to the point where such transferences may overdevelop, forming a block to further therapeutic progress. Stone and Gustafson (1982) wrote on that risk and made the important distinction between truly cohesive groups and others in which overidealization leads to a group without any real healthy separateness among the members or within each member.

An opposite, extreme view on idealization could be described as advocating "whenever you find idealization, wipe it out," assuming that is the way to deal with the underlying persecutory anxiety.

There is a middle-of-the-road approach between those two extremes. It considers the *timing* in interpreting idealization. There is an initial stage, during which idealization needs to be developed as a defense, without having its growth disturbed; but in a later stage it is necessary to deal with the hostility hidden beneath idealization.

Exploring the "bad mother" group images can prevent the stereotyping of an idealized "good mother" group, while the therapists or others are rigidly cast in "bad" roles. The mother group functions, good and bad, should become instead interchangeable in psychotherapy groups, fluctuating within the group as an entity, the therapists, one member or another, or another group. Achieving this fluidity of roles provides varied opportunities for the patients to meet and to solve their individuation difficulties. The group can be especially suited to contain and to receive projective identifications from its members, for holding, modifying, and eventually returning them to the projectors, helping their selves to blossom and to expand (Ogden, 1979). The patients often experience for the first time, while in group psychotherapy, these "container," essential maternal functions, since their dysfunctional mothers were unable to provide them with such interactions while the patients were growing up (Bion, 1964).

When the group as an entity is cast in the role of a "bad mother," therapists also feel relatively free to perform supportive, "good" maternal functions, responding more directly to patients' needs. Since focusing the anger and frustration on the group-as-a-whole "takes care" of the negative maternal transference, the therapist can interact with the patients, in other more caring ways, providing "good and bad maternal experiences within the group." When the therapists are cast instead in the "bad mother" role, their behavior is seen as a repetition of the really depriving maternal attitudes, whereby mothers demanded—for the child to survive—that their emotional needs be supplied by their child. Children of these mothers were used as selfobjects, with the children experiencing a resulting self-estrangement (Miller, 1981). Family therapists describe in this regard the special role of the active father as the "helping third," whose family role is to reclaim the mother and make the husband/wife relationship a primary one, thus setting the children free for their own separation-individuation (Skynner, 1976). Cotherapists of different gender widen the range of transferential targets, lending themselves to a replay of these families' struggles and solutions. The scapegoated member becomes the recipient of the group's "badness." It is possible to interpret the dumping on this particular person, of all groupmates' "badness," including the role of an infantile introject of the needy, fragile mother, now being displaced to this particular member. Sometimes more subtle expressions of scapegoating can be disguised as overprotection of a fragile, weak individual. For instance, groupmates apparently respond to minority members with lenient, superficial overprotection, while they really are contemptuous and jealous of minority members, who seem "too easily forgiven and protected from criticism."

From a psychological viewpoint the group is like a

dream (Anzieu, 1966) insofar as both group and dream images are submitted to the primary process functions of condensation, displacement, and symbolization. The "bad mother" group images can therefore have multideter-mined confusing meanings, because of undergoing dis-guising condensations and far-fetched displacements, across the several group transferential targets. What uni-fies those confusing, multiple, "bad mother" group images is a psychoticlike sadomasochistic style of relations be-tween the self and the objects. Following the complex metamorphoses of the "bad mother" group images be-comes important when exploring negative transference in group psychotherapy, in order to overcome the schizo-paranoid anxieties and defenses, searching to help the patients to achieve the depressive position.

CONCLUSION

The "bad mother" group images can become a hidden secret shelter where patients' hostility takes refuge and is likely to remain unnoticed and therefore unexplored. The existence of such a pocket of resistance may considerably limit the possible therapeutic results, since anger—a cen-tral psychopathological core—can stay unmodified. How to deal with negative transference is often considered the main challenge in psychotherapy. In the "bad mother" group, when and if absorbing a significant split, hidden hostility can undermine and boycott this basic psychother-apeutic work. The group-as-a-whole, cast in the "bad mother" group role, often becomes the rigidly fixed, unconscious target of the negative transference.

The mature integration of good and bad aspects of objects and of self-representations should, by contrast, ideally reveal the different nuances of ambivalence, in-cluding the exploration of anger at the group-as-a-whole.

Otherwise, the complete spectrum of various feelings undergoes splitting, promoting the idealization of the "good mother" group, while members may go on fighting their internal persecutory superegos through placating them with a false self.

Group psychotherapy outcome research is often based on the patients' evaluation of how helpful they found the group (Malan, Balfour, Hood, and Shooter, 1976). Unexplored negative transference toward the "bad mother" group can be mobilized when answering such evaluatory questions, casting serious doubts on the objectivity of results obtained by such methods. Former group patients' evaluation of group psychotherapy effectiveness can be severely biased by the relatively unexplored negative transference toward the "bad mother" group. The possibility that the group had unconsciously been maligned should be kept in mind. A "vilification" process—the opposite of idealization—may have silently taken place.

5

PSYCHOTICLIKE ANXIETIES AND PRIMITIVE DEFENSES IN GROUP ANALYTIC PSYCHOTHERAPY

RAMON GANZARAIN, M.D.

Clusters of psychoticlike anxieties were inferred by Melanie Klein as part of normal children's emotional development (Segal, 1973). She labeled them "schizoparanoid" and "depressive" positions. Defenses such as introjection, projection, denial, splitting, and projective identification were seen as being useful against these primitive anxieties.

Groups tend to regress to those early levels of mental functioning. Bion's "basic assumptions" (of dependency, of fight-flight, and of pairing) are group defenses against such psychotic anxieties (Bion, 1948–1951). His ideas on groups initially were only descriptive (Rioch, 1970). Later on he attempted to understand group psychology dynamically in terms of Kleinian psychotic anxieties (Bion, 1961;

This chapter was first published in *Issues in Ego Psychology* 1980, 3(2): 42–48, and it is reprinted with permission.

Grinberg, Sor, and Tabak de Bianchedi, 1975; Meltzer, 1978). He wrote: "Groups . . . in my view . . . approximate to the patterns of psychotic behavior. . . . Splitting and projective mechanisms—mainly projective identification—are typical psychotic defenses observable in groups" (1961, p.181).

Bion himself did not fully elaborate his attempts to develop this approach systematically (Parloff, 1968, p. 525). A lack of familiarity with Kleinian concepts makes it difficult to grasp the depth, richness, and relevance of these concepts to group analytic psychotherapy (Parloff, 1968, p. 513).

This chapter is an attempt to make these formulations, which were developed by the British School of Psychoanalysis, better known and easier to apply in our daily clinical practice of group psychotherapy. I will illustrate these concepts with clinical observations of therapy groups, and I will draw some general concepts based on these observations.

When I taught psychiatry at the University of Chile, the medical students were offered the option of being psychotherapy patients in groups formed exclusively by them. I was the therapist of one of those groups. I had to miss one of their weekly sessions. We had agreed that they would meet without me. They met in my absence, but with the presence, as at every session, of the observer-recorder.

When I returned to the group's next session, some changes were immediately apparent. None of the students, for instance, helped me to bring the extra chairs needed so there were seats for everyone, in clear contrast to their previous politeness, when several had volunteered upon entering the room to bring extra chairs. I had to bring the extra chairs. When I arrived at the office, I found my "official seat" occupied. I had difficulty finding a place for the last chair, my chair. Since there was simply no space left to put my chair on the floor, most of the students had to move to make room for me. I commented that they obviously did not want me back, as suggested by their nonverbal behavior, and I speculated that perhaps they had felt I abandoned them the previous week.

The student occupying my "official seat" inquired whether the observer-recorder had briefed me on the excellent session they had in my absence. There was a wish to please with their good work, hoping to be praised. I told them the recorder had already informed me about the good preceding session. But, I added, I could also hear the message: "We don't need you to have a good session." When I stated they were saying they did not need me, there was a tense silence. The student occupying my "official seat" pointed out after a while, "You see, this is what happens when you are present. Your comments produce these silences, and we don't feel at ease." I responded, "Maybe you were irritated by my absence, and needed to prove that you can have an excellent session without the therapist. Today, you felt I might have heard the information on your good previous session as if you had attacked me. You have also expressed your fear of me today by not letting me come back into the room, or allowing me to occupy my 'official seat.'"

Tense, even more prolonged silence followed my comment. It was again broken by statements like "You see what you're doing. We cannot have a good session with you." I responded, "You're hearing what I say as if I were criticizing you, taking revenge against you, or even spoiling your ability to have a good session now."

By then, the student occupying my "official seat" started covering his eyes with his right hand, and looking, again and again, outside the room, through a nearby window. He repeated these movements several times. He then said, "You keep repeating the same words in a monotonous voice, I thought you were trying to hypnotize me with such repetitions, and with your glances. I started to feel sleepy, as if I were about to fall into a hypnotic trance. I felt also an intense headache, which you intended to induce in me. I was scared and needed to protect myself from your glances, by looking outside through the window and covering my eyes." Intense anxiety and a certain surprise accompanied these comments.

Another student immediately said, "I felt something similar. I was convinced you wanted to cause the intense stomachache I am now having."

I elaborated on their conviction that I wanted to cause them pain; to attack their leader's head and make all of them fearful of me, as if I were returning their fantasied assaults against me. I reflected that the two who felt themselves to be targets of my assumed revenge were precisely the two who had led the group in my absence, and that one of them was sitting in my "official seat."

The group members looked at each other in surprise, having shared what was by then an intense emotional experience, now mixed with relief derived from an understanding of what had been going on. Time was up, we adjourned in the midst of relieved laughter. I heard several comments of amazement at what we had just experienced.

Two members experienced a paranoidlike "delusion of influence." More remarkable was how such delusional belief was quickly dismissed by interpreting its unconscious meaning, the underlying psychoticlike, paranoid anxieties. No psychotic behavior, thoughts, or feelings remained. They had evaporated after the emotionally shared understanding. None of these students was clinically psychotic before or after the session.

This group of medical students, particularly two of them, had a transient delusion of influence. They really believed I was intentionally causing them pain through hypnotic techniques, as if I were retaliating against them. They behaved somehow as Macbeth did, imagining too vividly the return of the king he had murdered. The intensity of their anxiety was considerable, especially in its nonverbal expressions: glances, hands covering eyes, avoidance of eye contact, tense prolonged silences, squirming in the chairs, and so on.

The hostile envious attacks against me, when the group felt abandoned, triggered their omnipotent triumph over me. These envious attacks led them to fear my return, trying to avoid it by leaving me out. The fear of my retaliation led them to feel criticized by me, as if I were not letting them work efficiently, and later on, as if I were intentionally causing them pain.

The next meeting allowed the group to reflect and to gain some deeper understanding of the previous week's experiences. The members realized how unconscious anger at feeling abandoned and taking over the functions of the therapist had made them very anxious. Someone commented that in order to diminish their intense anxiety, the leadership functions had to be carried on by two of the students, instead of just one; as if their mutual support in assuming the leadership function had partially protected them against unconscious fear and guilt.

In my absence they had indeed experienced a feeling of accomplishment, of triumph. They managed then not to feel the loss of the therapist, but felt instead, rather omnipotently, that they could have a better session without him. They were thus denying missing the therapist, denying depending upon him, and denying any anger against him. There was a triumphant feeling of hope that now they were able to become a really productive group. Their capacity to care for each other was dramatized by two of the members assuming the role of cotherapists. The session without the therapists went by, then, with a feeling of exhilaration, excitation, and triumphant achievement.

The session without the therapist stirred up hypomanic denial of feelings of being abandoned by him. The group defensively resorted to appointing a pair of members to successfully replace the therapist. Anger at having been postponed was also denied; what prevailed, instead, was a feeling of loving mutual understanding, which enhanced the conviction that they were breaking new ground. There could be hope then for progressively better and better group meetings. The group had resorted to the basic assumption of pairing, as described by Bion, to protect themselves from experiencing depression; they were instead feeling somehow hypomanic.

During the session after my return, the group was experiencing a paranoid anxiety; they were defending themselves mainly by flying away; they tried only fleetingly to fight the therapist; they attributed to the therapist the anger denied by the members. The group then resorted to casting the therapist in the role of an enemy, who should be either fought or avoided.

My return forced the group to be confronted with their unconscious guilt feelings for having taken over my role as therapist and having also experienced a triumph over me. Frequently, in the middle of hypomanic states, if the avoided guilt is brought out into the open, the individuals using manic defenses will feel persecuted.

Groups use the "hypomanic high" to feel good about themselves. They can then cultivate hope, based on the effect of omnipotent love. Magic pseudoreparation will take place, making up for previous loss or harm, without requiring the individual's sustained and prolonged efforts to amend his wrongdoings. Psychic pain is avoided. There seems to be no basis for anxious, persecutory guilt feelings, since individual responsibilities are denied. Reparation of the harm, which is fantasied as having been done, is entrusted to some external future change, which will be the magic product of love operating miracles. Such attitudes and feelings are characteristic of the "pairing basic assumption."

Although pairing refers frequently to a heterosexual couple, the sexual nature of the couple's link is not essential to the pairing's basic assumption. Pairing group assumptions can also be asexual, such as between an ideology and the group members advocating it; an emotional atmosphere of hope is thus also created.

Groups use the paranoid-schizoid phenomenon as a defense against depression, just as psychotic patients do. Guilt and sadness are then absent, since they are replaced by fights or withdrawal, that is to say, the fight-flight phenomena.

Let me now turn to clinical material from another group. Nine students from the University of Chile, about to graduate, had been functioning for a year as a psychotherapeutic group, meeting once a week in my private office. Eight (three women and five men, four married and four single) were resuming their regular meetings after a summer break; previously they had met for forty-two sessions. One member, Joe, had already graduated from the group, as well as from the University, and had taken a job and entered private practice in another city. The group was facing three problems: (1) the loss of Joe, a very active and popular member; (2) the possibility of bringing in a new member; and (3) a annual raise in their fees on account of severe inflation.

I will focus on the participation of Peter in the group. He suffered from asthma and neurotic depression. Peter missed Joe and described how Joe had been very important for him. He said, "I have difficulties in expressing my hostility and I identified myself with Joe. He spoke for me." Peter added that, through identifying himself with Joe, he was also getting the therapist's attention and affection. He noted that this was a pattern for him from childhood when he would bring home classmates who were nice fellows as a way of getting in better contact with his father. "Dad behaved very pleasantly when I brought these bright visitors," he said.

Peter was the spokesman for the group's emotional reaction to the loss of one of its most popular members. Sensing a mood of depression, the therapist helped them link the loss of their most popular member with the fear of the possible end of the group's existence.

Although the group had ambivalent relationships with Joe, they denied their hostility toward him and idealized him. Another member talked about a situation in which he felt guilty because he had taken over somebody else's job. While other members reassured him, the therapist interpreted that they felt guilty about the possibility or wish of taking over Joe's function within the group, because it would be like making him disappear from the group and stealing his role. Other group members could now establish a parallel with their own wish to take over the therapist's function.

While they were experiencing their greed to "incorporate" or take over somebody else's role, they began perceiving the therapist as greedy for money; they were angry at him because of his policy of raising the fees following the rate of inflation. The group expressed several metaphors in oral sadistic terms, such as being devoured, exploited, emptied by this greedy therapist, who was about to deprive them of many "goodies" by raising their fees. At this point the therapist interpreted the projective meaning of this perception of him; that is, they were avoiding acknowledging that they themselves were greedy, wanting to take over Joe's and the therapist's roles in the group.

In the following session two members identified themselves with Joe in a different way by considering the possibility of dropping out of the group. In response, other members acknowledged that they had felt abandoned by the doctor during his recent vacation. Peter pointed out that the group was important for him, but he had realized that both he as well as the others tended to deny the group's importance and to derogate it by resorting to humor. Furthermore, they devalued the group as a way of defending themselves against feeling sad or deprived because they had missed each other or the therapist while he was on vacation. When they started to acknowledge that they missed each other there was very active interchange of cigarettes among the members. All of them started to smoke simultaneously. While they were grabbing cigarettes from each other, one of them commented sarcastically, "You see we don't need each other, we don't need love from the other members."

Two group members identified themselves with Joe by deciding to start their private practice together as Joe had done. They presented their decision within a month after the group had resumed its sessions in the early fall. Starting their private practice was a result of allaying some of their guilt for charging for their professional services.

Peter then took a leading role within the group and acted as a therapist by focusing the group's attention on Paul's behavior, mainly his inhibition. Paul tried to relate his inhibition to his family's low socioeconomic background; he elaborated that when he started attending the University he had only one suit, one overcoat, one pair of shoes, and so forth. Paul reminded the group that he was born after his eldest brother had died, and that he was named after him. There was a family myth about how handsome and clever the eldest brother was. The therapist commented that Paul must have felt as if he were a thief, who had stolen his brother's identity, occupying a situation where he did not belong. Peter commented on Paul's excessive worrying about the amount of attention he was taking from the group and the amount of time that was being devoted to him. Other members reminded Paul that, when he had had an opportunity for a promotion at work (because of the departure of his chief, whose job he took) Paul had felt very uncomfortable. Paul elaborated on his constant feeling of having displaced someone.

I would like to emphasize how Peter was leading the group in accomplishing its therapeutic task with Paul: helping him to realize the inappropriateness of his under-estimating himself and relating his inhibition to his guilt about his greediness. Guilt was making Paul feel responsible for stealing the central role in the group. In the same way, he felt he had stolen his previous chief's job and his eldest brother's identity. While helping Paul to master his inhibition, Peter himself was overcoming the same conflict through his activity in the group. Peter was now confident enough to take the therapist's functions within the group, as well as to occupy Joe's previous role.

After the next session, Paul came remarkably better dressed; in addition, he told the group that after he had thought over the previous session, he realized how he devalued himself by his constant comparison with the idealized image of his dead brother. He also reported that he had had a series of nightmares. In all of them the central character was a ten-year-old child, who was in reality his nephew, "the child of the family." While taking care of that child, the boy's life was suddenly in danger from an earthquake. Paul was unable to run, to inform someone about the danger the child was in, or to rescue him. Ever since this dream, he had been scared and anxious.

Coming back to the present, he suddenly wondered why he had again been doing most of the talking. He apologized, saying that he needed it, that he did not want to lose the group's attention. He related his family's current pampering of his nephew to the way he assumed they might have treated his eldest brother. Paul emphasized that his fear, in the nightmare, was not that something might happen to him; his main concern was how to protect the child.

Several members praised Peter for his job as therapist. Peter responded immediately that he shared this problem with Paul, also tending to express his hostility in an indirect way.

I shall now deal with the question: How can psychoticlike anxieties be conducive to analytic work?

First let me clarify the meaning of the term *psychoticlike*. It underlines certain similarities between psychosis and certain anxieties in the style of dealing with objects and in the prevailing defense mechanisms used; that is, guilt about destroying a loved object and introjection of the lost object are "melancholiclike."

In the clinical material presented, there were several instances of working through a melancholiclike anxiety. Guilt centered around losing a loved object through fantasies of greedily "devouring" and "incorporating" that object's role. These guilt feelings were mainly elaborated around Joe's departure from the group and the wish expressed by several other members to take over Joe's role and function within the group. Peter and Paul reacted in that way to Joe's departure. Patients expressed guilt, too, about taking over the therapist's role. Several members verbalized their concerns about having taken over somebody else's role, both in their working situations or in their families. The working through of these guilts around fantasies of having "devoured" the role and functions of a loved object led the group members to work through some of the depressive anxieties connected with previously experienced mourning processes.

The melancholiclike guilt around greediness—an expression of oral sadism—was experienced by Paul around getting the group's attention which he described as "eating up all the group's time," while talking about his relationship with his dead brother. Other members were able to examine their guilt at asking for love and attention, both in the group and in their out-of-the-group lives.

There were several primitive, psychoticlike defense mechanisms mobilized against these depressive or melancholic anxieties. Greed and hostility were split and projected as a defense against guilt. Manic defenses were also operating: Dependence and guilt were denied, therapy was humorously devalued, some considered dropping out, implying they didn't need or value the group. Through dealing with these defenses the patients were able to experience guilt and integrate their previously split and projected parts. They moved from intrapsychic fragmentation to personal integration. This integration also brought out increased group cohesiveness: They worked harder to achieve their therapeutic tasks.

The patients tolerated their guilt over their oral sadistic impulses, accepting their responsibility for their hostile fantasies without disowning them through projection. Objects became, therefore, separate, differentiated individuals, and not mere containers of split parts.

The patients' view of reality was also modified. They developed a sense of psychic reality by acknowledging both dependence and ambivalence toward their objects. They modified their belief in the omnipotence of destructive and loving impulses. They discovered and practiced actual ways of affecting external reality through hard-working reparation, accompanied by means of effective therapeutic interchanges.

I have summarized the working through of the depressive anxieties in one group. Kleinian analysts value this working through as a crucial stage, both in group and individual analytic psychotherapy. This group was dealing with their depressive anxieties by resorting to a dependent basic assumption, presenting first Peter's claims for help and later on Paul's. When these two patients were at the center of the group's attention, however, they did not try to induce guilt in the other group members by threatening to kill themselves or to become completely disorganized. In other words, they did not behave as casualties of the group experience, as some group members present themselves in "laboratories" or "conferences" on groups. This group was expressing the dependency basic assumption to cope with their depressive anxieties by putting it at the service of the work group; that is to say, the need to be helped moved these members to understand themselves better, thus performing the primary therapeutic task of the group.

The dependency basic assumptions form a cluster of defenses against guilt induced by greed. Greed is an expression of oral sadism. It is manifested in group by behaviors which mean "we want more." Groups try to get what they want from the therapist by force through manipulative, exploitative maneuvers.

Group members avoid any awareness of their demanding hostility by defensively projecting their dependent infant self. Sometimes they project it onto the therapist, as in the dual or reciprocal of the dependency basic assumption (Bion). The roles are reversed then, and the therapist is perceived as the greedy one, who wants to be fed. Sometimes a group member is pushed into becoming a "psychiatric casualty" who could then try to force the therapist to give him extraordinary, special attention, while the other members get some vicarious gratification too. Sometimes therapeutic groups can display appropriate dependency, leading to realistically assimilating the help offered, and integrating it to foster the members' further emotional growth.

The dependency basic assumptions idealize the therapist as a source of everlasting omnipotent nurturance, transforming him into some kind of God. However, human nature's "thirst for the infinite will not be satisfied even with God's own richness," as St. Augustine confessed.

Bion also speculated about interactions between the basic assumptions group and the work group. In order for the work group to be effective it has to draw energy from the basic assumption that is active at that moment. However, the two modalities of group functioning may sometimes create a conflict by trying to move in opposite directions. A well-known example, where a predominant basic assumption prevents the work group from doing its task, occurs in psychiatric hospitals. When a patient perceives his relationship with the hospital as a fighting one, as if the staff members were his enemies forcing him to stay against his will, he fights back and does not develop the dependent attitude appropriate and necessary for a patient to receive help.

The work group uses verbal communications, while the basic assumption one uses, above all, nonverbal communications. Bion (1961) described it as follows: Frequently communications in the groups are nonverbal "in terms of short interjections, long silences, sighs of boredom, moments of discomfort, changes in the seating arrangement. This state of affairs in a group deserves close attention" (p. 185).

The basic assumptions group functions mainly in the realm of fantasy. Kleinian psychoanalysts working with psychotics and children have acknowledged, and systematically described, how human beings live in two coexisting worlds—the internal world of fantasy and the external one of objective reality. The whole set of images of our internalized objects, living in our fantasy world, forms an internal society within each individual, which he is constantly relating to and interacting with.

SUMMARY

I have presented clinical examples of psychotherapeutic groups where Bion's "basic assumptions" (of fight-flight, pairing, and dependency) were observable as group defenses against psychotic anxieties. Paranoid, hypomanic, and depressive anxieties were observable in the material presented.

How the two modalities of group functioning, basic assumptions and work group, relate to each other was also briefly explored.

SECTION II

TECHNIQUE: THE GROUP AS A TOOL

INTRODUCTION

. . . "If we were wise,
we would devise
ways to utilize
this mutual advice:
Attempting with kindness
to destroy
the great blindness
where each person
is by oneself."[1]

In general, patients in psychotherapy initially bring their problems and symptoms to their sessions often without paying any major attention to their interactions with significant others, the therapists, or their groupmates. Later on, when psychotherapy becomes effective, they are interested instead in their relationships, particularly in

---

[1] . . . si l'on
   etait sage
Ces avis mutuel seraient mis
   en usage
On detruirait par là, traitant de
   bonne foi,
Le grand aveuglement où chacun
   est pour soi.
From-Molière's *Le Misanthrope*, Act III, Scene 4, lines 965–968. In: *Molière-Théâtre Choisi*, ed. Ch.-m. Des Granges. Paris: Librairie Hatier, 1937, p. 390.

their group interactions (Garland, 1982). The focus on problems or symptoms is gradually replaced then by an orientation toward the examination of relationships.

Object relations theory is centered on relationships, mainly on those within our minds, those occurring in our internal world, in the realm of fantasy or psychic reality. Both spheres of interactions, the internal and the external, influence each other, but the dominant one is the internal, mental world. The terminology of object relations theory appears to be the "natural language" to communicate the patients' feelings, anxieties, and fantasies about their internalized relationships. Thus, the object relations concepts opened up to psychotherapeutic exploration the whole range of psychopathological expressions of the psychotic anxieties, including those of clinically nonpsychotic persons.

The mental representations of external objects are not their "real" picture or exact copy because affects and fantasies distort their images through subjectively modifying the person's attention, perception, and memory. Consequently, unrealistic assumptions and expectations about others are formed on the basis of such distortions. Psychotherapy aims at modifying the dramatic actions taking place on the stage of our minds by providing opportunities to change those internal images into more realistic and, one hopes, less threatening ones. Experiences in the context of the psychotherapeutic interactions provide the favorable conditions to re-negotiate the relationships between the self and the internal objects whenever deeply rooted assumptions or expectations are not corroborated or met by the therapists' or the groupmates' behavior. When their actual interactions are different from the patient's internal predictions and assumptions, contradicting them, that patient will review and gradually modify the views about him- or herself and others. When the patient's past is not automatically repeated in the person's current psychotherapeutic relationships, such a patient will naturally examine the current group interactions in order to change the up-to-then wrong and narrow views of what to expect from the others in relation to the self. When such reflections are taking place, the group has become a therapeutically effective tool, through analyzing this individual's transference (to the therapists, the groupmates, and the group-as-a-whole) in the here-and-now; the remote or "past" unconscious has become the "present" unconscious (Sandler and Sandler, 1984).

These clinical notes on technique include chapter 6 on countertransference, emphasizing how the therapist's affective responses can be put to use with group patients. Chapter 7 is on acting out, centered on how to help patients to understand their emotions, expressed nonverbally, or in actions. Likewise, chapter 8, on working through, describes how patients gradually learn from the repeated messages of their unconscious, witnessed by the groupmates.

An overview on the borderline problems, within the group context is also included in chapter 9. Finally a study of hypochondriasis in chapter 10 attempts to illustrate the unique technical strategies offered by the object relations approach to group psychotherapy.

6

COUNTERTRANSFERENCE WHEN INCEST IS THE PROBLEM

RAMON GANZARAIN, M.D.
BONNIE BUCHELE, PH.D.

As patients with a history of incest repeat within therapy contradictory interpersonal roles learned during their childhood, the therapists feel under pressure to assume the opposite reciprocal attitudes of these patients' mind-sets. They feel manipulated to play a part in these patients' fantasies, which is the typical effect of projective identification on countertransference. In this chapter, we describe some pairs of reciprocal roles, how they were assumed by the patients—in their past and in the group meetings—and our countertransference responses to them. We use the word *countertransference* here to mean the whole of the therapist's unconscious and conscious attitudes and behaviors toward the patient. This broader definition goes

This chapter was first published in *International Journal of Group Psychotherapy* (1986), 36(4): 549–566, and is reprinted with permission.

beyond the repetition of the therapist's own childhood and incorporates the therapist's specific responses to the patient's personality.

Clinicians treating patients with histories of incest experience intense, perplexing, contradictory feelings, such as horrified disbelief, excited curiosity, sexual fantasies, related guilt, need to blame, and wishes to rescue. These countertransference feelings affect how one treats these patients. However, there is virtually no literature on the subject of countertransference when treating adults sexually abused in childhood by their family members. To fill such a void, in this chapter we shall also report on how we as cotherapists (one female, the other male) used our emotional responses to understand these patients and to develop effective psychotherapeutic strategies in dealing with them in a group setting.

FORMATION OF THE GROUP

To form such a group, we invited individual psychotherapists to refer to us their adult patients (eighteen years of age or older) who were in individual psychotherapy and had a clear history of incest. We offered them a long-term, psychoanalytical oriented group where these patients could share their traumatic experiences about incest, while continuing their individual psychotherapies. Although there are no written accounts of having treaters of both sexes lead such a group, we believe that with this arrangement treaters could serve as a surrogate "parental couple," thus offering these patients additional transference targets.

Thirteen patients were referred to our group—twelve women and one man. All thirteen had started their individual treatments for a variety of psychological problems, and incest had been discovered only after weeks of treatment. We interviewed all thirteen patients, seeing them at least twice before deciding whether or not to include them in our group. We explained to them the additional psychotherapeutic opportunities offered by a group of peers with whom to share similar traumatic experiences. We informed them about the practicalities of the contract (schedule and fees) and told them they would have to attend at least 40 sessions. We also assessed their motivation to participate in such a group and the degree of their psychopathology, so as to verify both their interest and their ability to utilize what the group could offer them.

We have several reasons for prescribing group treatment for persons with histories of incest: The members provide a peer group offering opportunities to explore the meanings of their experiences with others who have been similarly traumatized. The transference is less intense than in individual therapy; this dilution is helpful in the management of strong, chaotic transference feelings which predictably occur with this population. Likewise, countertransference emotions are tempered by the presence of group members who can carry part of the burden when responding to emotionally laden group situations. Finally, the group-as-a-whole gives members a "good enough" mothering atmosphere where it is safe to be one's self.

When prospective patients were offered the possibility of entering our group, most of them initially responded with a feeling of relief. They would say, "Finally I shall meet people who believe me and who can really understand me," or "Now, I'll be able to talk about my awful secret with people who have gone through something comparable." However, some patients were reluctant to join the group, asking: "Would there be people in the group I know? Perhaps they are friends I have hidden from and now I'll be forced to share my shameful secret with them." A related response of shame was verbalized as:

"Well, if people know that I am a part of the group led by you two doctors, then everybody will know that I am a victim of incest. I will be publicly labeled in the community." Also fortifying their reluctance was their fear that joining the group would be a disloyal act and would result in their losing their "special" status.

Seven patients were selected for the group, which started in February 1984. All seven were women whose ages ranged from eighteen to forty-five years, and whose socioeconomic status varied from lower to upper class. The group met once a week for an hour and twenty minutes. No sessions were canceled and we met continuously without summer interruptions.

Reciprocal Roles

We shall describe a mixture of transference patterns and social attitudes expressed as roles, and explain how these roles influence countertransference, through projective identification inducing role suction and/or role reversals.

As transferences developed in the group, patients experienced with the treaters a reenactment of their parental relations. Multiple, contradictory roles learned during childhood came back in the context of therapy. Patients sometimes shifted from one role to its opposite (i.e., from "victim" to "favorite"), thus confusing the treaters. Each role had its reciprocal and, while a patient assumed a given role, she put pressure on the therapists to assume the complementary opposite one. We conceptualize these phenomena as the ways in which projective identification operates as a defense mechanism (Ogden, 1979; Horwitz, 1983).

Some roles these patients assume are familial. They fluctuate between being the parent and being the child.

Incest marks "The End"—the end of childhood and the beginning of a pseudoadult sexual life. If the incest partner is the father or the mother, that means the child loses the abusing parent who is no longer available to the child in his or her normal capacity. From then on, these children are pushed into a parental role. They are promoted to act as partners, not only sexually but otherwise. They are pushed into parenting their parents who feel inadequately parented themselves. Many examples of this type of interaction have occurred in the group. For example, when the male therapist, whose native language is Spanish, mispronounced a word, one member hastened, in a maternal way, to correct his error.

At home, incestuous persons become "favorites" through love and seduction or, just the opposite, become "victims" of violence and power abuse. Seduction is forced on them by enslaving them through their need to be loved and to gain approval. They feel like "possessions," "pieces of property," owned by the adults who seduce them. One woman who dropped out of the group early feared other group members would criticize her love from father and how much she liked her favored status within the family. She mainly feared being criticized for not stopping the incest. Being the favorite one in the family was very important to her.

Sometimes clinicians may feel that the adults who "victimized" these patients are to be blamed and forget that there is an intricate, ambivalent relationship between these incestuous persons and parents, with basically a close relationship. Although angry feelings may also be present, there is a background of loyalty. Failure to remember this paradox can, once gain, place these patients in an untenable position where they feel misunderstood.

Another pair of childhood roles assumed by these individuals are those of "rival" (either of the parent of the opposite sex or of the one of the same sex) and "dependent small child" who still needs protection and nurturance. For example, one patient sat in the female cotherapist's seat in her absence. The patient, feeling guilty about occupying the therapist's chair, as well as about acting as cotherapist with the male therapist, made many defensive statements to deny any rivalry implications. Two other patients abruptly left the group, almost as if they were small helpless children being forced to run away from home, replicating the way they had left their respective parental homes. Both felt financially exploited by their fathers who had sexually abused them; they left home after the fathers offered to support them financially if the daughters would continue to provide them with sexual favors. When these patients' dependency conflicts were stirred up in the group, they felt compelled to terminate the treatment. Not surprisingly, they believed treatment was too expensive and used finances as a pretext to leave the group precipitously.

One role fluctuation these patients experience is between being "perverts" or "normal" individuals. They tend to idealize the picture of normal sexual life as a rosy, romantic, "virginal" experience, since sexuality is perceived as unhealthy. For example, one woman reacted intensely to the sound of the male therapist's breathing. She connected heavy breathing with sexual arousal, remembering sounds made by the adult who sexually abused her. She implied that the therapist's breathing was perverse.

These adults oscillate between appearing to be "sexual experts," with extensive sexual experiences, and "shameful ignorants," who know nothing about sexual physiology and reality. As experts, they sometimes verbalize seductive messages. For example, when the male therapist complimented one patient on her appearance, she immediately said, "I'm free this evening." The same patient waited until the male therapist was absent from a session to ask about female sexual physiology; namely, whether being sexually aroused with a forbidden person is normal.

Sadomasochistic issues are important since there is an intertwining of love and power abuse by the adult who sexually seduces a child. There are issues of dominion and submission present. The patients actually were victims of forceful seduction in which they, as children, could do nothing except respond with a mixture of passive compliance and, later on, active exploitation. Passive compliance was the response of one patient who pretended to be asleep when she heard her father's steps as he came upstairs to her bedroom. She remained immobile while father performed his sexual acts. We heard many stories of forceful, active exploitation from these patients. One girl's father forced her at gunpoint to participate in family sexual orgies with him and her siblings. Another patient's father forced her to go to school and recruit little girls for the practice of his pedophilic perversion. A third patient felt exploited by the therapists whom she thought made her attend the sessions in order to keep the group going. She could not agree with another member's conviction that she still had important psychotherapeutic work to accomplish. She claimed instead her alleged achievements when confronting their incestuous offender.

Some other members thought that the therapists were "really" the ones who needed the group, not the patients! They relished pointing out and perpetuating the extremely tense, almost unbearable group atmosphere. They repeatedly stated how they wanted to spare themselves such discomfort by leaving the group. It was as if they were saying, "Mom wishes to cling to the illusion of us forming a nice, united 'family,' but the 'home' atmosphere is rotten!"

These reciprocal roles lead to an identification with the aggressor. For instance, the same girl who as a child was forced at gunpoint into family sexual orgies now as an adult baits and lures men, dominating and exploiting them, not at gunpoint but by being very seductive. She acts as if she were ready to take revenge at men by exploiting them as her father had exploited her.

Incestuous persons' sexual behaviors with appropriate partners are disturbed because of their previous experiences. These people may feel ashamed and perplexed at the difference in having sexual contact with an appropriate partner. They wonder whether to tell the truth about being victims of incest. They fear the absolute impossibility of ever reaching "normal" sexual relationships. And last, but not least, they suffer from unbearable flashbacks of the former perverse experiences. As in a severe traumatic neurosis, the scenes of the traumas are replayed.

In society, the person with a history of incest fluctuates between being "special" at home (or in court!) and an "outcast" with peers: The shift from being special to being one among many peers is like a demotion, a loss of status. Incestuous persons feel isolated from peers because of shame, guilt, and knowledge. Hence, the peer group is lost as a resource for their emotional growth. This role fluctuation is illustrated by the only male patient we interviewed. He chose not to participate in the group and openly spoke with dread about anticipating the loss of being special. He was apprehensive about friends knowing his incestuous secret. He said he was indeed his mother's favorite and that she had given him the privilege of being a special individual. He anticipated he would resent any criticism of her by other group members.

The loss of the peer group is important from the viewpoint of group psychotherapy. The rationale for prescribing group therapy as the treatment of choice for incest survivors is that it provides a surrogate peer group where members can deal with emotional difficulties derived from the incest and can catch up on some missed emotional growth.

In social situations, these persons fluctuate between judging themselves to be "chronic liars" and having fantasies of being "honest informers" who one day will "tell the truth": Being a "chronic liar" is like being a psychopath, like living a charade; being an "honest informer" is to become a traitor who will damage the loved one; and "telling the truth" risks being responded to with disbelief or, worse, with the conviction that this behavior should be reported and legal action taken quickly and dramatically. These multilayered conflicts culminate in a confused loss of the self.

Unfortunately, incest survivors are often disappointed with justice, perhaps only vaguely keeping a faint hope that something can really be done to correct their traumatic lives. One patient, after having been impregnated by her father and forced to have an abortion, realized that her father was starting to "fool around" with her younger sister. She then decided to take legal action. The mockery of justice was that father was placed on parole for only two years. However, this patient continues to advocate public education about incest so that injustices can be rectified.

Frequently, these patients' parents who have "dirty secrets" at home are seen by the community as model citizens. This hypocrisy, plus the limitations and clumsiness of the legal system, leaves these patients feeling that they really cannot trust anyone—that hypocrisy is pervasive.

These roles are reenacted in the group. The patients sometimes identify themselves with their aggressors. They also elicit in the treaters the complementary opposite roles, exercising on them a role suction (Redl, 1963), putting pressure on them through projective identification. Treaters can be pushed into assuming some of these roles. For instance, voyeur curiosity can be stimulated by the patients' stories, and conflicted responses can fluctuate between lust and repulsion. The male patient's seductive behavior with the female therapist made her wonder: "How good could he be in bed?" while the male therapist harshly condemned this mother surrogate for her unbelievable lust! Of course, these reactions are true across gender. Whenever the male therapist responds to the seductive messages conveyed by the female patients, the anger at the offender is reenacted in the female therapist's feelings.

COTHERAPISTS' COUNTERTRANSFERENCE RESPONSES

We have been treating these victims of incest with concurrent group and individual therapy because they often have brittle, immature egos and are prone to act out their hostile and self-destructive tendencies. Our concern is to protect them from such actions by providing them with different contexts in which to understand themselves and to verbalize their feelings rather than acting on them. Although concurrent group and individual psychotherapy may complicate matters by allowing an "institutionalized" external splitting of the transference, to reduce such splitting and to make therapeutic use of it we meet periodically with the other treaters. Sometimes we are able to achieve coordinated interventions with them.

When we started planning for the group, we struggled with what to call these patients. *Victims? Survivors? Sexually abused? Incestuous persons?* While each term seems to describe these patients, it may miss some other aspect of the incestuous experience. For example, *victim* overlooks the sadistic power that persons with a history of incest may exert over the people surrounding them. One patient in the group was certainly *abused*, but she also had become a powerful person in her family. She managed the household accounts and reigned as the favorite. The term *survivor*, by implication, compares the incest experience to being in a concentration camp. Most incestuous persons fight valiantly for psychological survival as their abusers forbid them any autonomy, but biological death is not usually imminent or threatening. Equating the threat of psychological death with that of biological death promotes an inaccurate view of the experience. There is also a judgmental message implicit in how they are labeled: The terms *excusing, forgiving, accusing them,* or *accusing someone else* tend to omit the loving, parenting, loyal aspects of the relationship between the victim and the offender.

Perhaps the most important emotional responses we started having toward the group members were those of revulsion and disbelief. In the history of the study of incest, disbelief is paramount. Many mental health professionals, when hearing about incestuous experiences, tend to disbelieve them. When one patient reported that her father sold her sexual favors (a farmer in a small community, he treated his daughter like another mare or cow), we could not believe her. We were shocked!

When starting the group, a sense of secrecy and confidentiality made us go to extremes in trying to hide who our patients were. We had fantasies that everyone in our office building was peering into the waiting room when our group started meeting. Our curiosity was also aroused about sharing secrets.

At the beginning, we also had rescue fantasies, similar to a manic reparation. We had sexual fantasies across gender, especially fantasies of possession, believing that these persons were really "sexually experienced" people. The male therapist thought, "Gee, this woman is like a refined courtesan"; while, as previously mentioned, the female therapist wondered whether a male patient would be a perfect lover. Both therapists experienced considerable countertransference guilt and anxiety about being lured by the seductiveness of these patients, who have been described by Herman and Schatzow (1983) as being "ripe for acting out with their therapists." Obviously, we were sad about their loneliness, realizing that these patients had had no effective parents since they were six or seven years old, and they thought no one would ever believe them. Also, we were angry at the offenders, a reaction described by Boatman, Borkan, and Schetky (1981).

We experienced confusion about where to place love and loyalty, questioning whether incest is only a matter of hate, abuse, and sadism (Gelinas [1983] refers to this same confusion). We also were surprised that the presenting complaint to clinicians is frequently one of depression, anxiety, substance abuse, sexual difficulties, and so on, and that clinicians have to actively find out about incest by asking direct questions.

After six months of group meetings, a feeling of frustration set in. We realized that there was only hard work ahead, a very slow working through of a complex problem. Our patients had to go through the complexity of a difficult struggle against pain, guilt, anger, and mistrust, but especially against denial. They needed to deny the loyalty, love, and enjoyment of their favored status; they needed to understand why incestuous acts sometimes had been fun; and they needed to work through their resentment at being rebuffed by the offender when he preferred a younger sister or some other woman. And then we had responded with our own mistrust (Poggi and Ganzarain, 1983), fearing that we could be at the mercy of the sadistic urges of the patients who would take revenge, betray us, and do to us what had been done to them, getting back at us as surrogates of those who had victimized them. The female/male cotherapist couple may become a transference surrogate of each patient's parental couple. The severely disturbed relations between their parents and between them and their offspring may be repeated in the group, providing opportunities for psychotherapeutic work.

The risk of disruptive competition between the cotherapists is minimized by jointly dictating notes about each group meeting and discussing them together; by planning together strategies dealing with possible interventions, decisions, referrals, other helpers, publications, and so on; and by frequently discussing feelings and differences with each other, but without sharing them with the group members.

During the sessions, the cotherapists do not openly engage in direct explicit verbal exchanges with one another, since that would likely interfere with, or unnecessarily complicate, the natural, spontaneous flow of the sessions. Instead, they explore their countertransference conflicts while discussing each session privately or with supervisors. Sometimes these discussions begin as individual reflections, which are later on shared with the other cotherapist.

As cotherapists, we have often felt under attack from both patients and other treaters who have tried to split us as a couple. We agree with Corwin (1983) that this tendency to split may have therapeutic advantages that can be used in the therapeutic relationship in the transference. We have experienced fears of the group disintegrating; that members will drop out, which is parallel to abruptly leaving home in anger or running away. We also tend to take shelter and refuge in our relationship with each other against the many anxieties that occur when working with these difficult patients.

Cotherapists are cast in gender-related roles in the transference. On the one hand, the female treater may replicate patients' mothers when experiencing "They're not telling me everything." She feels somewhat betrayed by the secret, hidden liaison going on between the female patients and the male therapist. She is surprised by the patients' absence of overt anger toward her, although there is considerable nonverbal competition about clothes, hairdos, and perfume. She also senses that the patients devalue her and cast her in the stereotypical role of "Mommy," who should inform them about the facts of life. On the other hand, the male therapist feels that he is the target of these patients' anger against men, whom they see as potential abusers. Being angry, they indirectly rebuff him with statements such as "I would fix that steer," when talking about men who approach them. He feels he is the recipient of unconscious, nonverbal, seductive messages, an experience observed also by Fowler, Burns, and Roehl (1983).

Therapists, and possibly offenders, tend to deny, minimize, or excuse incest when the relationship is more distant than that of mother–daughter, mother–son, father–son, or father–daughter, as if because the relationship is less "forbidden" it is emotionally less loaded. The danger in such minimization is that the actual severe traumatic effects in those more distant incestuous relationships might be denied.

When doctor-patient incest occurs, it parallels the double betrayal of the "natural" incest in the sense that the initial contract is broken; as a result, the helping relationship is lost. Later on, there is usually another betrayal when the love relationship ends. There is initially the same secrecy, guilt, and excitement at becoming a favorite.

OTHER HELPERS' RESPONSES TO INCESTUOUS PERSONS

Concurrent helpers (legal professionals or treaters such as individual psychotherapists, hospital team members, and so on) frequently respond to the influences group psychotherapists have over incestuous persons with competition and jealousy. There is competition among all the helpers, including the group psychotherapists, about who controls and possesses the case. Competition also occurs about who is the most effective, the most comprehensive, the most understanding, the most knowledgeable helper. Because they have been raised in homes where they were "special" in many ways, these patients have characteristics of the "special patient" syndrome so aptly described by Main (1957) and may encourage splitting and promote competitiveness among their different treaters.

Jealousy can be the by-product of this competition. Incestuous persons often stimulate feelings of exclusion as they attempt to cope with their own sensitivity to being excluded. They may replicate in the therapeutic relationship a parallel to the family situation in which these issues of inclusion became paramount—the reversal of a situation across generations whereby children were excluded from the secrets of their parents' bedrooms.

Family therapists may have a special response to the incestuous person. To promote open communication within the family system, they may encourage the incestuous person to confront the offender in front of the entire family. Since such confrontation is a revenge fantasy frequently entertained by incestuous persons, they may accept the family therapist's recommendation for an intra-family confrontation out of a wish for revenge.

It is debatable whether incestuous persons should talk directly only with the offender, should share their secrets with no one, or should reveal them to the entire family.

This subject was a matter of frequent discussion in our group. The consensus was that the decision belongs to each individual patient. However, a dramatic confrontation with the whole family frequently does not work because the offender probably will deny any wrongdoing, or the other members of the family might take sides with the offender, criticizing the victim or accusing him or her of being "crazy." Some family therapists recommend a step-by-step exploration of the incest situation: First, the victim should talk with other siblings who have been victimized; then the matter should be discussed with the excluded parent; and, last, this "hidden secret" should be talked about in a meeting with the entire family.

DISCUSSION

Mental health professionals frequently respond with disbelief to patients disclosing incestuous experiences. The allegation that Freud labeled such confession as "mere fantasies" seems to support such disbelief.

In our view, Freud's ideas have often been misunderstood. He did not specifically conduct a systematic, explicit study of incest; he did, however, acknowledge that seduction really occurs during childhood: "Actual seduction . . . is common enough; it is initiated by . . . someone in charge of the child who wants to soothe it . . . or make it dependent on them. When seduction intervenes it invariably disturbs the natural course of the developmental processes, and it often leaves behind extensive and lasting consequences" (Freud, 1931, p. 232). While Freud wrote more on seduction than on incest, his broader, more important discovery of inner psychic reality, the life of fantasy, as a determinant of mental symptoms seemed paramount to him. His shifting attention from the disclosure of incest to the discovery of psychic reality has indirectly reinforced mental health professionals' spontaneous tendency to ignore incest. Recent publicity in the press and in scientific publications has forced a reexamination of Freud's "seduction theory" (Masson, 1982).

The phenomena, actual incest and incestuous fantasies, are not mutually exclusive: Both incest and fantasized conflicted wishes for it can coexist, although incestuous fantasies are not usually accompanied by actual occurrences of incest. When actual incest is the problem, treaters may feel confused by the many conflicting feelings that the person experiences. That confusion becomes unbearable for the treater. According to Jung (1946):

> The existence of the incest element involves . . . an emotional complication of the therapeutic situation. It is the hiding place for all the most secret, painful, intense, delicate, shame-faced, timorous, grotesque, immoral, and at the same time the most sacred feelings that make up the indescribable and inexplicable wealth of human relationships and give them their compelling power. Like the tentacles of the octopus, they twine themselves . . . through the transference, around doctor and patient. This binding force shows itself . . . in the patients's desperate clinging to the world of infancy or to the doctor. The word possession describes the state in a way that could hardly be better [p. 179].

In an effort to avoid chaos, clinicians may artificially narrow their focus and, instead of realizing the multiple kaleidoscopic views of the complex problem of incest, may adopt stereotypes in an effort to understand it. For instance, initially we referred to our patients simply as "victims," thus ignoring that they also had other experiences whereby they felt themselves to be powerful and the rulers of their homes. By emphasizing the masochistic aspects of victimization, we overlooked the sadistic power that persons with a history of incest may exert over the people surrounding them.

The description of the incestuous experience as trauma uses the conceptual framework of traumatic neurosis. Indeed, patients with a history of incest do experience "flashbacks" of traumatic scenes and suffer from other symptoms typical of traumatic neurosis.

Some incestuous experiences are not painful. In fact, most incest situations have some painless aspects. Specifically, incestuous relationships also include love and loyalty. In addition, mutual gratification may be involved, but both clinicians and patients have difficulty acknowledging that satisfaction may occur in incest.

Sometimes incestuous experiences do not cross the threshold necessary to trigger intense anxiety and defensiveness in the child, because pain is not necessarily present. The child may think that such sexual activity happens in every family, may feel torn between curiosity and surprise, and may comply with what is happening to her or him. When the trauma becomes chronic, certain dysphoric feelings predictably appear. The adult partner wishes to keep the child as is, without allowing growth. The child, however, gradually discovers that this situation is not "normal," struggles, and tries to become disentangled from a situation that has become habitual.

The complex network of interactions in the incestuous couple is repeated in the transference. Being blind to some aspects of the transference may promote the acting out of them. Acting out also may be stimulated by the therapists' countertransference reactions, preventing them from seeing the complete picture. If the countertransference reactions cause the therapist to be caught in a simplistic, categorizing view of what the patient's experience is, then what is omitted probably will be acted out. For instance, overemphasizing sexual behavior may lead to overlooking the sadistic component so that the patient acts out his or her sadism using sexual attractiveness to dominate the partner.

Although the evaluation of the therapeutic outcome of these patients' group treatment is not the purpose of this chapter, we can make some general observations about patients' progress. Two patients left after several months. They were then less depressed, expressing anger more directly at the offenders, and suffering less self-blame. One ceased mutilating herself by understanding the unconscious motivation of her self-destructive behavior. Both returned to improved marital situations.

Three resumed or continued their adult college education. Another three women who had serious physical problems took considerably better care of their health. Two became more comfortable, spending more money on themselves, buying better clothes, or vacationing abroad. We regard these changes as expressions of their improved self-images.

The member who made a serious suicide attempt has considered returning to the group. Another suffered a serious relapse in drug abuse while working through her depressive reaction to important losses.

Concurrent group and individual psychotherapy (as well as psychiatric hospitalization, when indicated) may externalize the intrapsychic splitting. Different aspects of the patient's pathology may be revealed in the various treatment modalities. If it is possible to establish collaborative relationships among the different concurrent treaters, the destructive consequences of the externalization of splitting may be counteracted. Then patients may have an opportunity to have a fully integrated view of the many conflicts involved in the problem of incest. Integrating the different aspects of the self will eventually occur within the patient's own mind.

SUMMARY

During the course of psychotherapy, the patients with a history of incest reexperience a number of pairs of contradictory and reciprocal roles related to their incestuous past. The therapists feel pressure to assume the attitude complementary to the one held by the patients. Some pairs of reciprocal roles are developed in the family, such as "parent/child," "favorite/victim," and "rival/small child." Other pairs of opposite reciprocal roles occur in the context of sexual life: "pervert/normal"; "sexual expert/innocent"; and, in a sadomasochistic pair, "possessor/possessed." Vis-à-vis society, opposite roles are also played out: "special person/social outcast" and "manipulative liar /honest informer." The patient assumes all of these roles at various times, thus exerting pressure on the therapist to take the opposite stance. The role suction exerted on the therapist is powerful, fluctuating, and ultimately confusing.

Psychotherapeutic work with incestuously abused persons generates strong feelings. An initial response is to protect these "victimized people." Therapists struggle to find the appropriate label for the patients but none captures the complete experience. Revulsion and disbelief are potent as patients tell their stories; rescue and sexual fantasies abound; sadness about their loneliness is also experienced. Therapists cannot tell whether their patients love or hate them, and may become frustrated at the long time it takes to work through these patients' deep-seated mistrust of authority figures.

The type of incest—sibling, parent-child, or other—influences the countertransference. Most therapists believe that parent-child sex is the most traumatic, so when individual cases disconfirm this belief, they are easily misunderstood.

Male and female cotherapists experience feelings related to their genders, paralleling the events in the patients' families of origin. The links between the cotherapy couple are the targets of the patients' attacks, who attempt to split them by fostering competition between them.

Multiple treaters are often necessary. Competition and jealousy over who knows the "real story" and who is in control of the patient are then stirred. Treaters may disagree, for instance, about the advisability of the patient confronting the abuser.

The authors discuss how actual incest and incestuous fantasies can be compared, the validity of placing the focus on the emotional consequences of incest as sequelae of trauma, and how clinicians—in an attempt to bring order to the chaotic clinical information—tend to oversimplify the complexity of incest.

The authors often felt numb and confused because of the patients' use of projective identification. The clinicians' tolerance for the ensuing ambiguity helps them to recover insight, and thus integrate new understandings of these difficult patients.

We wish to emphasize that it took considerable effort to sort out what these patients elicited in us. Our difficulties were somehow comparable to overcoming the effects of prejudice, but were stronger than racism and sexism. These patients had broken a taboo! Therefore, we could not remain indifferent to such a transgression. We kept wondering unconsciously whether they were victims, monsters, or heroes.

Revulsion and disbelief sometimes prevented us from asking or listening in an effective, helpful manner. Our guilt, fear, and discomfort combined to create resistances in communicating openly and empathically with these patients. In short, we felt, on and off, deskilled by our responses when treating the emotional scars of incest.

7

ACTING OUT DURING GROUP PSYCHOTHERAPY FOR INCEST

RAMON GANZARAIN, M.D.
BONNIE BUCHELE, PH.D.

Psychotherapists can expect acting out to be a likely "side-effect" while treating persons with a history of incest, because these persons need to master their traumatic pasts by compulsively repeating them through actions, often quite dramatic. A central portion of the repetition is "keeping the secret," by not talking. Thus, the stage is set for acting out. Group psychotherapy may additionally lend itself to staging new variations of the early traumas, both inside and outside therapy meetings, since group-mates may be available as accomplices in acting out.

There are few articles on acting out during group psychotherapy; fewer still pertain to incest victims. This chapter attempts to examine the problem of acting out

This chapter was first published in *International Journal of Group Psychotherapy* (1987), 37(2):185–200, and is reprinted with permission.

during group psychotherapy with persons with a history of incest. In our experience, we were initially prone to ignore acting out behaviors despite their worrisome nature.

Acting out refers to behaviors during psychotherapy characterized by the patients' acting instead of thinking, talking, or reflecting about feelings and attitudes. These actions take place primarily outside the therapy. But they may also occur within the therapeutic context. The proneness to act instead of reflect is then called "acting in."

Acting out and acting in both occur outside the patients' awareness of what such actions mean. Actions are impulsive ways of avoiding full awareness of an emotional problem, while simultaneously attempting to communicate messages about painful conflicts.

Psychoanalysis values insight over abreaction, but acknowledged early in its history that transference is essentially a repetition of early conflicts rather than the remembering of them. Psychoanalysis discovered thereafter the interpretation of transference as a potent therapeutic tool, which allows patients to recover their forgotten pasts, and offering them new opportunities to choose new ways of behaving, after thinking and planning new solutions for old conflicts. Hence, acting out may be seen as a consequence of an incomplete analysis of the transference (A. Freud, 1968). The patients' actions occur outside the therapeutic context, because the impulses discharged have not been brought to the patients' scrutiny.

Patients use projection and splitting, respectively, to "externalize" or to "divide and conquer" transference-related mental responses (fantasies, feelings) they anxiously experience as unacceptable. Likewise, when mental pain such as shame, anxiety, guilt, or sadness threatens the patients' well-being, they may deny such pain by frantically resorting to impulsive actions. Some activities will make them feel "happily excited" (i.e., "partying," enjoying sex and drugs), instead of sad; others may bring them to angrily blame and fight "enemies" or offenders to protect themselves from self-reproaches or loneliness. In other words, hypomanic defenses such as omnipotent denial, or taking a paranoid stance, protect them from depression, experienced as sadness and guilt.

Victims of abuse frequently identify themselves with their offenders, actually behaving like them vis-à-vis other helpless victims, or adopting their abusers' attitudes and values. The defense mechanism of "identification with the aggressor" explains this paradoxical development.

Acting out has a bad connotation. There is a prejudice against it, as if it were *only* the product of faulty psychotherapeutic technique, or as if it were always to result in irreversible, serious, damaging consequences. The truth is that acting out is *also* an incipient attempt on the patient's part to communicate unbearable painful mental contents that cannot reach consciousness (Grinberg, 1968), but can only be discharged as spontaneous actions (O'Shaughnessy, 1983). Acting out is like a dream that could not be dreamt (Grinberg, 1968). From this viewpoint, acting out is a coded message from the patient's unconscious. Its content is elaborately disguised to pass through—to be "smuggled" across—the censorship that prevents these contents access to consciousness. Psychotherapists are trained to decode such secret messages from the unconscious but sometimes the codes used remain secret for quite awhile. Patients may hurt themselves in the meantime, before the secret code is deciphered. Such is the unavoidable drama of acting out. One can find, however, some consolation in thinking that specific actions will be repeated, in renewed attempts to get the cryptic messages across, until patients and psychotherapists alike are ready to deal with them.

Both patients and therapists need to reach a certain readiness to deal with the unconscious meaning of acting out. The oversimplified advice given sometimes at psychiatric hospitals to acting out patients to "put into words what you feel," instead of into "action" or "talk instead of acting," tends to overlook the patients' difficulties, or the impossibility, in choosing between actions and words to express their mental suffering. Verbalizing requires the sufficient working through of the depressive position. The depressive position is a major developmental achievement which makes symbolization and the labeling of feelings possible (Segal, 1973). Only after such mental growth has been achieved, can mental contents be "put into words" (O'Shaughnessy, 1983). If the patient has not yet reached the depressive position, the psychotherapist, breaking "the secret code of acting out," will find the patient unprepared to fully understand the messages from the patient's own unconscious, as translated by the therapists.

The patient then needs to translate the therapist's words into the patient's *own language*. To put the message into the patient's own words requires a new integration of the patient's mental contents. New integrations are a product of working through the depressive position. Insight without new mental integrations is only "pseudo" or "incomplete" insight, promoted by a limited, only intellectual, understanding by the patient of unconscious material. Pseudoinsight is frequently based upon the patient's "parroting" the psychotherapist's words without the translation into the patient's own language.

Working through deserves attention as the most effective solution to the problem of acting out. Working through is a sort of psychical work that allows the patient to accept certain repressed elements and to be free from the grip of repetition (Laplanche and Pontalis, 1973). It is necessary to supplement the focus on the intrapsychic obstacles, with a consideration of the therapist's specific contributions to carry on such process. As Melanie Klein (1961) wrote, the task of the analyst is to "draw conclusions from the analytic material as it reappears in different contexts, and is accordingly interpreted" (p. 12). The psychotherapy groupmates may contribute to each other's working through (see chapter 8).

ACTING OUT IN GROUP PSYCHOTHERAPY

Perusal of the literature on acting out in group psychotherapy reveals that publications on the subject are scarce. Current literature tends to take a "cookbook" approach, focusing on one or more techniques, which the author believes to be most effective in coping with this phenomenon. There is a general consensus that acting out should be interpreted in groups, as in any psychotherapy. There is some disagreement, however, regarding the setting of limits to inappropriate behavior. Levy (1984) maintains that interpretation by itself should suffice. Others (Ormont, 1969; Borriello, 1973, 1979) say that directly limiting acting out behavior is sometimes necessary. All concur, however, that acting out needs immediate attention. Borriello elaborates that the immediacy should include putting the affective experience into words. Soliciting assistance of group members to understand and interpret the acting out behaviors is recommended.

The special aspects of acting out in psychotherapy groups are seldom explored in the literature. For instance, the availability of the patient's peers in acting out is seldom discussed, although it seems logical that this facet of group treatment would have a direct effect on acting out behavior (Rutan and Stone, 1984).

There are a number of reasons for group psychotherapists' difficulties in discussing this subject. A popular notion about group psychotherapy is that it is an arena for wild sexual or aggressive behavior. Marmor (1972) refers to this belief when he states that some people come to group treatment consciously seeking erotic experiences. Hoping to disconfirm this mythology, group therapists may avoid discussing acting out altogether. Other authors may label some forms of acting out as "practicing" (Yalom, 1975), thereby not only dispelling the myth, but giving the behavior an adaptive connotation. Discussion of the issue may also be limited because the therapists may mistake a "flight into health" for working through.

When the authors began their psychotherapy group with victims of incest, they asked themselves: Will acting out become a problem in this group? Does incest produce a proclivity for acting out? Victims of incest frequently suffer from traumatic neuroses. Since mastery of the incest trauma occurs through actual or symbolic repetition, a proclivity for acting out seems likely. Bloch and Bloch (1976) have stated that acting out can be expected in many patients suffering from posttraumatic stress disorder.

The incest trauma leads to feelings of depression, which in turn are defended against by denial and avoidance. Jumping into action is an easily invoked type of avoidance. In short, these patients have a tendency to either become hypomanic deniers or to get paranoid and fight their wrongdoers, rather than becoming depressed and blaming themselves.

We shall discuss three areas of acting out: sex, power and sadism, and self-destructiveness. These three areas were chosen for discussion because they emerged in a natural but obvious way during the psychotherapeutic work. Their preeminence may be partially explained by the fact that they include the unmistakable mixture of the basic instincts of sex and aggression. One area does not necessarily predominate over the others; rather, predominance fluctuates in the course of the work. These three areas are not meant to be all-inclusive. This chapter is instead only an initial exploration, since to date acting out during treatment for incest is unexplored elsewhere in the literature. During the group's evolution there were numerous instances of acting out and working through. We shall describe some of them.

Sexual Fantasies

The issue of sexual fantasies is discussed less frequently than power or self-destructiveness but sexual concerns are ever present, especially nonverbally; for example, in styles of dress, flirtatious mannerisms, and postures. On at least one occasion, however, sexual fantasies were paramount and acted out in a striking way.

Four group members attended a male striptease show together. They reported about it in the following session, amidst laughter, a proud sense of achievement, and some embarrassment. It was an interesting group project, planned—outside meetings, of course—and successfully carried through despite members' traumatic memories.

The organizer of this "outing" had previously seen a similar show; at that time, she went through the trauma of being lifted onto the stage by a performer, who proceeded to simulate that he was raping her. The patient felt panic-frozen, so that she could not defend herself. She learned, soon after, that her boyfriend had planned the whole thing, as a practical joke. She had a counterphobic need to return to the male striptease show.

Other patients reported how they got back at men, by doing to the strippers what men have done to them: sadistically scrutinizing the sexual endowment of the performers. Making them feel self-conscious, by shouting things like "shake it baby" or other abusive commands.

Getting together to plan and to attend the show as a group was a way of acting out multiple wishes: to exclude the therapists; to ventilate anger against men; and to do something sexual together.

Betty organized this "outing." She had a history of sex among three with her best girl friend and her lover. He knew about the attendance at the strip show and did express special interest in having "the incest girls" to the house, so that he could "get to know them better." There were some clear innuendoes of possible group sex among five persons. The male therapist commented on this, helping the organizer to realize how she had been ignoring the implicit shared sexual fantasy. Betty then remembered her intense suffering when, as a consequence of the sex among three, she had lost her best girlfriend, because of her unbearable jealousy when her lover became sexually involved with her friend, while both excluded the patient.

The naive "going along with the adventure" of the other group members stopped. Then they were able to state their unwillingness to participate in the proposed plans to "socialize together." They clearly rejected such possible involvement.

Power and Sadism

In an effort to avoid chaos, clinicians may artificially narrow their focus and, instead of realizing the multiple kaleidoscopic views of the complex problem of incest, may adopt stereotypes in an effort to understand it. For instance, initially we referred to our patients simply as "victims," thus ignoring that they also had other experiences whereby they felt themselves to be powerful and the rulers of their homes.

They grew up learning how to stealthily use their power within the family. This power arises from many sources: control of the family stability by maintaining the incest secret, including the possible blackmailing of the abuser in order to remain as "father's mistress" or "favorite"; occupying the parenting role by being the caretaker of parents and siblings; identifying themselves with the abuser, who has sadistically used his power to get his way. Because the use of power was covert in the family, the behavioral manifestations of power abuse are also subtle, but pervasive within the group. Many instances of a wide variety of the acting out of power and sadism issues have occurred during the group's life. The authors will describe just a few.

Karen was known among her friends as a master at intimidating people. She also controlled the other group members, convincing them that the therapists were the enemy, after they brought up her possible relapse into drug abuse. She refused to establish eye contact with the psychotherapists; she sat beside the male therapist turning her back on him. She was, however, also furious with Ana, a newcomer, cast in the role of her critic; Karen distorted Ana's comments as being callous, stupid, and irritating. Anger was being displaced onto Ana instead of expressed against the therapists. Later Karen tried to approach Ana as they were leaving the building. Ana did not hear the invitation to talk. Consequently, she moved away toward her car. Karen then felt victimized. The feelings elicited by this exchange were brought up in the next group meeting, examining what both participants had experienced. Karen claimed Ana behaved exactly like Karen's father, expressing anger by remaining silent. Karen was projecting onto Ana her own intimidating techniques of ignoring other persons. The group then learned that Karen's nonverbal abusive ways of intimidating were a replica of her father's behavior toward her.

Intimidating as an abuse of power was also expressed verbally by Betty. She cast the therapists in the role of being uncaring, arrogant, and stupid. She raised serious doubts about their credentials and criticized their group techniques. Betty presented the therapists' behavior as a caricature of an old-fashioned, disreputable method of group treatment. She was joined by Wilma in stating that "whatever good was coming out of the group, came actually from the other group members, who were giving to each other, but nothing good was coming out of the therapists' interventions." This violent devaluation of the therapists culminated with Betty making calls to other agencies, inquiring whether their programs also offered group therapy for incest victims. The patients were considering leaving as a group, going to another agency, because the therapists were unqualified to treat them.

During this period of bitter power struggle against them, both therapists felt cornered, controlled, that anything they said would be twisted, and taken as a sadistic attack against the patients. Communication was then distorted to such a point that it sometimes seemed impossible. The therapists started doubting their own ability to use their clinical skills to help the group during this intense paranoid crisis.

The therapists themselves became confused regarding the future of Karen, suspecting her relapse into drug abuse. They assumed she would soon be forced to leave the group because of her life circumstances. They felt such a possibility as a relief from the control and immobilization exercised by Karen through her intimidation. However, they realized later on that she might be able to stay in the group.

Working through issues of sadism is central in the resolution of basic conflicts induced by incest. The therapists' realization that the intense period of paranoia was a replica of similar exchanges between abusers and victims helped them to understand that Karen was identifying herself with her father in feeling betrayed, and, above all, controlling the group by intimidating everyone, abusing her guilt-inducing power, and unconsciously imitating her father.

Self-Destructiveness

Persons with a history of incest are prone to be self-destructive because of a need to expiate their guilt for incestuous activities through self-inflicted punishment. They are also inclined to use self-destructive behavior to extract attention and support from their environment.

Most patients with a history of incest struggle with feelings of love and hate toward their abuser. The guilt resulting from their awareness of their love can serve as a trigger for self-destructive behavior. In early group stages, the necessity for these persons to deny their love and instead parade their hate for the offender can intensify the internal self-reproaches of group members. The more vulnerable patients may then become self-destructive, even to the point of attempting suicide.

Jane joined the group several months after its beginning. Group members were still proclaiming their hatred for their incestuous partners, while Jane had currently a good relationship with her father. The group accused her of denying her anger against father. She felt like an outcast, because she did not share the other members' hatred for the offenders. She presented herself provocatively, as having already overcome the hatred for the offender, thus eliciting the other members' criticism and ostracism. She was unconsciously punishing herself for loving father, offering herself as the group scapegoat. This pattern of interaction continued for several sessions. Her symptom of self-cutting was recurring in the meantime.

Wilma had considerable difficulty verbally acknowledging her guilt, but repeatedly acted in self-destructive ways. Following an argument with her boyfriend one dark evening she defiantly hopped on her bicycle and rode a long distance on a winding country road; she was fully aware of the danger involved. Her self-destructive tendencies attempted to deal with her unconscious guilt, the awareness of which she usually avoided by projecting it. However, Wilma was gradually able to realize, with the group's help, that whenever she was "waging wars against male enemies" she was indeed struggling with an internal guilt over being very much like her father, who had sexually abused her.

WORKING THROUGH

Working through is the solution to the acting out. Several successive steps can be described in the working through of acting out:

1. The translation of acted out impulses into some meaningful interactions within the group, so that those interchanges can be discussed, and then reflected upon.

2. Putting the meanings of behaviors into words that make them understandable. Therapists or patients may verbalize the newly discovered meanings.

3. Spreading self-understanding, with each patient translating someone else's words into the patient's *own* language and realizing how the same behavior reappears in different contexts.

4. Arriving at "advanced" new reflections of the re-

peated interactions of the patients with themselves, with other group members, with outsiders.

5. New integrations within the patient's mind bring about new views of self and of others, which may facilitate permanent behavioral changes.

Our patients have just begun to work through the issues underlying their acting out. But some members are in relatively advanced stages of working through their conflicts about sex, power/sadism, and self-destructiveness.

Working Through of Sexual Conflicts

Sex as a matter to laugh about, and take revenge at men with, was followed months later by a need to seriously work on some of these patients' actual difficulties in enjoying sex with their partners. Wilma reported she was anorgastic and felt very inadequate as a woman. Betty had a severe anxiety attack when a dentist put an anesthesia mask on her mouth; she then had flashbacks of the intrafamily offender putting his hand over her mouth while sexually abusing her, so that nobody could hear her in their small and crowded home. Later, she could understand why she had difficulty in accepting sex at night with her husband: incestuous contacts had always occurred at night before she went to sleep; she reflected on this with her husband and got him to better understand her avoidance of sex at night.

Anger at themselves for their sexual responses was particularly explored in connection with feeling bad when they had lubricated and even had several orgasms during incest. Some hated their bodies for having a normal physiological response to sexual stimulation, in a situation where mentally they were rejecting the incestuous sexual partner. The automatic, independent responses of their bodies, regardless of their emotions of anger and revulsion, made them hate their own bodies.

Working Through of Power and Sadism

Intimidation as an abuse of power was illustrated with the vignette about Karen. She was not aware of her ego syntonic character traits. Karen's impulse to control the group had been gaining momentum for months. She would come late, leave early, and glower in silence, or have outbursts of anger at both therapists. She occasionally gave evidence of her perception that the therapists were ignoring her, rather than vice versa. Furthermore, examining her exchanges with Ana revealed that Karen was accusing Ana of abusing her with silent indifference, exactly as her father used to do. Karen's identification with the aggressor then became evident. The therapists diagnosed these unconscious defense mechanisms, in a private discussion, precipitated by their frustration with this patient's controlling behavior. They realized that any intervention made by the male therapist would be rejected by the patient; consequently, they agreed that the female therapist would confront Karen with her intimidating behavior and the group with their fearful response. They hoped that would start the working through process.

In the next session, Karen continued her angry, controlling behavior. As the therapists attempted to interact with her, she furiously arose to leave the room. The female therapist then told Karen that she was intimidating everyone with her behavior. Karen halted with her hand on the doorknob. She had an expression of astonishment at the use of the word *intimidation*; finally, she left silently. Just as Karen hesitated at the door, there was a remarkable relief of tension in the room. As she left, everybody commented, for the first time ever, how intimidated they had been by her. Other group members agreed with the therapist's confrontation and elaborated on it with a noncritical and understanding attitude. The matter-of-fact tone of the therapist's confrontation was a model for them.

Following sessions were not characterized by an atmosphere of intimidation. Karen initially participated silently. She said she would now be able to remain through the entire sessions adding: "I shall eventually be able to talk with you but right now do not talk to me, because I may not yet be able to take it." Although her words were addressed to both therapists, nonverbal indications were clear that she was talking primarily to the male therapist. The other members accepted and supported Karen without fear of her; they were not controlled by her any more.

Working Through Self-Destructiveness

Self-destructiveness is an expression of self-hatred. These patients hate themselves because of reproaching themselves for their sexual activities with family members and for being like their abusers.

Betty deprived herself of many possessions that would have been financially available to her. When she tried to buy herself something, she felt undeserving and a panic attack usually resulted. Betty gradually began to connect these reactions with her past: She revealed that her brothers paid her for her participation in sex with them. Sometimes they charged admission to neighborhood children to see her doing explicit striptease. Betty became friendly with several prostitutes who lived next door. Therefore, having money available to her reminded her that she had been paid for sex. As she shared these details of her past with the group, Betty also realized that her inability to buy things for herself was related to hating herself for feeling as if she had sold her body in the past. Once she realized this, Betty was able to interpret to herself the meaning of her conflict about buying, to the point of from then on stopping incipient anxiety attacks.

Wilma went through the three major forms of acting out that we have described—sexual, sadistic, and self-destructive—when she caught herself in a flirtation with a younger man. She wished to seduce him as a way of overcoming her doubts about herself as a woman. But when Wilma realized that she was attempting to do with this man what her father had done with her, she hated herself because of the realization that she was "like her father," her abuser. She was indeed using a young man to bolster her self-esteem, and, by showering him with special attention from a mature woman, she was making him feel important. Her becoming the source of his self-esteem gave her important leverage to dominate him. On the other hand, the more this young man seemed interested in her, making her feel the center of his universe, the better Wilma felt about herself. Later on, however, her self-hatred for psychologically abusing this young man increased to the point of her becoming intensely depressed, unable to concentrate at work for a few days. Some evenings Wilma needed to get drunk to feel better with herself, obliterating her preoccupation with the young man; later on she would catch herself driving drunk and recklessly, or even sometimes causing the neighbors to be concerned for her. Although it was not really the case, Wilma felt as if she were planning to abuse a minor, just like her father.

The therapists interpreted her self-hatred as anger at the part of herself which was like her father, and explained her suicidal fantasies as a wish to get rid of "the abuser within her." As a response, she cried stating she did not want to go on living.

The fear of being like the hated offender is a specific common concern of incest victims. It is peculiarly combined—because of an identification with the aggressor—with struggles to overcome also the perpetrator's unbearable guilt for the abuse. Wilma was displaying this drama in the group's scenario; while striving to expiate her own guilt and to be pardoned, she implicitly was simultaneously pleading forgiveness for her abuser, whose internal tragedy she shared. Since such tragedy is well known to incest victims, the group members were able to empathize with Wilma, like no other group could probably do. They helped Wilma in forgiving herself, through understanding her narcissistic needs, her unfulfilled sexual wishes, and her need to be domineering with persons that she cared for. The group members succeeded in getting Wilma to understand herself. As soon as she stopped being devastatingly harsh in judging herself, she was able to put herself in her father's shoes and to diminish her condemnation of him. The group's love for Wilma helped her to forgive.

Feeling loved usually bolsters self-esteem, but this is particularly so during incestuous experiences, for both persons involved. The abuser utilizes the admiration, fear, and love of the victim to increase the perpetrator's low self-esteem. In this context, the victim becomes the abuser's nurturing person, with a motheringlike function. Wilma had also cast her young man in this role. Her groupmates supported her by acknowledging and "legitimating" these narcissistic exchanges between her and the young man, also by partially meeting her needs to feel good with herself.

The working through process was expanded when later on Wilma realized the displacement: that she planned to meet with the young man whenever she felt frustrated either by the individual psychotherapist, by the group male therapist, or by her age-appropriate boyfriend. Through realizing the displacement and substitution of the frustrating therapists or the ungiving boyfriend by this idealized romantic relationship, she understood a deeper meaning of her acting out. She was casting her young man in a nurturing role, comparable to the functions she had herself assumed as a child for her lonely, deprived, insecure father. She used her own words to describe her realization that she was repeating her father's "typical behaviors" in different contexts.

DISCUSSION

Acting out is a special resistance to doing exploratory psychotherapeutic work. Acting out can occur during treatment for a variety of psychiatric diagnoses. Hence, it is impossible to have overriding rules for the management of it. Instead, a case-by-case assessment is necessary. Sometimes the therapists must directly limit acting out behavior (Ormont, 1969; Borriello, 1973, 1979) such as when the behaviors are seriously self-destructive, are illegal, or severely curtail psychotherapeutic work. Some forms of acting out, on the other hand, do have an adaptive connotation and may be therapeutically productive as the "practicing" of new behaviors (Yalom, 1975).

The therapist's preferred theoretical model guides the approach to acting out. The existential model, for instance, advocates practicing new behaviors in every "new encounter" (Yalom, 1975). Behavioral modification uses techniques of punishment and reward to modify acting out. The psychoanalytic model strives to develop an understanding of the patient's actions. "Complete" working through of acting out is seldom attainable. Usually acting out behavior will alternate with periods of reflection and new insight during psychotherapy.

Acting out is inevitable in the treatment of persons with a history of incest because taking action is essential in mastering their traumatic experiences. Furthermore, acting out is a style of relating within their families of origin. Hence, working through will not stop acting out but will gradually modify it. Talking about their experiences may be especially difficult for these adult patients because of their belief in the omnipotence of words. It is as if talking about the experience will equal reliving it.

The therapists' intense countertransference, vividly experienced, is a major response to these patients' actions. Cotherapy is helpful in working through the therapists' feelings, so that it is possible to think together about the messages expressed by acting out. Each patient can be helped to understand the unconscious communication of the acting out behavior. The assistance of group members in achieving this goal is clearly advantageous. Developing the patients' willingness to examine the meaning of the acting out behavior is the real product of effective psychotherapeutic work.

A natural proclivity for acting out is not a contraindication for group psychotherapy with these patients. Realizing that the patient is attempting to communicate some meaningful unconscious material may focus the work more sharply, facilitating the translation of those actions into words.

8

WORKING THROUGH IN ANALYTIC GROUP PSYCHOTHERAPY

RAMON GANZARAIN, M.D.

Working through is at the core of the changes induced in patients by psychoanalytic treatment, done individually or in groups. The concept of working through was developed in the context of individual psychoanalysis, closely related to the notions of transference neurosis and regression. The extrapolation of those three concepts from individual psychoanalysis to groups may be questioned. Some authors even believe that neither transference neurosis nor regression develops in group psychotherapy with the systematic unfolding or the depth required for their therapeutic use, mediated by the working through processes. Others, including the author, think it is correct to use all those concepts in analytic group psychotherapy, since the phenomena they describe are clearly observable

This chapter was first published in *International Journal of Group Psychotherapy* (1983), 33(3): 281–296, and it is reprinted with permission.

in our clinical practice with groups. I shall briefly review the literature on working through and describe some of my relevant clinical experiences (Ganzarain, 1974; see also chapters 3 and 5).

Laplanche and Pontalis (1973) defined working through as "a sort of psychical work that allows the subject to accept certain repressed elements and to free himself from the grip of mechanisms of repetition" (p.488). They emphasized that, although it is a process constantly present in psychotherapy, "it operates more especially during certain phases where progress seems to have come to a halt, and where a resistance persists despite its having been interpreted" (p.488). The authors stated that, technically, "working through is expedited by interpretations from the therapist which consist chiefly in showing how certain meanings in question can be recognized in different contexts" (p.488).

Working through enhances the idea that the patient carries out certain work during the treatment. Such working through applies to resistances. It generally follows the interpretation of a resistance with apparently no effect; the appearance of a period of relative stagnation of progress may, in fact, conceal eminently positive work in overcoming some resistances. The patient's working through permits him "to pass from rejection, or merely intellectual acceptance, to a conviction based on lived experience (erleben) of the repressed instincts which are feeding the resistance . . . by becoming more conversant with these resistances, the patient is enabled to carry out the working through" (Freud, 1914b, p.155). Although working through is based on repeating old patterns, interpretation helps to modify them and thus facilitates the patient's freeing himself from the repetition mechanism.

Glatzer (1969) summarized Freud's (1914b) concepts

on working through by saying that there are "difficulties in achieving the transition between intellectual insight and genuine change in feeling and action . . . because the three unconscious areas of the id, ego, and superego involved in the reactions to the working-through process are not only in resistance to this process, but are in conflict with each other and within themselves" (p.292). She did a systematic study of the resistances of the ego, id, and superego to the working through in analytic group psychotherapy. Glatzer (1969) considered "the superego resistance to be a major block to therapeutic progress. The transformation of the superego from a corrupt ('bribed with pain . . . to accept the disguised id wishes') to an incorrupt state is one of the decisive points in psychotherapy" (p.294).

Glatzer (1969) described the "varied and subtle" resistances of the unconscious ego as trying "to preserve the neurotic balance and to defeat effective interpretations" (p.295). She emphasized that "the infantile ego wants to cling to the fantasy of megalomania" and resents "any imposition of reality by interpretations" (p.295), especially if they come from the group therapist, cast in the role of the archaic witch, the feared and hatred preoedipal mother image.

Freud (1914b) related working through to "the id's resistance." The compulsion to repeat, characteristic of the unconscious, is the basis of the necessity for working through.

Working through is treated in the Freudian text as a form of the work accomplished by the analysand. Other authors have also clarified the part played in the process by the analyst. Melanie Klein (1961) wrote, for example: "It is only by drawing our conclusions from the analytic material as it reappears in different contexts, and is interpreted accordingly, that we gradually help the patient to acquire insight in a more lasting way" (p.12).

"Psychoanalysts underlined the patients' difficulties in translating insight into change" according to Langs (1974). Novey (1962) stressed both the working through of affective experiences and the actual corrective experience in the relationship with the analyst as factors in the working through process and "took into account concepts derived from learning theorists, such as the need for trial and error, and for experimentation outside of the analytic sessions" (p.672).

It seems necessary to supplement the focus on the intrapsychic obstacles with a consideration of the analyst's role, especially in terms of specific interactions with a patient. In analytic group psychotherapy one has to include also the specific relations with the other group patients and with the group-as-a-whole, since there the interactional opportunities for working through also come up, making the therapeutic experiences in groups significantly varied and complex.

Greenson (1965) saw working through as involving specifically those processes that lead from intellectual insight to significant and lasting behavioral changes. In a wide sense the concept of working through can be related to virtually all aspects of the analytic process, but in its narrowest sense it alludes to one specific component: the step from insight to structural and behavioral-symptomatic change. "Since affect makes insight more believable . . . it is what produces the therapeutic results," commented Glatzer (1969, p.292).

Brodsky (1967) stressed the contributions of working through to the mastery of anxiety and other painful affects. Other authors have insisted on that special function of working through.

Ekstein (1965) related it to the termination process. "Termination is seen primarily as an important aspect of working through, and thus a process, rather than as an arbitrary or ideal ending point" (Ekstein, 1965, p.76). The work to master anxiety and to try new behavior, that is, the product of working through, continues in an ongoing self-analysis, after the actual termination of the visits to the therapist has occurred. "A kind of reeducation takes place, and the repetitions of failure are replaced by the repetitions of mastery" (Ekstein, 1965, p.68)

Melanie Klein (1961) conceived working through as including "Bringing about the consistent analysis of paranoid and depressive anxieties" (p.12–13); ultimately this leads to greater integration" (p.13). The elaboration of the depressive position allows the development of the capacity to make reparation, thus fostering love to prevail over hate in the patient's dealings with his objects. The successful elaboration of the depressive position thus promotes the full use of the ego's capacities to assess reality, both internal and external, and enhances creativity and sublimation.

Abse (1974) stated that the distinction between psychoanalytic group therapy and other modalities is centered on time duration and the presence of working through and integration in the therapeutic process. Nonanalytic groups tend to be briefer than analytic groups, sometimes considerably shorter. The working through processes require, by definition, considerable passage of time.

Some psychoanalysts who also practice group therapy express doubts that detailed working through processes can ever occur in group psychotherapy. Anthony (1971) believes that "although . . . a transference neurosis can develop within the group, it does so only to a limited extent. . . . The group situation, by its very nature, impedes the regressive movement required for full reactivation of the early . . . relationships" (p.107). For him, the psychoanalytic work favors regressive transference, but the group situation focuses on the progressive. He adds, however, "This is not to say that regression does not occur in groups . . . but it does not take place to the same degree" (p.107). Anthony (1971) seemed to agree with Spanjaard (1959) when he summarized, without any criticism, Spanjaard's viewpoint as follows: "The limitation is imposed by the mutual rivalry for the therapist engendered by the group situation so that the regression reaches and remains at the post-oedipal level—that is, the level of the 5- to 7-year-old or of the adolescent attempting to wean himself from parental dependency" (p.107). For Anthony, the transference manifestations are diluted in groups. As Slavson (1950) stated, "Transference . . . cannot be as intense in groups as it is in individual treatment, because of the dilution brought about by other members."

Bion (1961) and other analysts who also practiced group therapy believed, on the contrary, that deep regressions do occur in groups, facilitating the development of intense preoedipal transference to the group-as-a-whole (frequently felt as a mother surrogate), to the other group members, and to the therapist.

I myself have observed transference neuroses develop in psychoanalytic group therapy, with deep regressions that allowed for the working through of early psychotic-like anxieties and primitive defense mechanisms. I shall describe clinical material supporting those statements.

Working through is the essential characteristic of psychoanalytic group therapy that distinguishes it from other group treatment modalities. Nonanalytic group psychotherapies attempt to promote abreaction or catharsis, rather than working and learning, the two main elements implicit in working through.

CLINICAL ILLUSTRATIONS

What follows are clinical illustrations of the working through done by two patients I treated in groups.

Daniel was forty-year-old man who, when he started his treatment with me, had been married for twelve years. He had been in another group for ten months. He and two other patients of that old group formed a new group, together with five new members.

Daniel's personality was described by his previous therapist as masochistic. He became the scapegoat of the group. She described him as an unrewarding patient "going downhill." I saw Daniel in three individual interviews before starting my group. I tried then to dissuade him from continuing treatment, having in mind his previous therapist's gloomy prognosis. However, he wanted to accomplish something he had not yet achieved. He therefore insisted on being included in my group, and I finally agreed.

In the sixth session, Daniel told the group that he was impotent. He had not offered that information during his previous therapy. He had suffered from ejaculatory impotence since puberty, being occasionally able to achieve orgasm. He related his lack of ejaculation to his fear of impregnating his partner.

He had also been suffering from lack of erection since he had a vasectomy three years earlier. He had that operation with hope of losing his fear of impregnating his partner and thus becoming sexually freer, "a bed-hopper" who would have as many affairs as possible. To his dismay, however, he had lost his erections.

The other three male group patients had coincidentally also had vasectomies; however, none of them had afterward suffered from impotence. Daniel was thus confronted with the fact that his lack of erection was not a necessary anatomical consequence of the vasectomy; his impotence was, instead, psychological.

Lucy reported that her husband had also suffered from impotence after a vasectomy. Lucy had insisted that her husband should see a urologist; she made an appointment for him and even went with him to see the urologist. Lucy's husband received brief hormonal treatment and some supportive comments. He recovered his potency shortly thereafter.

Lucy's response to her husband's problem stirred up in Daniel the wish to be taken care of by his wife. He would have liked his wife to demonstrate such an active interest in his sexual potency. The group confronted him with his overdependent stance and suggested that he himself could make an appointment with a urologist.

Daniel regressed to a dependent attitude when he wanted his wife to take the initiative and to arrange his appointment with a urologist. He was also regressing by depressively pining for his wife as a lost sexual partner and seeing her with a paranoid approach: If she did not take the initiative to help him overcome his impotence, it was because she probably never really loved him but had simply been after his money.

Daniel then explored his relationship with his wife. He felt that his wife did not love him anymore; he suspected that she had married him for his apparent wealth. The group confronted Daniel with his conflicting wishes to be taken care of by his wife while deeply mistrusting her.

In session 16 Daniel reported in a sheepish, self-effacing way that he had been to a urologist and had been able to perform sexually with his wife. He apologized "for being so dependent upon his wife." He spoke about their satisfactory sexual intercourse, almost as if he were displaying a sign of weakness—needing to be loved by his wife. He had actually been extremely tentative and indirect in stating his sexual needs to her. (He wrote down on a piece of paper, "I love you," and placed it on his wife's mirror; he placed bottles of beer in the refrigerator, since their past pleasant sexual interactions were accompanied by beer drinking. His wife picked up the messages and responded so that they could again enjoy sexual intercourse.) In the following sessions Daniel was happy and boastful about his restored masculine capacity.

Between sessions 17 and 50 we reviewed his shame at depending upon women. He was his mother's favorite, but now he never took the initiative of writing or calling her. He waited for her to initiate their contacts. There was a conflict between his relish in being his mother's favorite and his need to act like a tough he-man who did not need anyone. The old-group patients remembered in session 12 that Daniel had a peculiar reaction when their former therapist announced that she was leaving town. Daniel stopped coming to the group, actually missing the last two months of group meetings. He stated defensively, "I had a pretext," intending to say, "I had a good reason." The "pretext" was that his son was playing Little League baseball games at the same time that the group met. When he caught himself in the obvious Freudian slip, he said that he did not mind at all whether that doctor was going to stay in town or leave. He tried to name her, but he forgot her name. His fellow patients helped him to realize that he was acting defensively, denying his previous doctor's emotional importance for him while angrily wiping her out of his memory. There were parallels between his reactions to the separation from his previous group therapist and his responses to the feared loss of his wife: He had denied his wishes to depend on those women, reacting with anger against and distancing himself from them, frustrated by both his wife and the female group therapist.

The report that a female patient's husband had over-

come his postvasectomy impotence helped Daniel to recover hope and offered him a clearer view of his
psychological conflicts with his wife. The presence of three
other male fellow patients who did not become impotent
after vasectomies reinforced his newly acquired conviction
that his impotence had psychological causes.

The unfinished business around the separation from
his previous therapist became very significant. The fact
that there were other old-group patients provided a continuity that allowed him to acknowledge his style of
separating from women when he felt hurt and angry
about losing them.

Daniel's transference neurosis developed in the two
therapeutic groups, so that he responded to the loss of his
previous therapist with the same cluster of defenses that
he used to cope with loss and separation from his wife and
his mother.

Daniel denied the emotional importance for him of
female therapist, wife, and mother. He tried to delete
them from his life. He actually left his previous therapist
before she left the group. He feared he had lost his wife,
and he behaved in ways that created distance between
them. The hypomanic denial of her feared loss was
followed by a paranoid mistrust and a schizoid turning
away from her, thus avoiding dealing with mourning her
anticipated loss. It was impossible for him—without specific outside psychological help—to break that vicious
cycle; the depressive reaction caused by the loss of an
important woman was being denied, together with his
internal psychic reality of needing and missing her. He
perpetuated the psychic reality of such a loss by denying it.

Daniel turned away from his woman therapist and
from his wife, feeling omnipotently above the weakness of
needing them. He was convinced he could regulate how
emotionally important they were for him and had felt

triumphant over them through devaluing them; that is, his son's Little League baseball games were more meaningful to him than seeing his group therapist and saying goodbye to her.

The denial of mourning for the losses (feared or real, past or future) of important women prevented him from facing, dealing with, and elaborating those mournings. Coming to terms with them, accepting those women's emotional value for him, and accepting also his denied wishes to restore his relations with them was the specific working through that allowed Daniel to start repairing his relations with his wife. Daniel did learn and succeeded in practicing new behavior after elaborating a pathological mourning for his wife and for his woman group therapist. The presence of two other members of his first group made it possible for Daniel to establish a continuity in working through his abnormal reactions to separations, creating a bridge between the current group and the previous one.

I have limited the description of Daniel's working through by focusing only on the overcoming of his impotence. I examined, in a published paper, the working through processes in another case, discussed in even greater detail in chapter 10.

Working through her help-rejecting complaining attitudes allowed Laura to develop a new self-image. From feeling worthless and being content with a menial, backup, part-time job when and if called to replace a missing worker for a few hours, she moved into learning skills in a field of medical technology. She learned how to do EEGs,[1] thus reversing her hypochondriacal anxieties by having her clients anxiously worried about how their brains were

------

[1] I have slightly changed the actual nature of Laura's work to disguise her identity.

performing. It was almost a tailormade way of dealing with her own hypochondriacal anxieties by projecting them onto her clients.

Laura renewed contact with a half-brother. She called him over the phone, exchanged photographs and correspondence, and entertained fantasies of meeting him when she realized that he looked exactly like her father. The fact that she was making up for all her anger against her father, and attempting to recover him through such a specific surrogate, speaks of her willingness to establish a good internal relation with her father; that favorable predisposition expressed her internal change, vis-à-vis his father image.

On the cancellation of a session, Laura regressed, first to a state of confusion and later on to a schizoid withdrawal and turning away that was characteristic of her. She did not bother to explore reality; that is, asking the building's receptionist what was happening with her group meeting; neither was she able to see her groupmate's car. She reacted to the absence of the group and the therapist as if she had been abandoned, in a dramatic repetition— within the fully developed transference neurosis—of her former experience of being deserted by her mother. Laura was flooded with anxiety, which prevented her transiently from using her memory or her perception of external reality.

She ventilated her anger and envy of the doctor in the next meeting. She started mastering the experience of abandonment by turning the tables and imagined reversing the situation by threatening the therapist with his losing the group if fired by the angry patients.

Laura also used role reversal by taking care of her mother in a nursing home. The same psychological interplay underlay her choice of new, specialized work. She has learned new ways of behavior in dealing with other persons and with her own anxieties. Laura substituted the repetition of failure by the repetition of mastery.

The repeated evidence of transference distortions detected by several group members adds emotional impact to the insight gained, and we know how affect makes insight more believable.

Daniel bribed his superego by offering his impotence as self-punishment for his wishes to be sexually promiscuous while remaining emotionally uninvolved with his sexual partners. He planned his vasectomy to enjoy an absolutely free sexual life, with the paradoxical result that in his mind the vasectomy caused his impotence. The other group patients helped him to acknowledge—without self-destructive guilt—his wishes to become sexually very active; his group peers did not let him go on thinking of himself as impotent to justify in his own eyes his passive defensive stance of renunciation, out of guilt over his sexual satisfaction.

WORKING THROUGH IN GROUPS

Fellow patients have, during the life of the group, stored memories of each member's recurring attitudes. The multiplicity of remembrances can be put to therapeutic use, with the added value of consensual validation that is, having everybody else in the group helping someone to realize being again in the grip of the compulsion to repeat.

Working through may help to contain within the group sessions the patients' tendencies to act out by limiting those tendencies mainly to interactions during the therapy meetings. The repetition of behavioral patterns can bring even acting out under the analytic scrutiny. As Fried (1961) wrote, the patient in group psychotherapy is apt to express feelings directly in reactions and actions as opposed to merely reporting them.

The group offers its members a variety of opportunities to experiment with new boundaries, using the group as a testing ground to try out, during its meetings, patterns of interaction that are different from the old ones.

Other group members become "reinforcers of the incorruptible superego," wrote Glatzer (1969), for whom the "superego resistances are . . . the major block to therapeutic progress" (p.305).

The quality of the anxieties to be mastered in groups by working through is of a special kind. Early psychoticlike fears, described as schizoid-paranoid, are soon brought to center stage, as are the manic defenses. Regression then acquires a primitive flavor. Remember, in this regard, Daniel's hypomanic denial of his needs for his former group therapist and for his wife. Remember also Laura's intense persecutory fears of doctors and her help-rejecting complaining, coupled with her hypochondriacal anxieties, leading her to the conviction of being on the verge of losing her mind; sometimes she withdrew, felt disorganized, confused, and experienced derealization, as when a group session was canceled.

The fact that therapeutic work is basically accomplished by the patient leaves the part played by the therapist in the process reduced to being a catalyst of new integrations crystallized in the patient's mind. Such catalytic functions may also be performed by the fellow members, acting transiently as cotherapists. That possibility offers important avenues to solve the problems derived from the envy of the therapist's power—the witch preoedipal mother image (Glatzer, 1969)—since it allows each group patient to feel helpful and needed by the fellow members. They may benefit, too, from the transient cotherapist's newly acquired capacity to love and to do reparation.

The narcissistic anxiety caused by the effective interpretations formulated by the therapist is thus lessened in the group by the effective interpretations by peers or fellow members. The group also offers the opportunity for role reversals, such as when a patient can discover and point out in a group peer the same conflicts that have been previously interpreted to him. Glatzer (1969) wrote clear examples of those phenomena and commented that the "greater activity of the group therapist (as compared to the individual analyst) makes him a more available object for constructive identification" (p.297).

Glatzer (1969) also wrote of the help other members afford the therapist, giving him "a respite to regain his objectivity," particularly when a "stubborn, masochistic patient may involve the analyst" in a transference–countertransference tug-of-war.

Daniel and Laura were both stubborn, masochistic personalities. Both provoked, devalued, and distrusted significant persons in their lives, including the group therapist; both presented themselves as pitiful victims of fate or of somebody else's wrongdoing; both occasionally dragged me into potential power battles within the group setting. Then other group members did give me a respite to regain and keep my objectivity.

Conclusion

Working through is the essential characteristic of psychoanalytic group therapy that separates and distinguishes it from other group therapy modalities. The other types promote more abreactions of briefer duration than working and learning, the two main elements of working through.

Group psychoanalytic patients unfold a network of transferences, toward the therapist, their fellow patients, and the group as a whole, perpetuating in their interactions their malfunctioning intrapsychic worlds.

Separation anxiety is an important aspect of working through. It stimulates a progression to resolve the depressive position or the regression to schizoparanoid and manic defenses. If the depressive position is successfully solved, the capacity for reparation allows loving concern to prevail over hate for the patients' objects.

9

BORDERLINE PROBLEMS WITHIN THE GROUP CONTEXT

RAMON GANZARAIN, M.D.

The British School's psychoanalytic clinical studies of psychoses, groups, and children found psychotic anxieties to be part of normal emotional development, clustered in the schizoparanoid and the depressive positions. Psychotic fear for the endangered self (schizoparanoid) or for the fate of the threatened object (depressive) are defended against by using early defensive mechanisms, such as splitting, projective identification, and omnipotent denial. Fluctuations between these two positions or clusters of anxieties and defenses stay with human beings throughout their lives. We are all borderline from a dynamic view-

This chapter was first published in *International Journal of Group Psychotherapy* (1982), 32(1): 3–7, 57–60, and it is reprinted with permission. It consists of the opening and concluding remarks made by the author as Chairman and Convener of the symposium. Some Key Issues in the Group Psychotherapy of Narcissistic and Borderline Patients, AGPA Annual Conference, Los Angeles, 1981.

point, insofar as we all have a psychotic core in our personalities, combined with nonpsychotic parts.

The psychiatric descriptive viewpoint has long recognized a wide classification gap between neuroses and psychoses, filled with patients labeled "borderline."

How do the genetic and the descriptive viewpoints on borderline phenomena relate to each other? Pathological syndromes are known in medicine to be exaggerations or alterations of normal developments.

How to integrate the genetic and the descriptive approaches is problematic. The psychiatric descriptive viewpoint implies a value system, attempting to separate different degrees or levels of pathology. We implicitly use a scale of health-sickness evaluation. Borderline phenomena and defenses against them are, consequently, viewed as sick or primitive. They are alienated, estranged from normal human emotional life, and labeled as psychotic. If we assume that those phenomena belong only to the sickest level of the borderline spectrum, we shall not address our therapeutic interventions in every patient to include dealing with the psychotic parts of the personality.

The overemphasis in classifying the gap between neuroses and psychoses may lead to simplification of a complex subject, looking for pathognomic, that is, characteristically specific, symptoms, hoping that, whenever we find them, we may safely diagnose a "specific" pathology. The defense mechanism of splitting, for instance, has been abused in that way, when it is alleged to be pathognomic of the borderline personality organization. The defensive functions of splitting objects and/or the self are, indeed, used by everyone, not just borderline patients.

On the other hand, by addressing ourselves to borderline patients as if they were one category, we create some confusion. There are, no doubt, different types of borderline patients. Attempts have been made to distinguish those types. However, it is also possible to talk instead in general about borderline problems, as I am doing here.

Roth (1982) described a typology of borderline patients, expanding on Herbert Rosenfeld's (1979) efforts along those lines. I wish to comment briefly on his type 3 or false self personalities. Roth includes there patients who have joined our professional ranks. They have "an exaggerated external perception and . . . make . . . accurate mechanical remarks . . . about themselves or others" (p. 18). This defensive maneuver "serves to deflect attention from themselves and inhibits the sharing of their own infantile anxieties" (p. 18). That type of patient behaves in group psychotherapy as a doctor's assistant. Alice Miller (1981) described this type of false personality in her book *Prisoners of Childhood*. Emile Ajar (1979) is a French Jew from Arabic Argelia who has gone through quite a borderline identity conflict. His 1979 book *King Solomon's Anxiety* (L'Angoisse du Roi Solomon) deals with King Solomon who was a tailor. He became king of the ready-to-wear trade (*pret-à-porter*). He later organized a twenty-four-hour telephone service to provide emotional help. His staff of volunteers provided ready-to-wear psychotherapeutic advice over the phone. Ajar's (1979) King Solomon said: "It is out of egoism that I think about the others, in order not to think about myself, which is what I fear the most in this world." King Solomon is a type 3 borderline person. He carried helping others to an industrial scale.

Of course, some persons are more overwhelmed by the continuously operating psychotic substratum of our personalities.

The clinical diagnosis of borderline distinguishes those persons whose egos are unable to protect them from confusion. However, the point here is that technique with a borderline patient need not be sharply separated from clinical work in general. . . .Utter destructiveness exists, along with love and creativity and if the therapist admits this aspect of insanity she/he will be impelled to work directly to counter the harm of it [Rush, 1982, pp. 52–54].

One essential problem in dealing with borderline patients is the intense hostile component of their transference which frequently prevails, although sometimes they develop transference psychoses that seem highly eroticized. I shall elaborate on this essential clinical problem in treating borderlines further below.

Groups tend to regress to primitive levels of mental functioning. Intense psychoticlike anxieties shake then the normal infant's incipient ego, as they do the patient who starts in a group, making both first fear for the annihilation of her or his own self (schizoparanoid anxieties) and later on for the destruction of her or his loved object, carried on by the infant's own hostility (depressive fears). Thus, entering a group reactivates unconscious threats and anxieties, while early "introjective-projective reactions are revived with a special strength" (Greenacre, 1972) and the "individual's self-boundaries are loosened" again (Scheidlinger, 1974).

Bion described his "basic assumptions" as group defenses against reexperiencing early psychotic anxieties, whereby splitting, projective identification, projection, denial, and introjection are mobilized to protect the group members' egos from such primitive fears. He stated that "groups would, in Freud's view, approximate to neurotic patterns of behavior, whereas in my view they would approximate the patterns of psychotic behavior" (Bion, 1961, p. 181). He added: "I very much doubt if any real therapy could result unless these *psychotic patterns* were *laid bare* [emphasis added] with no matter what group. In some groups their existence is early discernible; in others, work has to be done before they become manifest" (see chapter 2).

Bion's program to deal with group patients' psychotic anxieties may of course not be that attractive. His method has been criticized as inflicting too great a narcissistic injury on individual group members (Gustafson and Cooper, 1979).

The transferences of borderline patients have intense hostile components, which frequently prevail, although sometimes the transference psychoses seem highly eroticized. Kohut (1968, 1971), Kernberg (1968, 1974), and Rosenfeld (1979) agreed basically on the disturbing influence of anger in those patients' transference relations. All three authors tried to deflect the so-called negative transference by focusing on the hostility occurring somewhere else or in a different moment than in the immediate here-and-now of the therapeutic relationship.

Kohut (1968, 1971) approached anger in past relations, mainly with the mother, in an implicit revival of the traumatic theory of neurosis. Kohut (1968, 1971) agreed with the patient that the mother did not provide enough or timely empathy. The therapist's empathic behavior fosters an idealized transference, and hostility against the therapist is generally ignored. The patient gets from the therapist the emotional understanding that his mother deprived him of. If anger is acknowledged, it is placed in the context of the therapist's being unempathic, just like his mother in the past. The therapist avoids examining the distortions of memories and perceptions by unconscious fantasies regarding the past or the present; these facts are ignored. Memory is selective in what it remembers, according to the prevailing affects, and perceptions are distorted by the way emotions color them. Such systematic analysis of unconscious fantasies was not dealt with by Kohut.

Kernberg (1968, 1974) focuses mainly on the hostility expressed in extratherapeutic relations of borderline patients. He avoids dealing with the anger against the therapist. He suggests this strategy because of the risk of inducing a transference psychosis, which may disrupt the patient's weak ego and cast the therapist in the role of a persecutor. He has a concept of transference psychosis as ego shattering. Kernberg's therapeutic strategy in dealing with anger ends up rejecting the patient as bad (for being hostile) or with a defective ego (for being weak) and conveys implicitly the message that nobody can cope directly with the patient's anger.

Rosenfeld (1979) postponed dealing with hostility within the transference, when anger reached the white-heat level of paranoid distortions. He waited for a near future in coming therapeutic sessions when the patient's observing ego regained its reality assessment. The patient is able by then to take full responsibility for his mental contents, instead of projecting them onto the therapist, as he did before. Rosenfeld's (1979) important contribution to dealing with borderline transference was his strategy of avoiding shoving back the patient's projected bad contents by not interpreting projection. He correctly observed that, if projection is interpreted while the patient is extremely paranoid, it will lead to a tug-of-war and to a therapeutic impasse. Transference psychosis is not necessarily ego shattering. I agree with that viewpoint.

Can Rosenfeld's psychoanalytic techniques be applied to group psychotherapy? We can also avoid shoving back the patient's projected contents at a moment in which the patient needs to disown them. The therapist and the group can become the *containers*, in Bion's (1967) sense of the term, of the patient's anger. By giving a vivid example of how to cope with hostility, the therapist and the group provide good mothering and a meaningful experience of being understood and cared for, thus facilitating a later introjection by the patient of those models of tolerant understanding of himself.

In analytic group psychotherapy the patient can project his mental contents into many recipients—the group-as-a-whole, each fellow patient, the therapist. The patient is encouraged to describe his current perceptions of the persons in the group without having his projections interpreted. Instead of interpreting projection, the therapist can encourage the fellow patients to examine what they have done to the group member suffering from paranoid distortions. Such a discussion may help the disturbed patient acknowledge how his or her perceptions and judgments were transiently altered by fear and anger. I have observed both narcissistic and borderline patients in group analytic psychotherapy being able to take back, admit ownership after a while, of their angry projected mental contents and develop their egos, integrating parts of themselves that they were previously forced to anxiously disown.

Hostility is the main source of human anxiety that threatens to disrupt the cohesiveness of the self, to erode the ego capacity to assess reality, or the patient's ability to benefit from psychotherapy. Rosenfeld's (1979) observations in dealing with pervasive paranoid anxieties can be applied to group analytic psychotherapy and may help borderline patients, sometimes.

10

AN OBJECT RELATIONS APPROACH TO HYPOCHONDRIASIS

RAMON GANZARAIN, M.D.

This study is about the object relations of hypochondriacal patients, as observed within group analytic psychotherapy. It includes excerpts of treatment sessions, transcribed from edited videotapes, to illustrate the hypochondriacal patient's characteristic style of relating and some effective psychotherapeutic strategies.

DSM-III defines hypochondriasis as an "unrealistic fear or belief of having a disease persisting despite medical reassurance and which causes impairment in the social or occupational functioning" (American Psychiatric Association, 1980, p. 249). Hypochondriasis raises many problems: Is it a medical or a psychiatric subject? Is it an independent syndrome with clearly established diagnostic criteria? Are there effective therapeutic approaches?

Most researchers on hypochondriasis are psychiatrists (Nemiah, 1985), who "see only a small and unrepresentative subsample of hypochondriacal individuals: those who

177

find their way into the mental health care system" (Kellner, 1985, p. 822). Most hypochondriacal cases receive care from internists. Yet, more than half of the patients seen by U.S. physicians in their offices suffer from primary hypochondriacal symptoms or from minor somatic disorders with a hypochondriacal overlay (Kellner, 1985, p. 822). However, with narrower definitions, the prevalence figure is reduced to about 9 percent of all patients in a family practice clinic (Kellner, Abbott, Pathak, Winslow, and Umland, 1983).

Hypochondriasis may occur without any other mental disorder or secondarily to a preexisting psychiatric illness. The connections with major psychoses—affective disorders and schizophrenia—alternate with those related to anxiety, placing this disorder in a vaguely defined "borderline territory" between psychosis and neurosis. The status of hypochondriasis as a diagnostic entity therefore seems far from firmly established. Hypochondriasis, like hysteria, has been recognized since ancient times; both disorders have sometimes been confused or denied a significant place in a diagnostic psychiatric manuals. Some clinicians conclude that the false belief of suffering from a physical disease is the most important part of the psychopathology of hypochondriasis, so that concurrent neurotic symptoms are secondary to this belief. From another viewpoint, treatment rarely helps and often produces complications, side effects, or new symptoms (Barsky and Klerman, 1983, p. 279).

Hypochondriasis can be understood from an object relations theory viewpoint within the context of psychotic-like anxieties such as paranoid mistrust, the schizoid use of defensive splitting, or pining over depressing losses. The Kleinian theory on envy contributes to an understanding of hypochondriac behavior as that of a "help-rejecting-complainer" (Frank, Margolin, Nash, Stone, Varon, and

Ascher, 1952), also suggesting a possible psychotherapeutic strategy to treat these difficult patients.

Hypochondriacs focus their attention about themselves almost entirely on their bodies. Their selective, increased perception of their somatic sensations is often coupled with alexithymia (which literally means "no words for mood" [Sifneos, 1972]). They have an uncanny ability to describe their physical symptoms, coupled with a lack of capacity to connect them to significant emotions and an inability to label their feelings. Hypochondriacal anxiety concentration on the bodily functions is based on a cleavage, or splitting, between the perceptions of one's own body and the perceptions of one's own mind. Fears of being seriously ill physically preempt any possible preoccupation with mental malfunctioning. Therefore these patients resent doctors who tell them that "there is nothing wrong" with their bodies, that "the problem is all" in their minds. They believe that such doctors not only fail to understand their physical complaints but also threaten them with madness. Since these patients have long histories of somatic symptoms and poor responses to medical treatments, they are frequently resentful of, and mistrusting toward, doctors. A physician's explanations generally fail to convince hypochondriacal patients, who know that they have distressing bodily symptoms; explanations only persuade them that they have an undiagnosed disease. Some patients become angry, apparently because of unmitigated distress and their belief that they encounter impatient, rejecting, or hostile physicians. The "physician may be frustrated because the patient refuses to accept (medical) explanations, fails to benefit from repeated reassurance, and makes irrational, egotistical demands" (Kellner, 1985, p. 826). Physicians often react with irritation, attempting to get rid of such patients. Some internists, however, are particularly caring in dealing with hypochondriacal patients, developing a prolonged relationship with them, and frequently scheduling regular visits and meticulous physical examinations to reassure the patients.

Freud (1914a) classified hypochondriasis as an "actual neurosis," whose symptoms are essentially contentless and unanalyzable. He believed the genesis of the symptoms is toxic, a direct physiological transformation of sexual energy or libido, which was blocked from discharge. Freud remained uncertain, however, whether hypochondriasis was of somatic or psychogenic origin. In 1912 he wrote to Ferenczi, "I always felt the obscurity in the question of hypochondria to be a disgraceful gap in our work" (p. 453). In 1914 Freud explained hypochondriasis as a withdrawing of libidinal cathexis from objects with a turning of it onto the self—as a transformation of object libido into narcissistic libido. But he kept his "toxic" hypothesis active as well as his idea that hypochondriasis is more medical than psychological.

According to Kohut (1971, 1977) and his followers (Richards, 1981), hypochondriasis is the product of the lack of a cohesive self because of the mother's failure to respond adequately and empathically to the child's bodily and emotional needs. Thus, it indicates a disturbance in the self or self-representation. In Kohut's (1971) *The Analysis of the Self*, he states: "Viewed metapsychologically the deeply frightening feelings of fragmentation and deadness which the child experiences are a manifestation of the fact that, in the absence of the narcissistically invested self-object, the cathexis is withdrawn from a cohesively experienced self and regressive (autoerotic) fragmentation and hypochondriacal tensions now threaten the child" (p. 99). He draws an analogy between an adult's "hypochondriacal concerns and the vague health worries of a lonely child," explaining how such an analogy may facilitate "the patient's grasp of the deeper meaning of his present condition as well as its genetic roots" (p. 137). Kohut identifies an excessive preoccupation with one's own body (a normal occurrence in physical illness) as "a manifestation of increased narcissism" (p. 215). Yet in psychotic (or prepsychotic) hypochondriasis, "individual body parts, or isolated physical or mental functions, become isolated and hypercathected" (p. 215).

Hypochondriacal symptoms also have been explained as a form of "separation anxiety" whereby the patient produces symptoms to convince the caregiver that the patient still requires attention and should therefore not be left alone. Some therapists have pointed out how this "separation anxiety dynamic" viewpoint not only explains the hypochondriacal behavior, but also suggests a possible therapeutic approach (Perry, Frances, and Clarkin, 1985).

If these patients are concerned about being abandoned and use physical symptoms to maintain an attachment, it follows that they would be more relieved if "guaranteed" a prolonged relationship with a physician. Thus therapists may consider planning a lifelong therapeutic relationship rather than an open-ended one, to reassure these patients of maintaining such an attachment. Hypochondriacal patients are frequently lonely persons in search of some surrogate maternal care from their caregivers. Laura, the patient whose group psychotherapy course I shall report in detail here, had been abandoned by her father when she was four and by her mother when she was sixteen (*some* aspects of this case were discussed in the previous chapter and there is some inevitable overlap). She often seemed to be saying, "have pity on me" and was consequently nicknamed "Pitiful Pearl" by her groupmates.

Sometimes the precipitating event that precedes the development of hypochondriacal anxiety is the death of a loved person with whom the patient has identified. Consequently, the patient may have developed a fear later on of getting the same terminal illness that killed the lost loved object. Some authors report "hypochondria paranoides" as a rare disorder (Stenback and Rimon, 1964; Austrup and Noreik, 1966; Ladee, 1966; Hansen, 1968; Retterstol, 1968). Hypochondriasis is similar to paranoia insofar as the patient has a delusional system: The patient is convinced that physical illness is the cause of the distress, rather than it being the result of external persecution. The concept of the "internal persecutor," as a modality of paranoid anxiety, constitutes an explanatory bridge connecting hypochondriasis with paranoid states. I'll elaborate on this point later. The Kleinian theory on envy also contributes to an understanding of the interrelationship between paranoia and hypochondriasis. Envy generates the "need to spoil" the envied qualities of caregivers, first promoting their devaluation and subsequently experiencing the fear of being revengefully persecuted by them. They are perceived as being hostile and irritated, or alternatively as an internal object within the patient's mind, following an identification with the devalued, lost caregiver.

The characterological pattern of the "help-rejecting complainer" was described within the context of group psychotherapy (Frank et al., 1952). These patients relish complaining and use the group time to present their litany of complaints, while rejecting any help offered. They unconsciously use complaints as weapons to devalue the envied caregivers. Some authors have consequently labeled them "untreatable" (Mally and Ogston, 1964).

Our clinical experience with hypochondriasis is based on treating eight such patients: four men and four women. These patients included four single and four married persons. Four were without any bodily disease, and four had some somatic illnesses. Four were in individual psychoanalytically oriented psychotherapy, three were in analytic group psychotherapy, and one was a control case in a research project on biochemical treatment of depression. The youngest one was thirty, and the oldest fifty. My reflections on their hypochondriasis are based mainly on clinical observations made during group psychotherapy.

INDIVIDUALLY TREATED CASES

Using individual psychoanalytically oriented psychotherapy, I treated four hypochondriacs who had concurrent somatic illnesses. To briefly summarize these cases: Ann was blind, Arthur was arthritic, Alice had acne, and Irene had tuberculosis.

Ann became blind after an accident destroyed her right eye and the other "dried up" because of "sympathetic ophthalmia." She delusionally believed she suffered from lupus erythematosus, an untreatable disease. Arthur suffered from chronic rheumatoid arthritis, which made him an invalid. He was forced to stay at home, where he dominated and controlled his aging mother (devoted almost entirely to taking care of him). I saw Arthur briefly only for a psychiatric evaluation.

Alice was an eighteen-year-old who suffered from a mild acne, polycystic ovaries, and severe depression; she required psychiatric hospitalization. She had a hypochondriacal preoccupation with her facial skin. Although her acne was mild, she was convinced it seriously disfigured

her. She developed washing rituals. Preoccupation with
her face had begun when she was eighteen, and her
mother became psychotic. Her mother's insanity made
Alice feel that she herself had "lost face" socially. She then
started overvaluing the appearance of her facial skin,
localizing her anxiety there, to deny her psychiatric condition. She rejected the part of herself that identified with
her mother. Regression to body/self-fragmentation had
occurred (Ganzarain and Buchele, 1988).

Irene was a thirty-five-year-old survivor of tuberculosis, who had had two thoracoplasty operations to surgically
immobilize half her thorax and thus collapse the tuberculosis caverns located in that lung. Because of peritoneal
tuberculosis,she was also sterile. Several of her siblings had
died of tuberculosis. Irene suffered from neurotic depression (connected with a survivor's guilt syndrome) plus
hypochondriacal anxieties leading her to visit doctors
frequently. She married a professional man, fifteen years
her senior. Irene was referred to me for depression by her
internist, who took appropriate care of her: He offered
periodic visits to check on her bodily health; during each
visit, he meticulously checked her physical condition. He
encouraged her to expand her artistic interests and he also
became a genuine friend of the couple, with whom he
shared common interests. The development of her paint-
ing talents gave Irene a new life goal that made her feel
good about herself. The internist's attitude was skillful,
both as a physician and as a psychotherapist.

This chapter is based, however, mainly on clinical
observations made during group psychotherapy; all the
sessions were videotaped. The excerpts of transcripts
come from those tapes. I shall now deal with the psychopathology of hypochondriasis, its description and psychodynamics, and, later on, with some psychotherapeutic
strategies, their rationale, and results.

PSYCHOPATHOLOGY: DESCRIPTION AND PSYCHODYNAMICS

Paranoid Phenomenon

The epitomy of mistrust and anger at doctors can be described as the "negative placebo effect." I observed it in a control case, while working on a research project testing a psychopharmacological treatment for depression. The control cases were given injections of distilled water, while the experimental cases received an active psychopharmacological substance. A man in his early forties responded to the injection of distilled water by feeling poisoned; he returned to the clinic threatening to sue the doctors and stating that "he had never felt worse in his life." Like paranoid patients who are afraid of being poisoned, this man expected doctors to give him harmful substances.

I also observed a basic mistrust of caregivers in another patient who was blind. I treated Ann with individual psychotherapy. She had lost her sight after a childhood accident that caused the physical loss of one eye. Her doctor's poor treatment caused the loss of the other. The vision in her unharmed eye was lost because her ophthalmologist did not immediately remove the destroyed, traumatized eye to prevent "sympathetic ophthalmia." Ann consequently developed a bitter mistrust of doctors, needing to prove them wrong, to vengefully devalue them.

I shall describe here three cases treated with group psychotherapy: Laura, Jill, and Jerry.

A HELP-REJECTING COMPLAINER ACTS OUT THE GROUP'S ANGER

Laura was a depressed neurotic with hypochondriacal symptoms, anorgasmia, and a masochistic personality. She had been going from doctor to doctor and strongly mistrusted them. As noted previously, when she was four years old, her father disappeared, abandoning the family. Her mother left home when Laura was sixteen, forcing her to take care of her younger sister and the household payments. In the thirteenth session, Laura became the spokesperson for the group's anger at the psychotherapist. In this group of eight married, white, middle-class outpatients all had at least graduated from high school. I had individually interviewed each patient three times before forming the group, which met for seventy-five minutes twice a week. During session 13, Laura reported her recent visit to a neurologist. Here is an excerpt of that session's transcript:

Laura: I don't feel like I'm making progress; I feel like I'm going down.

Robert: Maybe that's when you are making progress?

Sharon: Something's about to happen!

Robert: Yeah.

Sharon: You're getting close to something.

Robert: The more frightening it gets, the closer you're getting to what you don't want to get, although I don't have any idea what it is, or anything. I'll wait for five minutes and ask Laura what she found out yesterday because I was thinking about that.

Laura: I feel like I should talk.

Jill: But, do it!

Robert: You should go ahead and do it!

Laura: It makes me so embarrassed! It's hard for me to start. I went to the doctor yesterday, and I hope Dr. Ganzarain doesn't get mad at me for saying what I'm going to say, but I'm so fed up with doctors at this point I could scream!

Dr. G.: Do it please!

Laura: You have these feelings and you go to the

doctor to get help and then he tells you, "There isn't anything wrong!" He did also say, "You're no candidate for group therapy." He said: "You should have private sessions" and he meant what he said.

Daniel: Is he an M.D.?

Laura: Well, he is a neurologist with the Menninger Foundation.

Robert: Did you say it was Doctor Y.?

Laura: No, Doctor X. He's a good doctor and I believe what he's telling me and all, as far as that goes; but I have had such a fear of losing my mind, of losing my ability to think straight! I'm actually afraid of people! I don't care who they are. I've had to work the last three days. I think this afternoon got the best of me. Of course, they always excuse you; they always, you know, find excuses. Well, they can do this, but I can't for myself. I went home last night and my children were even worried. I never heard hardly a word out of any of them. Of course, my husband is really very upset too. He'd do anything to help. Well, he wanted me to go see a doctor at Menninger's, which financially we can't afford.

Dr. G.: Who is this that he wanted?

Laura: Doctor X.

Robert: Aren't you seeing a psychiatrist at Menninger's?

Laura: Not privately. He wants me to go privately. He said, "You need all the attention, and in a group you can't get all of the attention, you can't." So . . . the doctor just would like to try and help me, if he can. He's still going to have me take medication, although he cut it down.

Jill: What's the medication for?

Laura: Well, it's. . . . What is it? Dilantin.

Sharon: What's it for?

Laura: Well, he says, "I have an irregularity" and from what I gathered I still couldn't get him to really explain what "an irregularity" is. Well, from what I gathered last night it's really not all that serious, not all that big of a problem because the brain scan came out quite normal. But as I say, you've got these problems and yet they say you're fine and this is the most. . . . (*Cries*)

Wally: You're fine physically is what you're telling me?

Laura: Yeah, he said that I was really—as far as physically—I was. . . . He didn't say "tip-top," he said something like excellent or something.

Robert: Probably everyone in this room is physically in pretty good shape.

Laura: But anyway, finally I said, well, go ahead; I didn't know what my husband was going to think.

Wally: Would you have felt better had he found something wrong?

Laura: Yeah, I'd go for surgery. Now that sounds stupid and idiotic, but at least you can go through surgery and cut a part out and get healed up and go on your merry way. Mentally, you can't do that! I can't even see well. . . .

Robert: You have to do you own surgery mentally.

Laura: I have worked on this problem for so many years! And I never, never felt like I would like to feel. I'd like to have light shoulders; I'd like to go on about my business; I'd like to be happy.

Daniel: What do you think you worked on this problem? . . .

Laura: Oh, I have gone over to the Family Service and Guidance Center for therapy all the way back . . . I can't remember . . . ten—maybe not that long—years ago. I went over there for a year, maybe two years, I can't remember that either . . . I really felt like I was making headway. Well, I did for a while, but all of a sudden I started sliding back. As I saw, I'm to a point where I'm afraid of people! I don't know whether it's what they think of me or how I act or the response I'm going to get, or what. But nonetheless I went home and told my husband and he asked why we couldn't go through the Family Service and Guidance Center, instead of Menninger's because it wasn't quite as expensive. Well, I got kind of upset, because I would have really liked to have gone to Menninger's because the doctors there are a little more experienced.

Wally: You have the same doctors at the Family Service and Guidance Center. Don't they, Dr. Ganzarain?

Dr. G.: I would like to hear more. . . .

Laura: Well, anyway I have the feeling that I've never forgotten the feeling of this other doctor giving me this medication, and for three days I really hardly knew what I was going through. It made me dopey and sleepy, and I really wasn't that alert and I don't want to experience that again. This doctor also said he could treat me too, as far as that goes, and I asked him how? He said, well, by drugs. I'm a little afraid of drugs! He asked me if I had ever taken, what do you call them . . . depressant . . . anti-depressant pills or something. My regular doctor, seven years ago, gave them to me, and I can recall my reaction to them. I spent three days doing nothing but crying. This was just the reaction to the medication! But the thing is, I am to the point I hardly believe there's hope! (*Cries*) I know I kind of relaxed my trying, but I'm so tired of putting on a front, of putting on a face that people think that I'm not! I don't know; I just really don't know what to do; I'm just in a vicious circle; I just can't even get my thoughts together! (*Cries*)

Laura was voicing the group's anger at the therapist for not giving them more individual attention. The other patients were fostering Laura's expression of anger and giving her the attention she demanded. Some of the group members identified with Laura more clearly than others,

voicing their own irritation at, and frustration with, therapists. A couple of patients, however, criticized Laura's
demands, helping her realize how she used complaining to
attract attention and to express anger.

Regarding the psychology of complaining, Jerome
Frank (Frank et al., 1952) described the help-rejecting
complainer behavioral pattern in group psychotherapy.
The study of complaining is enriched when this behavior
pattern is understood as an expression of envy of the
helper (Rey, 1961). The envy leads to a devaluation of the
helper's power, through proving that the provided help is
"no good." Laura developed a specific envious devaluation
of doctors. She needed them just as she had needed her
parents, but how could she trust them if they abandoned
her by saying she was "fine"—or by placing her in group
psychotherapy!

Laura's masochistic character led her to "collect injustices" (Bergler, 1949) inflicted on her by others, especially
by doctors. The other patients in the group recognized
Laura's "injustice collecting" attitude and confronted her
with her need to suffer, which was an attempt to induce
guilt in everybody, and to consequently dominate and
control everyone.

The groupmates were, in part, speaking through
Laura's mouth, while simultaneously seeing themselves in
Laura's conflicts regarding needs and anger. Laura was
like a mirror her groupmates could use to see themselves.
She was the spokesperson for their anger at the therapist,
for having "abandoned" them by no longer seeing them
individually, and for placing them instead in a group,
where they had to "share" him with other patients. The
loss of individual contact with the therapist might have reminded Laura of her parents abandoning her. She resentfully looked for another caregiver, the neurologist, who
might provide her with adequate help.

Laura defended herself against her intense mistrust of caregivers by readily idealizing each new helper. She consequently had a naive proneness to assume that each new doctor would immediately provide her with miraculous help. In spite of, or maybe because of, her many past disappointments with doctors, Laura always had high hopes about the help offered by each new doctor. Such idealization of the new helper was necessarily short-lived. The new caregiver would soon be devalued also! She thus hoped to be correctly diagnosed by the neurologist as having some brain malfunctioning and to be either operated on, or given a medication that would cure her. However, she made a slip of the tongue, stating that she expected the neurologist to prescribe her some "depressant" (when she intended to say "antidepressant") medication. She described her "negative placebo effect" when taking antidepressants in the past: She felt "worse than ever" the following three days immediately after starting the medication.

Laura expressed her passive–dependent wishes for nurturance from the caregivers, complaining that in group sessions she did not have "private" sessions, or "all of the doctor's attention." Laura also openly expressed her fears of losing her mind, of suffering a disintegration of her self, of becoming psychotic when stating: "I just cannot even get my thoughts together." Her concern with having a malfunctioning brain was a "somatized" way to express her fear of psychosis.

Hypochondriacal Anxieties During Mourning

Another member of this group, Jill, suffered the death of her father during her group treatment. She feared she would have the same fatal disease that caused her father's death, since both suffered from a familial disease called "polyposis of the colon." It is characterized by the presence of benign growths in the colon, which have the potential to become cancerous. Jill grew up having regular colon checkups. Her father's carelessness with these regular checkups caused the doctors to miss the transformation of the benign tumors into cancer. When he finally went to the doctor, the polyps had already degenerated into a malignancy, which had spread to his abdomen.

Jill was critical of both her father and his doctors for letting too much time pass without a checkup. She also resented the timing of her father's death, insofar as it happened when she had made significant psychotherapeutic progress. Mourning stopped her progress, her lack of self-confidence resurfaced. She experienced a pathological mourning, initially developing a hypomanic defensive reaction, while suffering nightmares that caused her to sleep poorly.

At one point, Jill reported a dream that dramatized her identification with her dying father. The setting of the dream was a hospital room. She saw herself standing beside her father's bed, pleading with the doctor to do everything in his power to help her father. She uncovered her father's body to show the doctor how emaciated he was and how his skin was covered by foul-smelling awful wounds that required some active intervention. Suddenly the scene changed, and Jill herself was the sick person in bed, pleading with the doctor for help. Her identification with her father was dramatized by her body replacing his in the dream. She associated to her fears of eventually also developing a malignancy from her benign tumors. But she complained mainly of doctors being careless, indifferent, and inefficient, saying her family doctor had reassured her father that "there was nothing wrong with him," when the malignancy had already started. She transiently feared that doctors were also careless in treating her.

Jill's identification with her dead father conveyed how the internalized father had become a "persecutor from within" her own self, threatening her with the potential for developing cancer and also dying a horrible death, as he had. There was a clear sequence from Jill's painful experiencing of her father's loss, to identifying with him, to him becoming an "internal persecutor," threatening her life with the risk of dying as he had. Jill was then unable to develop an "internal good object" that would provide her with reassurance, comfort, and self-esteem; she was instead prone to develop internal objects who persecuted and threatened her with the possible development of a fatal disease. Her identification with her deceased father left her oscillating between blaming him for not taking better care of himself and blaming the doctors for being inefficient and indifferent. When Jill became too intensely critical and angry at her father, she would shift blame to the doctors rather than continue to experience unbearable guilt for her anger at her father's irresponsibility vis-à-vis his own health. Thus mourning her father's death led Jill to develop several paranoidlike and hypochondriacal anxieties as transient complications to working through her depressive anxieties after her father's death.

Jerry was another hypochondriacal patient I treated in group therapy with unmarried persons. Jerry was forty and divorced. He suffered from depression following his mother's death. He needed psychiatric hospitalization because of a pathological mourning, and he was referred for group psychotherapy.

Jerry attended the meetings, carrying a pillow to sit on, because of his concern with hemorrhoids. Antidepressant medication caused him constipation, which increased his hemorrhoidal disturbances, which he frequently complained about.

As group psychotherapy continued, we learned that

Jerry's mother had suffered for years from uterine prolapse. Jerry had been told that his father wanted to have
another son after Jerry's older brother was born, so he
demanded that his wife postpone the surgical correction
of her uterine condition, which she did until after she
delivered Jerry. For this patient the prolapse of his hemorrhoidal veins was a concrete somatic identification with
his mother, because Jerry felt guilty about his conception.
He mourned his mother intensely, since he felt they were
much alike in personality. She was anxious about her
physical health and was also a help-rejecting complainer.
One of Jerry's groupmates, Tom, suffered from juvenile
diabetes. Tom was often preoccupied with losing his sight,
as a retinal complication of diabetes. However, Tom was
rather careless about his health; often not following his
regular diet or insulin injections. When Tom talked in the
group about his health preoccupations, Jerry, in spite of
his knowledge of diabetes, tended to ignore Tom's anxiety.
When Jerry and Tom talked about their physical health, it
became obvious that Jerry used his hypochondriacal anxieties to attract attention; he consequently resented attention given Tom because of his more serious physical
problems. As group psychotherapy made some impact in
Jerry's symptomatology, he became less concerned about
hemorrhoids. However, his hypochondriacal anxieties
were then displaced toward his vertebrae. Consequently,
the pillow was replaced with a smaller one located behind
his back to support his lumbar spine.

Envy and Hypochondriasis

As patients, the help-rejecting complainers seek help
from doctors, but reject their assistance. These patients

have an ambivalent relationship to their helpers, whereby they seek help only to prove their helpers' impotence. They use complaining as a weapon to first engage the helper in some interaction, and later on to devalue the helper's power. Since inequalities exist between helpers and patients, the differences can easily provoke a patient's envy of his helpers, who are perceived as being powerful because of their resources, which the patient needs, plus some specialized skills and professional degrees.

The inequalities between patient and helper may be a particular instance of envious comparisons between the "haves and have nots." Such comparisons promote envy; that is, the wish to have what one lacks either by stealing it or by spoiling the "goodies" that others enjoy. Complaining may be a weapon at the service of envy (Rey, 1961) that patients use to attack and devalue their helpers' power by spoiling their enjoyment of being helpful.

In *Envy and Gratitude* Melanie Klein (1957) described the infant's envy regarding the mother's breast as a dyadic relation between a "have" and a "have not." The mother's power to gratify the dependent infant's needs can be spoiled by envy. The inequality between the two is based upon the fact that the infant needs the mother (or her surrogate) for survival, but the mother can go on with her life without depending on the infant. A similar lack of reciprocity is present between the helper and those being helped, leaving room for envy to spoil their relationship. The help-rejecting complainer attitude is a product of envy. Understanding the relationship between help-rejecting complaining and envy is central to developing a grasp of the dynamics of hypochondriasis and to developing a rationale for effective psychotherapeutic strategies.

Psychotherapeutic Strategies With Hypochondriacs: Rationale and Effects

Rationale

Using the "natural" defenses against envy to overcome it

Since envy emerges when a person compares what he has with somebody else's possessions, the attitude of "me too" is an unconscious defense against envy. It has an equalizing effect through denying differences that generate envy (Klein, 1957). The equalizing effect to the "me too" attitude is somehow reinforced in group psychotherapy, since patients are encouraged and expected to eventually function as cotherapists. They gradually oscillate between being participants in the group—experiencing emotional conflicts and also responding to the group material—and acting as "observers" who reflect and offer observations, suggestions, and interpretations to group-mates who act transiently as cotherapists. Thus group psychotherapy promotes patients' identification with their helpers, offering opportunities to develop a healthy "me too" defensive stance, vis-à-vis envious reactions to therapists. Such identifications with the therapist form the basis of the "therapeutic alliance" in individual psychotherapy, helping the patient to "see things" as the therapist does. In group psychotherapy, a reversal of the roles between patient and therapist is even more explicitly encouraged. There is, however, the risk that some patients may exaggerate envious identifications with the therapists and behave rigidly and constantly as "a doctor's assistant," without being able to ever explore themselves as patients (Frank et al., 1952). This exaggerated use of the "me too" defense against envy is one of the most difficult resistances to group psychotherapy. However, unlike narcissistic personalities, hypochondriac patients do not usually become "doctor's assistants."

The fantasy of aggressively "taking away" the goods possessed by the envied person is another defense mechanism against envy. For instance, narcissistic patients may try to "steal" the power from the therapist, by "taking over" the helping functions. The behavioral pattern of the doctor's assistant will epitomize the violent acting out of these fantasies, to the point of role confusion (Klein, 1957), with the patient pretending not to act as a patient anymore. But within limits, the sharing of therapeutic functions in the group provides opportunities for patients to exercise intermittently some therapeutic functions while still being able to analyze their envious wishes. Envy is prominent in the patients' reactions to any exercise of power by the therapists, such as when making paramount "administrative" decisions affecting the patients' dependency (e.g., choosing not to meet, when to separate, when to bring in new patients, or when to consider possible terminations). Thus a particularly clear set of envious reactions may be explored.

Guarantee against abandonment

Since many hypochondriacal patients have been abandoned at an early age by their caregivers, it may be important for the therapist to offer a guarantee against again being abandoned, this time by their current caregivers whom they resentfully need. Some authors (Perry et al., 1985) suggest a long-term contract, with regularly scheduled visits to an internist, guaranteeing the doctor's prolonged availability as a way to soothe abandonment fears. Group analytic psychotherapy has a policy of planning for a somewhat prolonged contact (at least a year), between patient and therapist, which offers some guarantee against possible abandonment. The availability of group members as replacements for the therapists may also meet the need to look for new helpers. Each patient can defensively "turn away from the primal object" of dependency—the therapist—to rely upon groupmates (Klein, 1957).

Provide opportunities to correct paranoid distortions of helpers

Patients may view their helpers as revengeful, indifferent, and sadistic. Meissner (1982) suggests breaking the "paranoid vicious cycle" of distorted perceptions by exploring in detail and double-checking all the circumstances leading to the paranoid distortions. Such distorted perceptions escalate patients' views of continuous ongoing retaliations between them and their alleged persecutors, with themselves as victims (Meissner, 1982).

By carefully reviewing again and again all the details that led to paranoid distortions, the therapist can help the patient achieve reality assessment, and distortions give way. I did some such work with Laura after she forgot that the therapist had cancelled a group session, and came to the meeting place only to discover in shock that nobody was there! (See also chapter 8.) Laura had purposefully missed the previous session because the last time she attended, she left the group in anger. When she arrived for the cancelled session and realized that nobody was there, she thought everybody was furious at her and that they were getting back at her for her recent absence. With effort Laura later remembered that she had been notified of the cancellation. When she reported her response to the group's absence, Laura described her initially dramatic reaction, of feeling anxious, experiencing depersonalization, and remembering occasions when her parents had abandoned her. She sat down for a while to pull herself together enough to overcome her physical and mental anguish. When she finally remembered the phone call from my secretary canceling the session, she insinuated that she resented my not calling her. When I commented that she probably would have expected me to call, Laura responded, "I know that your secretary does all the work." The groupmates confronted Laura with her implication that my secretary does *all* my work, and we gradually moved on to exploring the group's feelings that doctors are so busy they can barely pay attention to their patients. When the group commented on the power doctors exert over their patients, I said that they seemed to resent my power to cancel a session or to bring up termination, as I had recently done. The patients then clarified that they also had power in interacting with me. After all, I was someone providing them with a service, like the young boys they hire to mow their lawns! The group patients would go on "hiring" me as long as they were satisfied, but they had the power to fire me, if I did not continue providing good services. They jokingly reassured me that so far I had provided good service. They felt triumphantly in control, so that despite my having cancelled a session, they had the final say about the future of our relationship. They were thus protected against being abandoned, and last, but not least, they provided Laura with an opportunity to correct her paranoid distortions about my canceling the session as a revenge for her anger at me and the group.

Provide occasions for the group to develop further reparatory skills or abilities

Help the patients practice "good mothering," by being adequate helpers to each other. Becoming important and efficient—through helping other group members—is a curative factor in group psychotherapy (Yalom, 1975). Searles (1973) described, as a central part in the psychotherapy of seriously ill patients, their attempts to help the psychotherapist through projecting into the therapist their most regressed needs, and later on by proceeding to help the therapist, whom they now perceived as in extreme need of help. Other group members provide similar opportunities for projecting the need to be helped into them; thus all patients in the group are offered the chance to develop helping skills and to therefore feel good about themselves, since they can effectively care for somebody else.

Psychotherapeutic Work

As the group started practicing their capacity to make reparation to their loved objects, Laura planned to invite her mother to visit. Her mother had twice attempted to live in the same town, each time with one of her daughters; on both occasions, the relationship between her and her daughters became intolerable, forcing her to leave town. However, Laura was now determined to give her mother another chance. Laura planned this time to have her mother occupy an apartment in a nursing home. She would then have independence, but at the same time she would be close to her two daughters. The group met for its 119th session two days before Laura's mother's arrival. The group had been meeting for approximately one-and-one-half years, with the same six members (plus two others who had been discharged).

"Can We Ever Get Rid of Our Mothers?"

Session 119 started with Jill complaining that the others did not appreciate enough her progress and her contributions to the group. Jill felt that she was being used by the others without being given to in return. Her complaints apparently applied to everybody in the group, maybe even including herself for not having conveyed her achievements more clearly. As the session unfolded, Laura became the center of attention:

Sharon: I don't know, this seems like some kind of a show-and-tell session or something . . . sort of bringing everybody up-to-date on how everybody feels. I think . . . it was just a few sessions back that you, Laura, said something about how you were doing, and everybody noticed that you . . . you know . . . you're so much better than you were earlier.

Laura: I feel . . . I feel much more com . . . I don't today because it's hard to focus my eyes. But. . . .

Robert: What's wrong with your eyes?

Laura: Oh, I've got the most terrific headache I've ever had . . . and I really didn't notice that I was dizzy until Sharon told. . . .

Sharon: 'til I said so. (*Laughs*)

Laura: And, really, I . . . all day long I haven't been able to see out of my glasses (*laughs*) and it seems like there's been things . . . you know . . . in my eyes and I've tried rubbing them out. I hope I'm not getting the flu (*laughs*). I don't feel bad other than that, but my head just feels like it's going to fly off. (*Laughs*) That's why I'm kind of quiet. I want to speak up but I'm afraid things might come out wrong. (*Laughs*)

Robert: Is there some reason for having a headache today?

Laura: I don't know. I've had it all day long, and I don't know why. (*Laughs*) It's even hard to smile. So . . . yeah . . . I have felt better. . . . I had felt stronger, both at work and even meeting new people in general. And I don't know, unless it's been a conviction that I have made within myself, that I was going to try to work at it. Maybe that's why. And I think I have tried!

Robert: I must be thinking about something that isn't important at all, but it really makes me wonder why you've got a headache today and why you're sick today?

Laura: I don't know. I have headaches once in a while, and I'm not going to bring up an old subject, but I've been having trouble with my teeth. I think this may be touching a nerve or something; maybe this is what's causing the headaches. I don't know. . . .

Jill: Maybe your mom is coming. . . .

Robert: That's why. That was what I was trying to get out of it.

Laura: But really, I've been trying to think very positive about that. I think about it. We go over to work on her apartment, and really and truly I'm so excited about the apartment that I forget about my mother's negative attitude. Really if she isn't happy, I'm afraid I just might get angry!

Robert: Why are you afraid?

Laura: What?

Robert: Why are you afraid you might get angry?

Laura: I don't want to say anything I might regret and I might say something I might regret! (*Laughs*)

Robert: I got angry with Norman the other night and I didn't say anything I would regret. I was mad and I just have to say what I stated.

Laura: You don't know my mother! (*Laughs*) Norman forgives and forgets, but I'm not so sure about her. . . .

Norman: I bet you're worried about your mother.

Laura: Well, I. . . .

Norman: Let me tell you why I say that.

Laura: Why?

Norman: Like Robert said, you've got a headache, but

when you're uptight and when nervousness really takes you over, you laugh at things that aren't funny. You do your giggling thing, and now really you're doing it today.

Laura: Am I doing it today?

Norman: Yes. You'll say something serious, you know, Laura. Like, "I haven't been able to focus my eyes and I've had this headache." You're doing today the nervous laughter type thing that you do, and the more uptight you are the more you do that. So maybe Jill, or whoever said it, was right. Is it this weekend your mother comes?

Laura: Saturday.

Norman: Well, that's this weekend.

Sharon: Two days from today!

Robert: Just about time enough to get sick, so you can be in bed when she gets here!

Norman: It might be more significant than you want it to be. When you're relaxed if you're talking about your husband, your work, yourself, this group, you don't do your giggles then, but it kind of gives you away; to me it does.

Laura: Well, I will admit I'm a little bit reluctant because I don't know what to expect.

Norman: I'm sure you don't.

Dr. G.: You do and you don't, because you have already told us that probably she is going to express her complaints (*Laura agrees with an "ummm"*); and she's going to say that she's not happy; and you know her, she's going to do it! You also know yourself, so what are you going to do with that? The illusion that she's going to be very pleased with her apartment is unrealistic, given her character.

Jill: But there's sure an unbelievable change in you, the way you have been toward her! If she comes and she doesn't like it, that's just tough luck; I've tried my hardest!

Robert: You might even get mad at her! That's very positive.

Laura: I've made up my mind I'm not going to let her tear me up, like she tore me up the last time.

Jill: She won't; I'll bet she won't!

Laura: Furthermore . . . I guess I don't want my husband to have to step in and do something that I should do and, therefore, I think I should try to be a little stronger and let her know where I stand. (*Sighs*)

Dr. G.: As difficult as it is! In Laura's case, there is also another side that she should watch: The little-girl side of herself may be expecting mother to be very grateful, to give you straight A's in how well you have done. The need to be evaluated very positively by your mother is what may get you, in terms of expecting her to praise you and to be grateful. All of those things that she's probably not going to do.

Laura: No, I don't think she's going to do that and I'll tell you why. She's going to think we went too expensive, as far as furnishing her apartment and we didn't, but she's going to think it's outrageous. But it's very neat, very "homey" and I wouldn't do it any other way. I wanted it to be pleasant. If it was up to her, she'd have an old chair here or. . . .

Jill: Can we ever get rid of our mothers!! (*Everybody laughs.*) I'm having problems with my mother. Nothing that's going to kill me, but I wish that I could get along with my mother, to the point where I could stand up for myself and know that whether or not what I tell her how I live is right or wrong, it's me. I'm saying it, and it's my decision. She can get me so messed up that, when I try to talk about something that's me, it's as though she just doesn't believe it.

Sharon: You go home feeling guilty and bad and wrong.

Jill: She just got me into hysterics the other night about the group. She does half the time. I've never seen me like my mother. If I'm like that, I won't have kids!

Laura: This is one thing that I'm going to have a battle with my mother over. She doesn't believe that I need to come over to group therapy and she's continuously harping, "Why are you doing it? Why are you doing it?" (*Sharon, softly, without interrupting Laura:* "You are driving me crazy, Mother!") (*Everybody laughs.*) I'm not going to tell her what I'm going to be doing, but this is eventually what I'll be hearing.

Robert: You only hear it, if you put up with it!

Jill: You must have had a different kind of mother.

Sharon: (*Repeats louder*) You drive me crazy, Mother! That's why I have to go to group therapy. You know, you don't have to tell her why or care what she thinks. You can tell her, "It's something I want to do; it's something that makes me feel better and that's why I'm going."

Robert: It's the whole thing of what Jill was talking about, that we all react to our mothers as mothers, instead of reacting to them as people, as adults, and we are adults and we should be able to say to our mothers, "Okay, I'm going to group therapy, because that's what I think is best for me and if you don't like it, bug off, I don't want to talk about it. I won't argue." Not in these words necessarily. . . .

Jill: I could use those words!

Norman: You're bad if you do it!

Robert: Who says you're bad?

Norman: Society does.

Robert: The Commandment is to love thy mother and father or honor them. Yeah, that's one of the Commandments, but to love or to honor doesn't mean to put up with a bunch of shit!

Norman: That's true.

Robert: You can love somebody adult as to adult and not obey their every command, because they're as neurotic as you are or even worse. . . . You're feeding their neurosis! Jill is, by putting up with her mother.

Jill: No, I don't put up with it! Okay, I don't put up with it anymore, because I've learned a lot, you know, but it's just that she can get me so mangled up! What I feel, I feel, but I can't ever say this is why I feel this, mother; this is why I go here, mother, because she thinks. . . . It's just what she can do to me! I guess I'd rather, but. . . .

Robert: Have you ever told her what you just said?

Sharon: She can say two or three words and just . . . you know . . . and make you feel terrible!

Dr. G.: The crux of the matter is whether you let her do it! And probably that's the thing Laura has to watch—and each one of you in your struggles to be more assertive and more independent. You still need mother in that kind of role, and there is still a childish part of yourselves that wants to cling to that image and not let go of mother and still look for her—or for a surrogate of her, like the group—for support, for encouragement, for a pat on the back; or are you growing out of that need? And in that regard, there is a parallelism between mother and some of your feelings toward the group. (*Jill nods her head.*)

Laura: I've got to say something. First of all, I want to thank you really. I don't have my headache anymore! (*Expressions of joy by several, such as through smiles and cheers.*) I don't really! And I honestly didn't realize that it was . . . mother.

Dr. G.: (*Laughs*) Mother strikes again! (*Everybody laughs.*)

Jill: That's just because you're getting loose.

Laura: Well, it's because I can talk about it.

Robert: It came out in the open and you got it out of the inside, and got it out in the open.

Laura: But I honestly didn't realize that that was what was getting to me. . . .

Robert: We all knew it wasn't nerves in your denture!

Laura: Well.

Robert: Well, I just got to feeling like Jill did, right off the bat, that it was your mother.

There were several observable changes in Laura during this session. She had obviously developed a new attitude toward her mother and was now willing to run the risk of having her in town and interacting with her on an everyday basis. She wanted to repair the relationship with her mother and to exercise her responsibility as a daughter. During the session, Laura moved from her usual seat, to the left of the therapist where she had always sat, to sit opposite him. The groupmates noticed her new seat and commented on it as something significant. More importantly, Laura was able to use the group's help to acknowledge the connection between her current headache and her fear of her mother's move to town. Even more remarkable was her acceptance of the group's help, and her expressions of gratitude for that help. She had begun to overcome her envy of the helpers and consequently was able to acknowledge their caring.

In the videotapes of this group session, one may observe how Laura made nonverbal identifications with her mother. For example, when Laura talked about her mother's complaints about her eyesight, she would rub her own eyes as if trying to clear her vision. Her concerns with loss of sight and the attempt to "clean her eyes" dramatized Laura's identification with her mother, who suffered from cataracts. Laura was also planning to "mother" her own mother by becoming her helper. A role reversal was taking place, as Laura prepared to welcome her mother. By becoming her mother's caregiver, Laura was now "in charge, in power" vis-à-vis her mother. From now on, she would be mothering her own mother. Since her mother was now in need, she would be prone to feel envious of Laura's power over her. Laura could therefore defend herself against her own envy, through "stirring up others' envy"—her mother's or someone else's (Klein, 1957). But then Laura became anxious regarding her mother's possible envious attacks. Now envy was outside Laura, on someone else's mind! As a consequence of such role reversal, Laura was now anxious about her mother possibly rejecting her help and ungratefully attacking Laura for not being good enough. As Laura cast herself in the role of a helper, she worried about her mother's rejection; she was foreseeing her mother's help-rejecting complainer attitude and was afraid of getting angry at her mother. She thus inadvertently stepped into the helpers' shoes and identified herself with them.

This role reversal was also a prelude to Laura's change of job. Her previous job was as a "surrogate" employee, on call when regular employees were absent and a substitute was required. Somehow Laura accepted this low paid, relatively marginal employment as an expression of her low self-esteem; likewise, obtaining better paying, more skillful employment that required technical qualifications was another indication of her improvement. She had decided to get some technical training of electroencephalography (EEG), and finally obtained a job as an EEG technician. As a member of a medical staff, she was testing patients' brain waves, a situation that promoted her disowning, or projecting, her own hypochondriacal anxieties onto the persons she tested. Laura's new job helped consolidate her improvement from hypochondriacal anxieties. It quite naturally helped her get rid of her anxieties by projecting them onto her clients!

During the 119th session, a similar role reversal occurred in Jill: She started by complaining about the group not appreciating her significant changes, then behaved like a complaining patient. However, later in the session Jill was the one who was able to correctly diagnose Laura's conflicts: "Maybe your mom is coming. . . ." A few minutes later it was also Jill who interjected, "Can we ever get rid of our mothers?" She was certainly tuned in with Laura's conflicts in dealing with her mother. Jill used her identification with Laura to effectively help her, thus taking a significant step forward in overcoming her own dependency stance as a patient, and acting instead as a cotherapist, effectively understanding Laura's conflicts. After helping Laura, Jill felt pleased with herself, leading her to greater self-reliance through the group.

There were other opportunities where the groupmates identified themselves with the therapist vis-à-vis Laura, mainly when she reiterated her litany of complaints and the other members felt free to express their boredom, impatience, and anger. By openly stating their emotional reactions to Laura's attacks on their help, her groupmates contributed significantly across time to Laura's own understanding of the consequences of her constant complaining. Upon the arrival of her mother in town, Laura was anxious about how to deal with her own impatience, irritation, and anger at her mother's envious rejection of Laura's help.

FOLLOW-UP

During the 280 group psychotherapy sessions that Laura attended, she was able to work through conflicts connected with her fears of abandonment, her mistrust of objects, and her tendency to masochistically "collect injustices," thus trying to control her objects through guilt. Laura's attempts to repair her relationships with her objects led her to also inquire about the fate of her father (who abandoned his family when Laura was four). She found out that her father had remarried in another state and had fathered several children with his second wife. Laura discovered that the oldest son of her father's second marriage was then living in her own state. She wrote to him, sending him a photograph of herself, and requesting contact between the two. She was excited when she received her half-brother's photograph. She found him "just like her father." For her to establish contact with this brother was a significant substitution for her missed relationship with her father. Laura's ability to improve her relationships directly with her mother, and indirectly with her father, combined with her role reversal in her work activities, produced an impressive change in her outlook on life.

DISCUSSION AND SUMMARY

Conclusions drawn out of treating only eight hypochondriacal patients are obviously not statistically significant, but some clinical observations and therapeutic results may be of interest. In particular, consider the rationale for certain psychotherapeutic strategies used to achieve significant changes in the lives of these hypochondriacal patients. "The 'separation anxiety' dynamic . . . explains the behavior and . . . suggests a possible therapeutic approach for some patients" (Perry et al., 1985, p. 230). The help-rejecting complainer (Frank et al., 1952) group behavioral pattern, coupled with the theory on envy (Klein, 1957), explains characteristic styles of object relations and likewise suggests relevant therapeutic approaches. The remarkable match between Frank's clinical group observations and Klein's theory, developed from the practice of psychoanalysis, exists despite Frank's basic disagreement with psychoanalytic theory. To guarantee a prolonged relationship with a caregiver allays the fears of abandonment experienced by most hypochondriacal patients. And using the defenses against envy of the helper's power to protect hypochondriacal patients from sabotaging help facilitates their use of therapy. Group psychotherapy promotes a sharing of the therapist's power; it uses the "me too" or equalizing defense against envy, by inviting each patient to become a cotherapist of the groupmates (Klein, 1957). Becoming a helper is simultaneously a role reversal: Through taking the helper's functions, patients may project and discard their envy by "stirring up others' envy" (Klein, 1957). This role reversal can be extended beyond the psychotherapy group members to help to take care of someone outside the group, either within the patient's family (e.g., an aging, semidependent parent) or the patient's workplace (e.g., clients or patients). Object relations theory explains the defensive use of splitting as an attempt to localize persecutory fears in the body and thus protect emotionally important relations from paranoid distortions. Since persecution would then be, by definition, from within the patient's body, the individual's interpersonal relations would remain unthreatening. Likewise, if fears of stirring up someone else's envy do occur as a by-product of role reversal, a detailed checking (again and again) of the ensuing paranoid distortions provides opportunities to correct the distortions by repeatedly inviting the weakened, persecuted, anxious ego to resume its good reality assessment, only transiently obfuscated.

Object relations theory explains how unconscious guilt for "spoiling" the loved object's envied goodness needs to be allayed or relieved through repairing the alleged damages inflicted upon loved objects, especially vis-à-vis a lost loved object who has died and with whom the hypochondriacal patient has identified. Group psychotherapy provides opportunities to work through these depressive anxieties, which are alternately mixed with persecutory ones. Psychiatric hospitalization or antipsychotic medication may unnecessarily scare hypochondriacal patients by not dealing with prevailing somatic concerns and forcing them instead to deal with the avoided fear of having lost their minds. Side effects of medication will likely be exaggerated or misinterpreted as damaging instead of helping (negative placebo effect).

The dynamic theories of separation anxiety and envy have an internal consistency; they "make sense" and also explain some effective psychotherapeutic strategies. The psychoanalytic theory on envy also offers a realistic prognostic approach to hypochondriasis, since it explains the likely failure in psychotherapy with hypochondriacal patients. A significant percentage of these patients would likely be unable to grow beyond their hostile-dependent object relations style, remaining instead in a "schizoid-paranoid position," unable to "work through their depressive anxieties" or to overcome their envy and attain the ability to experience gratitude. For instance, of the four hypochondriacal patients I treated with individual psychotherapy, only two achieved some limited, relatively stable improvement. These two patients experienced significant changes in their lives thereafter, but ideally there was still considerable room for improvement. The internist's skill in doing supportive psychotherapy was central in helping one of them. None of these four patients had the opportunity to test whether certain specific advantages of group psychotherapy, mentioned above, would have helped them overcome their envy and their subsequent need to spoil the psychotherapist's effectiveness.

On the other hand, Jerry (the patient I treated in a group of unmarried persons) achieved only limited improvement with approximately two years of group psychotherapy. Indeed, he had to interrupt his treatment because of external circumstances beyond his control. When he interrupted the group treatment, he still needed to enviously devalue his helpers and had difficulty developing good relations with significant persons in his life. The theory of envy also helps therapists understand the struggles facing these patients, and the likely failure or necessarily slow progress in their psychotherapy.

Internists can probably help a large number of hypochondriacal patients by understanding the basis of their emotional struggles. Psychiatrists may want to consider group analytic psychotherapy with some cases they treat themselves.

SECTION III

THE GROUP AS A TRAINING BASE

INTRODUCTION

The student's self-observation while being a patient (or participant) in a group has become the preferred method to learn about group psychotherapy. Experiential learning was first promoted in England by Bion. He "took" groups of trainees, who wanted to learn from participating in his groups. K. Lewin, Leland P. Bradford, and Kenneth Benne also conducted "training laboratories" for group development in Bethel, Maine, where the participants assumed the role of learners to develop skills and sensitivity to observe and understand human groups. The transfer of learning from these experiences to the various situations "back home" was facilitated by special consultations, sometimes called "application groups." "Sensitivity training" became then applicable to a wide range of human activities such as education, organizational and community development, personal growth, and so on.

This section begins with an overview of the training of group psychotherapists. Two chapters describe the psychiatric training of medical students, who were volunteer patients, during fifteen group psychotherapy sessions, while also regularly attending lectures on psychiatry and on psychotherapy. A chapter focuses on training medical school faculty members in the teaching-learning processes, within the context group human relations, to familiarize them with the methodology of teaching.

The chapter on sensitivity training presents a general overview of the subject, from its definition to its possible psychoanalytic rationale. I also describe here workshops to sharpen group psychotherapists' treatment skills, by being themselves patients, during a brief psychotherapeutic group experience.

Learning occurs within a relationship. The objective, external interactions between or among those involved in the teaching-learning process evokes and may reactivate the learner's subjective, fantasied relationships with the internalized objects. Hence, if the student is experiencing persecutory anxieties, a learning inhibition or examination fright may take place. Curiosity is an important stimulus for learning, but since it is emotionally linked to inquiring about childhood's "forbidden" topics (such as the "facts of life" or the many secret functions of mother's body), the search for knowledge can be interfered with or blocked by unconscious anxiety, related to fantasied fears of mother's disapproval, punishment, or retaliation.

Intense envy can also prevent learning or make learning difficult, when the "have-nots'" envy of "those who have" the knowledge elicit unconscious fears of "taking away" such knowledge, having to face later on possible risks of retaliation. All of the above enhances the importance of a nonthreatening, but friendly, supportive atmosphere in learning situations. For instance, teachers may cast themselves as partners or colleagues in learning, decreasing the student's possible struggles with envy. The learner's evaluation can be accomplished with no wounds to self-esteem, but as a starting point to plan the next steps in learning. If the students have an active participation in choosing what and how to learn about a topic, they will likely become better motivated than when passively ordered about it.

Personal experiences as a participant in small groups is

a never-ending source of meaningful discoveries about oneself, the teaching-learning process, human relations, and group psychology. Group mental life's spontaneous regression to deal again with psychotic anxieties and the primitive defenses against them provides ever important lessons about the human mind.

11

TRAINING GROUP PSYCHOTHERAPISTS: IDEOLOGICAL AND EDUCATIONAL ISSUES

RAMON GANZARAIN, M.D.

The field of group psychotherapy has grown so fast and in so many directions, that it has become very difficult to agree on a definition of it. Contingent upon the practitioner's ideology, or theoretical persuasion, certain techniques and concepts are preferred over others. Hence, we now use terms in the plural (psychotherapies) instead of in the singular. However, we still strive to reach some "operational" definition of a "standard model" of group psychotherapy to describe what the trainees shall learn. Variations can then be compared to the standard, still leaving room for different approaches.

From an educational viewpoint, I shall discuss the

The author is grateful for permission to quote from the following: Scheidlinger, S. (1982), *Focus on Group Psychotherapy: Clinical Essays*. New York: International Universities Press, pp. 6–7, 9, 13. Bowers, W., Gauron, E., and Mines, R. (1984), Training of group psychotherapists: An evaluation procedure. *Small Group Behavior*, 15(1):125–137.

objectives of training, the teaching methods, and the evaluatory processes to assess both whether a trainee achieved the desirable goals and how effective each method can be.

IDEOLOGICAL ISSUES

Scheidlinger (1982) called our attention to the need for the "strictest possible delineation between the spectrum of group modalities and traditional psychotherapy" (p. 6). With that purpose in mind, he distinguished four major categories of "people-helping" groups: (1) group psychotherapy; (2) "therapeutic" groups for clients in mental health settings; (3) training and human development groups; and (4) self-help and mutual help groups. Scheidlinger defines group psychotherapy as a specific field of clinical practice within the realm of the psychotherapies, a psychosocial process, wherein an expert psychotherapist, "with special additional group process training, utilizes the emotional interaction in small carefully planned groups to 'repair' mental ill health, i.e., to effect amelioration of personality dysfunctions in individuals specifically selected for this purpose" (p. 7). He emphasized that clinical orientation means each member is diagnostically assessed to evaluate problems and strengths and that participants accept the group's therapeutic purpose. By contrast, Scheidlinger described as "therapeutic" groups "all other approaches utilized by human services personnel (not necessary trained professionals), in inpatient or outpatient clinical facilities" (p. 7). Often these are auxiliary or conjoint missions to a primary treatment of psychiatric patients. The human development or training groups can be distinguished from the other categories insofar as the aim of these training groups is "*more in the realm* of affective and cognitive education than psychotherapy" (p. 8). Scheidlinger included here the NTL "T-groups," the self-analytic groups—first introduced at Harvard University (Bales,1950)—and the Tavistock Study Groups. Finally, there are the self-help groups dealing with problem-solving objectives, such as Alcoholics Anonymous, Synanon, or some other healing groups where mutual aid is put at the service of accomplishing a special purpose.

Abse (1974) underscored that the criterion for distinguishing between psychoanalytic group psychotherapy and the nonanalytic modalities is how long they last and the presence of working through at the core of the therapeutic process. Parloff (1968) distinguished three types of technical focuses, within the analytic group psychotherapies:

1. The "intrapsychic" modality treats "individuals in a group" and aims at exploring the unconscious conflicts within each individual. It is somehow comparable to doing individual psychoanalysis with a number of patients who take turns to talk about their psychological problems, in the context of a group. Some New York analysts (i.e.,M. Schwartz and A. Wolfe) practiced this modality by placing their individual psychoanalytic patients also in a group they treated, so that each person attended individual and group meetings with the same therapist.

2. The "interpersonal" approach is a modality that focuses primarily on the "interactions between members." It has theoretical connections with H. S. Sullivan's interpersonal school of psychiatry. E. Berne's (1966) "transactional analysis" (TA) and Perls's Gestalt therapy (or a combination of the two) also belong to this category, as does Yalom's approach (1985). However, Yalom utilizes more the interactions among members than do the other treaters mentioned above, who prefer (Goulding, 1972) to focus on the therapist's exchanges with one member at a time. The task is to diagnose the different ego states

(parent, child, or adult) characteristic of the patient's interactions, attempting also to identify the specific "game" played and the unconscious "life plan," which each patient might have chosen early in life. The purpose is to help the patient to become able to shift planfully from one ego state to another.

3. The group-centered, holistic, or integralistic psychoanalytic approach, studies the group forces, or group dynamics, ever present in the background, while also focusing on the foreground interactions among individuals. This school promotes the "therapy *of* the group" or "*by* the group." Bion (1961), Ezriel (1950) in England, and Whitaker and Lieberman (1964) in the United States represent this orientation.

Foulkes and Anthony (1957) developed group analysis in England, borrowing concepts from Lewin's field theory. For instance, Foulkes focused on the dynamics of the here-and-now which depend on current forces rather than on past experiences. According to Lewin's "principle of contemporaneity," the group's "childhood is contained in the present" (Whiteley and Gordon, 1979, p. 19). Foulkes's technique was not therapist centered, hence he preferred for the leader to take a covert role, "behind the scenes" as a "conductor." "He is both a part, yet apart from the group, and his interest is in the group not the self. He is the servant of the group" (Whiteley and Gordon, 1979, p. 21). Foulkes coined the term *group matrix* to design the network of interpersonal communications in the group; each individual reacts to this matrix from his or her own unconscious, with the person's own "resonance." Interpretations may be directed to an individual or to the group; as the members become more experienced they make more interpretations to each other. Therefore, Foulkes's approach is a mixture of an interpersonal with an occasional group-centered focus.

In the group-centered variety, the common group tension is often the subject of the therapist's commentaries focused mainly on the here-and-now process. Once this modeling by the therapist is learned by the patients, they will also gradually act more and more as therapists with each other. The treater may remove him- or herself into the background, whenever the group is adequately performing its therapeutic task. Interventions will be required only when and if the group gets stuck. The therapist acts then as a catalyst. "I judge the occasion to be ripe for an interpretation, when the interpretation would seem to be both obvious and unobserved," wrote Bion (1961, p. 143). These tasks naturally require additional skills, besides those developed while learning to do individual psychotherapy.

The situation of the group psychotherapist could correctly be compared with that of an overloaded computer, often flooded with excessive input. The therapist will frequently be perplexed wondering which one among the many subjects going on should first be addressed. Ezriel's concept of a common group tension helps to diagnose where the meaningful emotional action is at a given moment. Learning to observe and to read the many nonverbal communications in the group is a paramount skill in group psychotherapy. As Bion wrote, "Groups communicate basically through nonverbal exchanges which express the primitive, pre-verbal layers of the mind" (Bion, 1961, p. 185). There is also a continuum of techniques varying according to the therapist's ideological persuasion, going from psychoanalytic group psychotherapy to behavioral modification orientations, with different approaches in between. Pinney, Wells, and Fisher (1978) listed the orientations of group psychotherapy in the United States as follows: psychoanalytic, interpersonal, group process, group dynamics, gestalt, transactional anal-

ysis, and behavioral. Prochaska and Norcross (1983) conducted a national survey of the various orientations among
contemporary U.S. psychotherapists' orientations; they
listed: Adlerian, behavioral/learning theory, cognitive, existential, gestalt, humanistic, psychoanalytic, psychodynamic, Rogerian, Sullivanian, and systems orientations.

Neither of these lists includes psychodrama, which is a
modality practiced in the United States and in many parts
of the world. There are also Jungian group therapists.
Combinations of group and art therapies are also used to
stimulate artistic creativity as a way to explore the patients'
minds.

These wide ideological variations promote a meaningful exploratory attitude, searching for more effective
psychotherapy methods, but they also can create confusion among trainees. Sometimes the intense competitiveness among different orientations creates some true
believers' rigidity.

Practical preferences about how frequently or how
long to conduct groups, coupled with different views on
how therapeutic change happens, may lead to wide practical variations from an extended weekend "marathon" to
once- or twice-a-week group sessions, over a long period of
time; these differences can become another source of
confusion.

In order to avoid conflicts and confusion, some technical group psychotherapy modalities have created their
own scientific associations and training institutions where
they offer to teach their specific approach. Organizations
to promote the practice and teaching of psychodrama are
an example of such development. Gestalt and TA associations have also constituted their own organizations. Similarly, associations for behavioral therapy have been
formed. We are moving into developing several modalities
of group psychotherapies. However, the American Group

Psychotherapy Association (AGPA) still offers itself as an "umbrella" organization, covering many diversified theoretical orientations. This is a commendable attempt to keep the standards of practice and the scientific exchanges among group psychotherapists unified in one common organization, in the middle of the explosive, sometimes chaotic, growth of the field.

How may the current trends in the delivery of mental health services affect the group psychotherapists' practice and training? Some emphasized the financial realities: "The name of the game is cost containment" (Dworak-Peck, 1987). Mental health institutions look therefore for "cheap labor," hiring less qualified professionals or even nonprofessionals to deliver some services. Emphasis is on maximum utilization of professional time, which may superficially seem a golden opportunity to spread group psychotherapy. However, the "cost-containment" criteria for indicating group psychotherapy is based fallaciously on stereotyping it as a "low-cost treatment." As a left-handed compliment, it does not give credit to the specific advantages groups do offer for patients suffering from personality disorders, regardless of the short-sighted cost considerations.

Quality control of mental health services is now exercised by the insurance companies. Health professionals consequently have doubts regarding the quality of health services now delivered. Mental health professionals have responded to these financial realities with two prevailing attitudes: with attempts to adapt to such recent trends, or with efforts to influence and modify them. Some group psychotherapists' efforts to adapt are well represented by Yalom's book on inpatient group psychotherapy (1985). He successfully advises on how to do groups under time pressure, since often inpatient treatment lasts only a few days. Yalom also wrote with coworkers a discussion on whether to train nonprofessionals on how to do group psychotherapy (Ebersole, Leiderman, and Yalom, 1969). There is a trend to somehow change the role of qualified group psychotherapists into becoming supervisors or consultants no longer being involved personally in doing actual group work. This seems a most efficient response to the cost-containment goals, together with emphasizing problem-centered therapy, short-term treatment focused on crisis intervention, and so on. But "service follows funding, with a high risk of losing a sense of personal and human caring" (Dworak-Peck, 1987).

Different levels of sophistication available among mental health services should ideally be adapted to the diverse patients' needs or psychopathology, looking for a specific modality of group psychotherapy to meet a patient's needs. Which type of group gets recommended may vary according to location, finances, or therapists' ideology. Perhaps the "more specialized" services could be reserved for treating personality malfunctions with psychoanalytically oriented group psychotherapy, while leaving other modalities for relatively less serious psychopathology or for mutual support among patients.

Education: Objectives, Methods, and Evaluation

The goals in training group psychotherapists are: (1) to acquire learning of the basic knowledge about psychotherapy and groups, from their dynamics to the rationale for the different modalities of psychotherapy; and (2) to develop skills to efficiently do group psychotherapy.

The AGPA guidelines for training specify the basic knowledge required prior to entering training in group psychotherapy: development and personality theories, psychopathology and diagnosis, principles of individual psychotherapy, group dynamics, social and cultural factors.

Skills required to do group psychotherapy include the ability to observe and to listen to what goes on in the group (empathic observer); the capacity to facilitate events within the group (facilitator); the talent to reflect and to clarify such events (clarifier); and the ability to understand and to link group events to the current context of group dynamics and to the individual's psychopathology and treatment goals.

Developing these skills is conducive to facilitating the group's spontaneity, making patients feel comfortable to express feelings, while simultaneously promoting their curiosity to reflect about how those emotions affect them and their groupmates. The relationships among groupmates and the different subjects of conversation may then unfold naturally, without interferences. The ability to observe nonverbal messages exchanged among groupmates, helping to put such signals into words, makes communications meaningful, moving them toward more open verbal expressions.

Bowers, Gauron, and Mines (1984) described a list of the group psychotherapist's skills, which includes the ability to express feelings; a nondefensive attitude; empathy; and nurturance-caring (See the list of seventeen skills and the description of each one in this chapter's addendum).

Bowers's rating scale specifies the basic skills needed to efficiently conduct psychotherapy defining each one. He developed an objective evaluation procedure, since the scale has an interrater reliability significant above the 0.5 level. Bowers and coworkers conducted regular evaluations of their trainees, whereby BPSRS facilitates the supervisors', the cotherapists', and the peers' perceptions about how each student is doing and also invites the trainees to set regular personal learning goals by themselves, thus reinforcing the selfdirectiveness in their training program in group psychotherapy.

The *methods* for learning about group psychotherapy include personal participation in a group, observing skilled therapists, personal practice with groups, supervision, and also intellectual learning from readings, lectures, and seminars.

Personal experience is the most important method, whether as a group patient, as a student of group dynamics, as a psychotherapy group's observer, or as a therapist. Being a patient in a group can last a relatively long time or be limited to a weekend. Battegay (1983) described the value of analytic self-experience groups in the training of psychotherapists, stating that "the self-experience group leads to an enlargement of the individual analytic experience in the social-interactional field," offering to the beginner an orientation about what occurs in psychotherapeutic groups (p. 200). He emphasized that being a member of one of these groups is an important "complement" to the individual training analysis and described how colleagues "make acquaintance with sides of their personality different from those seen in the dyadic psychotherapeutic situation." The different sides are mainly narcissistic disturbances and problems of power, often unsufficiently explored in individual psychotherapy. Besides, "the group situation activates unresolved personal conflicts linked with the family situation of childhood" (p. 211).

Giving the "T-group" more educational goals can help it serve better as a source of learning about small-group behavior. Alonso (1984) underscored that the T-group model protects the beginner from undue regression and avoids narcissistic injuries, while bonding with other trainees may increase the probability of group therapy becoming part of the professional identity. Likewise, attending the "group relations conferences," organized by the Tavistock and the A. K. Rice Institutes, promotes learning on leadership and authority or group dynamics. Placing psychiatric residents in groups to train them has evolved from initially offering vaguely defined "group experiences" (see chapter 12), to offering "T-groups," and to later on promoting trainees' participation in two successive stages: first in small study groups to learn about group dynamics and later on to be a cotherapist in a group oriented specifically to treatment proper. The Karl Menninger School of Psychiatry followed these different stages, gradually defining more clearly the learning goals and methods in training residents to do group therapy. However, beginning therapists tend to imitate initially the small-group consultant's style by focusing only on the group dynamics, without paying enough attention to the patients' individual therapeutic needs. The supervisors often struggle to correct the confusion between group dynamics and psychotherapy.

The observation of skilled therapists can be done with the observer silently sitting in the room, becoming like the psychotherapist's supervisor, or having a dialogue with the treater after the patients leave the room. If two cotherapists treat the group, the observer can join their exchanges about the just-finished session. It is also possible to observe behind a one-way screen or study videotapes of actual sessions. When the session is over the observers come out of the hiding place, behind the screen, and discuss details of the meeting with the therapist. If videotapes are used, they can be stopped and replayed or edited to underline some interesting points. Practicing individual psychotherapy should precede doing group psychotherapy. It is also possible to have prior experience as a group dynamics consultant before being a cotherapist, preferably with a peer with the same level of experience.

Supervision can be done one-to-one with a supervisor, together with a cotherapist, or in a group of peers; often various couples of cotherapists can discuss their treatment of comparable patient populations in various groups. With psychiatric residents at the KMSP, I have discussed groups of adolescents. The common age-related problems such as rebelliousness, needs for clear limits, difficulties in leaving home or in dating, and so on were common subjects in these groups supervised together.

I occasionally conducted phone supervision both in individual and/or in group psychotherapy. To my surprise, the absence of visible nonverbal communications was somehow replaced by a refined attention to the voice intonations. The supervisee and supervisor also sharpened their efforts to communicate verbally as completely as possible. Since the supervisees who contacted me by telephone were excellent learners, however, my experience may not be generalizable.

There is a scarcity of qualified supervisors in certain geographical areas. The AGPA is gradually developing a "mentors' system" imitating, in part, traditional British teaching through "tutoring" but mainly making available strategically located qualified supervisors who could be contacted by the trainees. This learning can be supplemented by accumulating credits earned while attending AGPA annual conferences.

The intellectual learning from reading, lectures, and/or seminars is self-explanatory. The ideal curriculum could be discussed forever. In general, reading on basic group dynamics, principles of psychotherapy, different special patient populations, problems of indication or contraindication, different modalities of technique, and so on are included. In the seminar on group psychotherapy that I taught for staff members of the Menninger Foundation from 1973 on I purposefully reserved half of the available time of each teaching session to discuss clinical material. During the first months I presented and discussed in detail edited videotapes of groups I had been treating. After a few months, the participants in the seminar were invited to present clinical material from groups they were either observing, cotreating, or treating by themselves. I found it very important to teach the concepts about group psychotherapy, tying them as closely as possible to actual clinical experiences to prevent a tendency present in some mental health professionals to overintellectualize and remain caught up in abstract conceptual views of psychotherapy while avoiding getting in touch with the feelings that arise from the psychotherapeutic situation.

Being a patient in a group is not always accessible to a trainee who wishes to become a group psychotherapist. In small communities, fears of mingling with a group of persons, who later on may become the trainee's social or professional relations, hinders the use of this modality of learning. Such is the case in Topeka, Kansas, where residents eager to be group patients have as an option mainly the possibility of being patients among their classmates or other psychiatric residents. In larger cities, the availability of many group therapists makes it possible for a trainee to become a patient in an "ordinary group," among nonprofessionals, while having seminars and supervision with other therapists, different from the one treating the trainee. Fears of appearing incompetent or of losing prestige among classmates make participation as a patient more difficult when the group is formed exclusively by mental health professionals. The fact that relations have started before the therapy group was formed and that they may continue after discharge also complicates these groups' functioning. Problems related to issues of confidentiality and acting out may compound the difficulty.

A LEARNER'S REVIEW

If I look back to my own training in group psychotherapy, I realize how valuable was my personal participation as a patient in the group formed by candidates in training analysis with Ignacio Matte-Blanco where intense sibling rivalries, power/narcissistic, reality/fantasy, and dependency/hostility struggles colored our sessions. I also remember especially my "T-group" in Bethel, Maine, where false self issues, self-esteem pains, and power-hunger anxieties taught me about the "rough sailing" in groups. Attending a Tavistock Institute Residential Conference in Leicester, England, gave me the opportunity to have Robert Gosling as my small-group consultant, allowing me to appreciate his tactful sensitivity, his creative poetic imagination, and his ability to work efficiently. Irvin Polster's brief workshop at the Menninger Foundation offered me a chance to experience his gestalt/TA technique, delivered through his warm, refined, elegant clinical style and I reviewed again false self issues. The Sirokas taught me about psychodrama at the Dallas AGPA annual conference, where I learned how to use sociometric tests to assign dramatic roles and also appreciated their candid caring transparency, making masterful use of their own life struggles to empathize with us patients in their group. But since those were personal experiences they are not necessarily meaningful or easily conveyable to everyone else.

Next, I value within my training experience the exchanges with a congenial colleague about recent group sessions just attended by both, either as a cotherapist couple or as team of observer/therapists. Having "been there" together, yet seeing things from different perspectives, provided me with great opportunities to learn. Likewise, when a group of colleagues supervises clinical material from a group I treated, I always gained new clinical understandings.

Replaying the group session, either in my own memory or from videotapes, also gives me the chance to be my own supervisor. Even though I may run the risk of being alternately too harsh or too lenient with myself as a therapist, I can rectify both exaggerations by replaying the supervised session again and again. To edit videotapes such replaying was essential, a sine qua non. The painful effort of choosing which segment to keep and the many to throw away was often made lighter by the concomitant learning opportunity to see again what I had missed, or overreacted or mistakenly responded to. The fact that videos offer us the possibility of self-supervision should be welcomed; for us they have the same importance that audio recordings have for musicians wishing to improve their performances. The conceptual tools I learned from my teachers were basically psychoanalysis, with a Kleinian flavor—imported from the United Kingdom—and Lewin's field theory with a touch of learning theory, as offered by the NTL, in the United States, during the 1960s. Leland P. Bradford, Kenneth Benne, Warren Benis, John Glidewell, and Edgard Schein where some of those who helped me to learn how to "shift gears" when possible from my deeply rooted psychoanalytic framework to a sociopsychological approach.

The same struggle existed in 1948 when, as an analytic candidate, I started doing group psychotherapy. I attempted then to "solve" these conflicts by magic imitation: I adopted Foulkes's 1948 book on group psychotherapy as my passport to enter a new territory. My passport was after all stamped in Vienna and in London, since Foulkes, like Sigmund Freud, practiced psychoanalysis and groups in those two psychoanalytically "kosher" cities. The new edition of Foulkes's book, with James Anthony as coauthor, explicitly borrowed Lewin's concepts. So did the NTL training as I said. Therefore, "shifting gears" seemed not to be as difficult, after all.

However, when Bion's Kleinian concepts on groups entered my mind, I realized that it was essential to understand the psychoticlike anxieties and the primitive defense mechanisms in order to work efficiently with groups. Since Foulkes did not accept those ideas, I had to go beyond his efficient but somehow simplified technique. I read more Bion and had the chance to be supervised by him. He mainly taught me that "the answer is the misfortune of the question" and invited me to cultivate questions. I continue searching for them.

ADDENDUM.

Bowers Psychotherapy Skills Rating Scale (BPSRS)

Wayne A. Bowers[1]

Person you are rating_____

1. *Expression of Feeling*: Will show verbally and nonverbally when angry, happy, sad, etc.; tells feelings spontaneously.

———1 not at all (0–5%)   ———4 some (41–60%)   ———7 all the time
———2 very little (6–20%)   ———5 much (61–80%)   (96–100%)
———3 a little (21–40%)   ———6 a great deal (81–95%)

2. *Nondefensive Attitude*: Accepts criticism and negative feedback; will listen without making excuses for self; will not verbally attack when being questioned on personal behavior; accepts consequences of his or her behavior including others personal reactions; clarifies statements of others.

———1 not at all (0–5%)   ———4 some (41–60%)   ———7 all the time
———2 very little (6–20%)   ———5 much (61–80%)   (96–100%)
———3 a little (21–40%)   ———6 a great deal (81–95%)

3. *Self-disclosure*: Talks about personal details; shares personal material (about home life, family, etc.) with others; talks about self.
———1 not at all (0–5%)   ———4 some (41–60%)   ———7 all the time
———2 very little (6–20%)   ———5 much (61–80%)   (96–100%)
———3 a little (21–40%)   ———6 a great deal (81–95%)

4. *Personal Flexibility*: Willing to try new behaviors suggested by others; willing to follow through on homework assignments to foster self-growth; self-institutes new behavior.
———1 not at all (0–5%)   ———4 some (41–60%)   ———7 all the time
———2 very little (6–20%)   ———5 much (61–80%)   (96–100%)
———3 a little (21–40%)   ———6 a great deal (81–95%)

5. *Empathy*: Ability to understand, share, and experience the emotions of others; able to experience the feelings of another person; able to get others aware of additional feelings.
———1 not at all (0–5%)   ———4 some (41–60%)   ———7 all the time
———2 very little (6–20%)   ———5 much (61–80%)   (96–100%)
———3 a little (21–40%)   ———6 a great deal (81–95%)

6. *Personal Involvement*: Offers to help others; helps others spontaneously relate on a personal level.
———1 not at all (0–5%)   ———4 some (41–60%)   ———7 all the time
———2 very little (6–20%)   ———5 much (61–80%)   (96–100%)
———3 a little (21–40%)   ———6 a great deal (81–95%)

7. *Nurturance-Caring*: Is willing to personally stand by others who are trying new behaviors; will allow others to contact him or her to talk over problem situations; protects others at times of personal stress or trauma; offers feelings and/or physical contact spontaneously; comfortable being touched.
———1 not at all (0–5%)   ———4 some (41–60%)   ———7 all the time
———2 very little (6–20%)   ———5 much (61–80%)   (96–100%)
———3 a little (21–40%)   ———6 a great deal (81–95%)

8. *Confrontiveness*: Will point out inconsistencies in verbal and nonverbal behavior; will respond verbally to nonproductive behavior.
———1 not at all (0–5%)   ———4 some (41–60%)   ———7 all the time
———2 very little (6–20%)   ———5 much (61–80%)   (96–100%)
———3 a little (21–40%)   ———6 a great deal (81–95%)

9. *Need for Closure*: Problems must always be solved; always ready with an answer; problems must have a logical progression.
———1 not at all (0–5%)   ———4 some (41–60%)   ———7 all the time
———2 very little (6–20%)   ———5 much (61–80%)   (96–100%)
———3 a little (21–40%)   ———6 a great deal (81–95%)

10. *Regression in the Service of the Ego*: Able to fantasize; able to be silly with others; can daydream easily; can be childlike.
———1 not at all (0–5%)   ———4 some (41–60%)   ———7 all the time
———2 very little (6–20%)   ———5 much (61–80%)   (96–100%)
———3 a little (21–40%)   ———6 a great deal (81–95%)

11. *Work Ethic*: Must have a goal in every activity; must always be doing something; prompts others to keep working; uncomfortable when not working.

————1 not at all (0–5%)   ————4 some (41–60%)   ————7 all the time
————2 very little (6–20%) ————5 much (61–80%)   (96–100%)
————3 a little (21–40%)   ————6 a great deal (81–95%)

12. *Tolerance for Ambivalence*: Is comfortable with confusion; expresses own confusion; comfortable when questions go unanswered.

————1 not at all (0–5%)   ————4 some (41–60%)   ————7 all the time
————2 very little (6–20%) ————5 much (61–80%)   (96–100%)
————3 a little (21–40%)   ————6 a great deal (81–95%)

13. *Responsibility*: Urges others to make decisions; respects decisions of others; gives others responsibility.

————1 not at all (0–5%)   ————4 some (41–60%)   ————7 all the time
————2 very little (6–20%) ————5 much (61–80%)   (96–100%)
————3 a little (21–40%)   ————6 a great deal (81–95%)

14. *Individualism*: Does not yield to group pressure; will stand up for own ideas.

————1 not at all (0–5%)   ————4 some (41–60%)   ————7 all the time
————2 very little (6–20%) ————5 much (61–80%)   (96–100%)
————3 a little (21–40%)   ————6 a great deal (81–95%)

15. *Extroversion*: Talkative; will socially mix; enjoys a group; is willing to talk to others; is center of attention in a group.

————1 not at all (0–5%)   ————4 some (41–60%)   ————7 all the time
————2 very little (6–20%) ————5 much (61–80%)   (96–100%)
————3 a little (21–40%)   ————6 a great deal (81–95%)

16. *Life satisfaction*: Enjoys living; sees life as worthwhile; feels life has treated him or her well.

————1 not at all (0–5%)   ————4 some (41–60%)   ————7 all the time
————2 very little (6–20%) ————5 much (61–80%)   (96–100%)
————3 a little (21–40%)   ————6 a great deal (81–95%)

17. *Energy*: Is physically active; enjoys participating in sports/recreation; encourages others to be active.

————1 not at all (0–5%)   ————4 some (41–60%)   ————7 all the time
————2 very little (6–20%) ————5 much (61–80%)   (96–100%)
————3 a little (21–40%)   ————6 a great deal (81–95%)

[1]Permission has been granted by the author for reproduction of this scale.

12

GROUP PSYCHOTHERAPY IN THE PSYCHIATRIC TRAINING OF MEDICAL STUDENTS

RAMON GANZARAIN, M.D., HERNAN DAVANZO, M.D.,
AND J. CIZALETTI, PH.D.,
WITH THE COLLABORATION OF
IGNACIO MATTE-BLANCO, M.D., GUILLERMO GIL,
M.D., F. OYARZUN, M.D., AND M. KELLER, PH.D.
PSYCHIATRIC CLINIC, UNIVERSITY OF CHILE,
SANTIAGO, CHILE

INTRODUCTION

There have been two main ways of using group psychotherapy in teaching psychiatry: (1) the students' attendance at groups formed by patients, with the purpose of commenting on the psychodynamic material presented; and (2) the constitution of groups formed by the students

This chapter was first published in *International Journal of Group Psychotherapy* (1958), 8:137–153, and it is reprinted with permission.

themselves, using the psychodynamic supplied by them, in the theoretical discussions. Several authors have commented on the first type, among them Hadden (1947), Semrad and Arsenian (1951), Votos and Glenn (1953). In the second category are Warkentin (1954), Whitaker (1954), Peltz, Steel, Hadden, Schwab, and Nichols (1955). Berman (1953) and Sutherland (1952) have used psychotherapy in groups formed by postgraduate students. One of us has devoted a paper to this (Ganzarain, 1955) and reported some observations in another (Ganzarain, 1951). The clinical material quoted in these papers suggests the great value of group psychotherapy in teaching dynamic psychiatry. A fundamental purpose in research on this subject is to demonstrate that value in a progressively more scientific way, for instance using adequate control groups and more objective methods for evaluating results.

Fey (1955) considers Whitaker's experiment the basis for teaching what he calls "personal psychiatry." He defines personal psychiatry, which he opposes to technical psychiatry, in terms of the emotions that occur between doctor and patient, emphasizing that "every patient needs his physician psychologically, as a person, and most of them need him medically, as a technician, as well" (p. 97).

If group psychotherapy used in this way contributes to a better teaching of psychodynamics that occur in the doctor-patient relation, and also alleviates some neurotic symptoms of the future physicians, perhaps it would be justified for every medical student to receive its benefits.

The purpose of this chapter is to report a study based on two hypotheses: (1) that using the students themselves as subjects of group psychotherapy is a better way of teaching them some psychodynamics of the doctor-patient relation than another method frequently employed for this purpose—which here we call "psychodynamic seminars" (didactic hypothesis); and (2) group psychotherapy achieves improvement of some neurotic symptoms of the students (therapeutic hypothesis).

MATERIAL AND METHODS

During 1954 we had sixty-nine students in our course. The following tests were administered to them: Raven, Terman, Maudsley's questionnaire, Catell (ludic factor), Bell, and Rorschach (individually administered). In addition, we asked them to report in writing whether they had previously received psychotherapy, whether they had chosen any medical specialty, and, if so, to name it.

The students' ages varied from twenty to thirty years. There were twelve women and fifty-seven men among them. Their I.Q.s, according to the Raven Test, varied between 15 and 60 points (mean 50, standard deviation 6,14); and according to the Terman Test between 94 and 127 points (mean 113, standard deviation 7,6). Their neuroticism by Maudsley's questionnaire varied between 0 and 27 points (mean 11,27; standard deviation 6,14), and by Bell's test fluctuated between 8 and 93 (mean 37, 35; standard deviation 21, 61). Thirteen students had received psychotherapy before 1954; ten began the study of psychiatry intending to become psychiatrists; thirty-eight had chosen several nonpsychiatric medical specialties; and twenty-one had not yet made up their minds.

Two groups of students were matched for these variables. The experimental group included thirty-five students, while the control group had thirty-four (two of them withdrew during the course of the experiment). Naturally they did not know that some of them were experimental subjects while others were considered controls. We informed them that we had a special interest in comparing two methods of teaching psychiatry.

The thirty-five experimental subjects were divided by

chance into five groups of seven students each. Each
experimental subgroup was directed by the same conductor during the experiment. The five conductors were men,
medical doctors, psychoanalytically trained, with previous
experience in group psychotherapy and in teaching psychiatry.

We had nine hours a week allotted to teaching psychiatry, for seven months. We used one hour-and-a-half for
group psychotherapy or the activity of the control students.

The purpose of the "psychodynamic seminar" was to
study the psychodynamics of some patients who were
undergoing psychoanalytically oriented therapy, from a
purely intellectual or theoretical point of view. The doctors presenting these cases intentionally avoided any reference to the relations existing between the material
discussed and the psychological problems of the students.
They also avoided any comment about transference situations created within the group. Four doctors with different levels of training conducted these seminars
successively. They were matched with the conductors of
the experimental group to avoid the accumulation of the
more experienced in one of the groups. Each conductor
presented a case in about four sessions. In this way we
wanted to avoid a strong personal link between students
and instructors. As we wanted to reduce the possibilities of
emotional relationship among the control students, each
seminar session was planned so that all of the thirty-four
control students attended them.

In this application of group psychotherapy one has the
problem of offering a "treatment" to so-called "normal"
persons. On account of this we did not call it group
psychotherapy but "group activity." However, we hoped
that most of these students would discover in themselves

some neurotic symptoms, and therefore accept the therapeutic character of the sessions.

In addition to the possibility of therapeutic benefit, there was the didactic profit of observing emotional phenomena during the "group activity" sessions. The conductor generally pointed out such phenomena and their relationship to theoretical principles. The conductors did not develop any other teaching activity with the students of their therapeutic groups, however, so that their authority was not excessively underlined.

If a student had a special problem, he was free to change to the other type of group at the beginning of the year. Actually there were only four requests of control subjects who wanted to shift to the experimental group. Only two of these requests could be met without affecting the homogeneity of the groups.

Psychotherapy was analytically oriented following the technique described by Foulkes (1948). However, when necessary, the conductor invited his group to a discussion about the difficulties of beginning interpersonal communications and the possible ways of overcoming them. In most of the groups the students decided to make a biographical report as a basis for the initial interchange.

We prepared a special form for recording each group session. The form had the following items.

Date			
Conductor	*No. of Session*	*Attendance and positions in the room*	
Subjects, interventions, and interpretations	Individual and group emotions and attitudes	Transference and countertransference	Examples of psychopathological phenomena experienced; theoretical comments

There were nineteen sessions of group psychotherapy. The conductors met for an hour-and-a-half weekly to comment on and discuss the sessions. Protocols of each of these meetings were made.

In order to evaluate the results, we separated them as to their didactic and possible therapeutic aspects. We judged the possible didactic results by the following elements: (1) marks; (2) personal records (each student had a personal record and in it the instructors who had exclusively teaching functions recorded every two weeks any interesting observation about the student; the personal records had the following objectives: (a) to take note of any change; (b) to have observers not directly participating in the group experiment asking for their relatively more impartial cooperation); (3) protocols of the group sessions; (4) a "didactic" questionnaire comprising fifty-four specially worked-out questions that covered all the subjects theoretically taught during the year (this questionnaire was administered at the end of the year without previous warning, in small groups of eight students, letting them know that its results were not going to be considered as one of the elements of final qualification of their efficiency); and (5) a "questionnaire about the experiment." It consisted of twenty-nine questions that referred to phenomena that all the students had learned through their theoretical studies and some had also observed and experienced during group psychotherapy. They answered it anonymously, mentioning only to which of the groups—control or experimental—they belonged. We assumed that the experimental students who had the opportunity of getting a better understanding of these phenomena through group psychotherapy would produce better answers in comparison with the answers of the control subjects. The purpose of this questionnaire about the experiment was to substantiate this hypothesis.

We judged the hypothetical results by readministering the following tests: Maudsley, Bell, Catell, and Rorschach.

The latter was readministered by examiners different from those who gave the first tests. All the Rorschachs were interpreted by the same two persons working together. The second Rorschach was interpreted without knowing the students' identity, with the purpose of reducing the influence of subjective factors in the interpreters.

We also had some ways of evaluating the therapeutic results qualitatively: (1) the observed changes in the subject's behavior and attitude, recorded in the protocols of the group sessions; (2) personal records; (3) the results of a "special questionnaire" asking the students about which of them had experienced favorable changes during the experiment; (4) individual interviews with some of the students.

Results

Didactic Results

Quantitative

Marks, the "didactic" questionnaire, and almost all the items of the "questionnaire about the experiment" did not reveal statistically significant differences between the two groups. Only one question was answered in such a way that differences were found. This direction was: "Quote and explain an example of transference observed in yourself." We qualified the answers to this as "good," "fair," and "bad," according to an established criterion: The presence of repetition of attitudes or emotions of the past in the quoted example was scored as 1 point. The explicit or implicit, but sufficiently clear, recognition of having experienced them as something unconsciously determined was also scored 1 point. An answer that got 2, 1, or 0 points was graded as "good," "fair," or "bad" respectively.

One examiner graded all the answers three times, using this criterion. Another examiner graded them independently two times, using the same criterion. The agreement between both examiners was high: They independently graded 88 percent of the answers in the same way. Therefore the criterion used was sufficiently objective. Their discrepancies were never higher than 1 point and were afterwards solved. Naturally all the scores were done without knowing the identity of the subject whose answer was graded. Generally we also did not know to which of the groups the student[1] belonged. The frequency distribution in each group is presented in Table 12.1.

TABLE 12.1.

Frequency Distribution of "Good," "Fair," and "Bad" Answers to the Question about Transference

Group	"Good"	"Fair"	"Bad"	Total of students
Experimental	28	2	10	35
Control	8	6	18	32

The theoretical chi square of this distribution is 5,99 and the experimental chi square is 8,61 at the 0.05 level.

These differences indicate a systematic influence of group psychotherapy upon the learning of transference. To be able to quote good examples of transference observed in oneself would reveal a deep understanding of

---

[1] Some experimental students quoted examples observed in group psychotherapy referring explicitly to it, thus letting the examiners know to which of the groups they belonged.

the phenomenon. It is not necessary here to point out the importance of the understanding of transference.

Qualitative results

These were judged by the following elements: (A) personal records, which were not always useful for registering results, because some instructors did not fill them adequately; (B) protocols of group therapy sessions (of the expected 95 protocols we received 85). We checked the protocols summarizing: (I) the psychodynamic phenomena observed; and (II) the psychotherapeutic activities accomplished by the students.

I. *Psychodynamic phenomena observed during the sessions.* Some of them were theoretically commented upon by the conductor following a vivid example observed during the session. Sometimes the comment could not be made by the conductor for several reasons such as: (1) it might have broken the emotional vividness obtained at that moment of the session; (2) for dynamic reasons defensive mechanisms had to be respected; and (3) the student himself recognized and commented upon the phenomena before the conductor said anything.

There were psychodynamic phenomena pointed out and commented upon exclusively by the conductor; others were recognized only by the students, and finally some were first theoretically commented on by the conductor and in a later session recognized by the students.

Among the psychodynamic phenomena pointed out and commented upon exclusively by the conductor, the one most frequently observed was hidden aggression, especially submissiveness with unconscious rebellion, important in the handling and understanding of the student-teacher relation, as well as that between the doctor and patient. Most of the students had the opportunity of experiencing some fundamental aspects of the way in which psychotherapy works (conductors A, B, and C were able to exemplify what constitutes emotional understanding, and conductor E was able to comment on an example of corrective emotional experience).

Among the psychodynamic phenomena recognized exclusively by the students, it was observed that in the groups conducted by A, C, and E, the students were able to learn the reality and the consequences of infantile sexuality. It also could be stated that the students belonging to the groups conducted by B, C, and E had an opportunity to observe several manifestations of the guilt feelings provoked by aggression. It deserves special mention that in the groups conducted by A, C, D, and E, the students had the opportunity of observing the disappearance of a headache during the session, in direct relation with interpretation and catharsis of repressed emotion. This constituted a true experimental demonstration of the action of psychotherapy in a somatic symptom. It is also interesting that the students of the groups conducted by B, D, and E could observe in some of their members the influence of emotions in the production of somatic symptoms.

Finally, although it occurred only in the group conducted by A, there was a very interesting experience: the observation of variations in transference; in other words, the students were able to observe in one session how each of them looked upon the conductor in a different way, due to the fact that each one transferred his own parental image to him.

The dynamic phenomena commented on by the conductor and/or recognized by the students are presented in Table 12.2. The high frequency of discussions by the conductor and the recognition by the students of the transference phenomenon deserves special attention. This finding supports and perhaps explains the statistically significant differences in Table 12.1.

TABLE 12.2.

Psychodynamic Phenomena Commented Upon by the Conductor and/or Recognized by the Students

Psychodynamic Phenomena	Group										Number of times
	A		B		C		D		E		
	s	c	s	c	s	c	s	c	s	c	
Transference	11	2	5	6	4	2		2	3	4	39
Resistances	12	3		2	1	2		2		1	23
Problems of Dependence	2	2	4	10	1				4		23
Improvement of Interpersonal Contact after Interpretations	5	4	1					1	1		12
Projection	2	3			3	1			1	1	11
Inhibition by Aggression		3		1					4	2	10
Repression				1	2	1		1	1	2	8
Displacement			2	3		1	1		1		8
Inhibition by the Conductor	4			1				1			6
Identification		1	1	1	1	1				1	6
Rationalization	1	2			1					1	5

s = recognized by the students. c = commented upon by the conductor.

In four of the five therapeutic groups the following psychodynamic phenomena were studied: (a) resistances; (b) problems of dependence; (c) improvement of interpersonal contact after interpretations which constituted a kind of experimental demonstration of some psychotherapeutic results; (d) projection; (e) repression; and (f) identification.

In three of the five therapeutic groups the following phenomena were observed: (a) inhibition by aggression; (b) inhibition by the conductor, interesting in the student-teacher relation and in the emotional attitude toward authority in general; and (c) rationalization.

II. *Psychotherapeutic activities accomplished by the students during the group sessions.* Interpretation, one of the most complex psychotherapeutic tools, was very frequently used. It was employed sixty-nine times by twenty-five subjects, which reveals a remarkable degree of practical psychotherapeutic learning. Another psychotherapeutic tool frequently employed was confrontation. It was used sixty-five times by twenty-five students. Objectivization of defenses was used sixteen times by thirteen students; and support, fourteen times by nine students; thirteen students displayed leader initiative and led their groups during some sessions.

Final inquiry of the students about their impressions regarding psychotherapy. In the "questionnaire about the experiment" the following questions were included: (a) "My impressions about group activity were . . ."; and (b) "My impressions about psychodynamic seminars were. . . ." Each student had to answer about the activity in which he took part. We graded their opinions as "good," "fair," and "bad," respectively: (a) when the activity in question was approved without mentioning any defect; (b) when the student listed both positive and negative aspects of his activity; and (c) when, without mentioning any positive quality, the student criticized the defects of his activity. Table 12.3 presents the frequency distribution of each type of answer. It demonstrates that the students' judgment was clearly in favor of group psychotherapy, although they did not ignore some favorable aspects of psychodynamic seminars. (The differences are significant, although it is not possible to treat them statistically on account of the low frequency that appears in this table.)

TABLE 12.3.

Frequency Distribution of "Good," "Fair," and "Bad" Opinions about Group Psychotherapy and Psychodynamic Seminars

Activity	"Good"	"Fair"	"Bad"
Group Psychotherapy	22	10	3
Psychodynamic Seminars	1	12	19

At the end of the year we had a forum in which the students discussed the methods of teaching them psychiatry. They stated that thanks to group psychotherapy they had obtained a better understanding of themselves, and consequently of their patients. Many were enthusiastic about group psychotherapy, stating that it was "the best part of the course."

Therapeutic Results

Quantitative

The scores obtained by the tests of Bell, Maudsley, and the designs of Catell permitted the comparison between

the results of each subject at the beginning and at the end
of the year. The differences of the scores between the two
groups were not significant.

Qualitative results

These were estimated by several procedures; The
"questionnaire about the experiment" included the following question: "Could you observe noticeable changes in the
behavior of your fellow students during this year? (If the
answer is affirmative, write their names.)"

In Table 12.4 we considered only those subjects who
were named as improved by three or more fellow students.
We thought it would be interesting to see whether the
student who noticed the improvement belonged to the
experimental or the control group, because the improvement was easier to register by the coparticipants of the
same psychotherapeutic group. For this reason it may be
supposed that, within certain limits, the improvements of
experimental students registered by the control subjects
might indicate very striking changes.

We interviewed all the students appearing in Table
12.4. It is remarkable that the only control subject included in this table informed us that he married during
1954, thus better adapting himself emotionally than before. This would prove the ability of fellow students to
register some rather intense behavioral changes in their
classmates. Among the six experimental subjects of Table
12.4, five informed us that there had not been any
important events in their life during the said period. One
of them had also married but not under very favorable
emotional conditions.

Table 12.5 includes the students considered as improved by only two of their fellow students. We interviewed everybody appearing in this table. It is also

TABLE 12.4.

Students Named as Improved by Several Classmates
in the Special Questionnaire

Students	Number of Experimental Classmates Naming Them	Number of Control Classmates Naming Them	Number of Classmates that Registered the Improvement
XIV	5	3	8
V	5	1	6
XXI	5	0	5
IV	4	0	4
I	3	1	4
IX	3	0	3
XIV*	2	1	3

*XIV belonged to the control group.

interesting that the only control subject informed us that he was undergoing psychoanalytic treatment during the experiment, while one of the experimental subjects was in the same situation.

Twenty-one of the thirty-two control subjects answered the question by not naming anyone who had improved. One of them offered a possible explanation of this phenomenon: "No, my friends have not changed; maybe those belonging to group activity can notice it better among their fellow students."

Rorschach. We judged the Rorschach protocols through the presence or absence of neurotic signs and worked out a special method to evaluate the variations of each test on a scale of improvement and impairment (Ganzarain and Davanzo, unpublished). The results obtained are summarized in Table 12.6.

TABLE 12.5.

Students Named as Improved by Two Classmates
in the Special Questionnaire

Students	Number of Experimental Classmates Naming Them	Number of Control Classmates Naming Them
XVI	1	1
XXVII	0	2
XXX	1	1
XXIX	1	1
VI	2	0
VIII	2	0
XXXI	2	0
XXVIII*	2	0

*XXVIII belonged to the control group.

TABLE 12.6.

Changes Registered by Rorschach Test

Changes	Experimental Group	Control Group
Unquestionably Improved	4	1*
Relatively Improved	20	14
Doubtful	2	4
Relatively Worsened	8	8
Unquestionably Worsened	1	2
Total of Students	35	29

*This subject was undergoing psychoanalysis.

The number of improved experimental subjects is higher than that in the control group, but the differences are not statistically significant. It is interesting to note that nine out of thirty-five experimental students and ten out of twenty-nine controls worsened. Neither of these differences is significant. This would allow us to think that, according to the Rorschach test, group psychotherapy had no harmful effect upon the students.

Protocols. Neurotic symptoms as well as subsequent improvement of some symptoms in several students appear in the protocols of the group therapy sessions. No protocol was made of the meetings of the control group; therefore, no comparison between both groups could be made from this point of view.

Neurotic symptoms most frequently observed as vivid clinical phenomena were: subjective feeling of anxiety in sixteen subjects; depressive attitude in twelve subjects; expressions of distrust in eleven subjects; withdrawn attitude in eleven subjects; and guilt feelings on account of sex in nine subjects.

Improvements were observed in these protocols by the conductor, the subject himself, by other members of the same therapeutic group, or by another instructor whose opinion was recorded in the weekly meeting of conductors. It follows from all these records of improvements that twenty out of thirty-five experimental students improved some of their observed neurotic symptoms. Some of them improved more than one symptom. Symptoms most frequently improved were: withdrawn attitude (six improvements out of eleven students who presented this symptom); attitude of tension (four out of six cases); headache (four out of five cases); verbalized aggression (four out of six cases).

Among the other frequently observed symptoms the following improvements were registered: depressive attitude (five out of twelve); guilt feelings on account of sex (two out of nine); anxiety (three out of sixteen); distrust (one out of eleven).

Personal Records. The study of the variation in the intensity of the students' neurosis evaluated through these personal records did not reveal significant differences between the two groups. According to the results obtained by each student (at least in two of the following tests: observation of improvements at least by two classmates, Rorschach, and personal records), the number of improved subjects in each group was thirteen of the thirty-five experimental students and three of the twenty-nine control students examined. These differences were statistically significant at the 0.05 level of probability (experimental chi square: 4,89, and theoretical chi square: 3,84). The improvement of ten of these thirteen improved experimental subjects was also recorded in the protocols of group therapy.

It is a remarkable fact that two of the three control subjects considered as improved were undergoing psychoanalysis and the other one successfully married during 1954. The fact of finding these probable explanations in each improved control subject supports the impression that the employed criteria really detect, in some way, behavioral changes.

Discussion

In the present stage of experimental research about group psychotherapy in the psychiatric training of medical students, the working hypotheses were necessarily too wide.

The instruments used to measure the complex results of this experiment are rough. Validity and fidelity of some of the tests employed are rather low, therefore the homogenization and the therapeutic results are only approximate. In the statistical calculations we had to use the 0.05 level of probability, which is the acceptable minimum. Besides, some calculations were made difficult by the low number of subjects.

It could be objected that some of the results obtained were due to gathering students in small groups during the school year rather than to psychotherapy itself. This effect could not be obtained in a larger group such as the control group. To answer this question, we have to consider the fact that all the psychiatric clinical practice was done in small groups of four students. Besides, in future experiments we plan to have a control group divided into small groups in the same way as we divided the experimental one. Sustained contact of each one of these subgroups with the same instructor during the school year might be added as well.

There were also reciprocal influences between the experimental and the control students. At the end of the year some of the students already knew that we were experimenting with group psychotherapy. Therefore some control subjects felt "excluded" from an interesting experience, and some experimental subjects felt "privileged." We did not know in what way they were influenced by this emotional atmosphere. There was no less interest in studying psychiatry among the control students, evidenced by the fact that neither the "didactic" questionnaire nor the marks showed any statistical differences between the groups. There might have been differences between them in the way of undertaking their respective activities, influencing their appreciation of those activities. Following these considerations it might be asked whether Table 12.3 reveals only the greater interest of the "privileged" in their activity or expresses the better didactic quality of it, or both. This question is partially answered by the fact that during 1955 and 1956 all the students had to receive group psychotherapy, since we could not have a control group on account of the low number of students in these years.[2] They judged it very useful—in spite of not feeling themselves "privileged"—making such comments as: "the most practical teaching of psychiatry." These opinions were expressed in the students' forum that usually takes place at the end of each school year.

We could not exclude the covariance factor represented by the participation of some conductors in the experimental group and of others in the control group. Besides, these latter instructors had a brief contact of about a month with their students, while each conductor of group psychotherapy maintained contact with his students throughout the whole school year. We do not know in what way these factors have influenced the results. In a future experiment this hypothetical influence may be excluded by arranging the schedule in such a way as to allow the same instructors to direct both experimental and control groups.

Rorschach tests were interpreted according to a criterion worked out by Ganzarain and Davanzo in order to judge the variations between its first and second administration. This criterion was, of course, worked out following the already known rules of Rorschach's interpretation, but as a whole our criterion represents a new integration of the test data not yet proved.

Only three questions of the "questionnaire about the experiment" were useful (see Tables 12.1, 12.3, 12.5). The use of several questions about transference in future works is suggested.

The protocols of group therapy constituted a valuable

---

[2] During 1954 there were two professors of psychiatry in the University of Chile. A third one was appointed in 1955; therefore, each professor has had since then a smaller number of students.

methodological element. Although we planned to record sessions of the control group, we were not able to do so. For this reason we were unable to compare both types of protocols.

The conductors' weekly meetings contributed considerably to standardize the technique employed, to solve some countertransference problems, and to observe the general development of the experiment.

The didactic results would demonstrate the quality of group psychotherapy as a method for teaching psychiatry. The students judged it very superior to the psychodynamic seminars (Table 12.3).

To be able to quote good examples of transference observed in oneself reveals a deep understanding of this phenomenon. Modlin (1955) has demonstrated that its comprehension is difficult even for the postgraduate student. The activity of the control students did not greatly influence their capacity for observing transference in themselves, whatever the number of times they commented on it. Transference was the phenomenon most frequently commented on in group psychotherapy. It was observed in vivid examples experienced by the students themselves. Therefore we suppose that the difference in the capacity for detecting transference in oneself is due to group psychotherapy. This would constitute an indirect evidence of its usefulness. The good understanding of transference as well as any emotional maturity achieved with the therapeutic improvements constitute important contributions to the learning and improving of the doctor-patient relation.

It was possible to judge with some precision which student improved (in spite of the low number of sessions of group psychotherapy), some neurotic symptoms with the Rorschach test, the protocols of the group sessions, the personal records, and the "special questionnaire" about the improvements observed by classmates. However, the correlation coefficients among these tests were low: between protocols and Rorschach 0,245; between the "special questionnaire" and Rorschach 0,243; and between "special questionnaire" and protocols 0,188. The low correlations between these tests may be due to the fact that each one of them evaluates a different aspect of improvement.

The fact that some experimental subjects became worse might seem very serious. However, several control students did the same. The difference of frequence of impairments between both groups is not statistically significant. On the other hand, some control subjects improved. We have already mentioned the possible explanations for their improvements.

CONCLUSIONS

1. Only one of the eighty-three pertinent questions included in the questionnaires was a useful instrument to judge didactic results: It was the question asking participants to quote an example of transference observed in themselves. The experimental students answered significantly better than controls. This would support hypothesis I (see Table 12.1).

2. The students judged group psychotherapy as being significantly better than psychodynamic seminars. This would also support hypothesis I (see Table 12.3).

3. The Rorschach test and especially the observation of improvements by at least two classmates were useful instruments for evaluating therapeutic results. The "observation of improvements by classmates" registered twelve of the sixteen subjects considered as improved, according to a conventionally adopted criterion (see conclusion 4).

4. Thirteen experimental subjects improved against three controls, according to two tests of the series of three used. The differences are statistically significant. This would support hypothesis II.

5. Nine out of thirty-five experimental students, and ten out of twenty-nine controls became worse, according to the Rorschach test (see Table 12.6). The differences were not statistically significant. This would suggest that group psychotherapy had no harmful effect on the students.

6. All this proves the better didactic quality of group psychotherapy over the method classically employed in teaching dynamic psychiatry, which we have here called "psychodynamic seminars."

SUMMARY

Group psychotherapy has been used to teach dynamic psychiatry. Whitaker and Warkentin used the students themselves as subjects for psychotherapy. Since 1951 we have employed it in this way. In 1954 we wanted to verify two hypotheses: (I) Group psychotherapy is effective in teaching some psychodynamics of the doctor-patient relationship (didactic hypothesis); and (II) it improves some neurotic symptoms of the students (therapeutic hypothesis). For this purpose we divided sixty-nine students into two sections matched for I.Q., neuroticism, social contact, personality features, interest in becoming a psychiatrist, and the data of having received previous psychotherapy. The control group was formed by thirty-four students. They devoted an hour-and-a-half weekly to discuss cases psychodynamically. There were thirty-five experimental students. They were divided into five subgroups, each with seven students, and devoted an hour-and-a-half weekly to group psychotherapy sessions. During the

GANZARAIN—DAVANZO—CIZALETTI

school year they had nineteen of these sessions. All the students received identical instruction in the remaining seven-and-a-half hours assigned weekly to the study of psychiatry. Toward the end of the year we studied hypothesis I with ad hoc questionnaires, and hypothesis II with personal records of each student, observation of improvements at least by two classmates, and readministration of some of the tests, the Rorschach being the most useful.

The results would support our two hypotheses. Statistically significant differences were found: (a) in the understanding of transference; and (b) in the improvement of some neurotic symptoms of the students.

The students expressed the opinion that group psychotherapy was better than psychodynamic seminars in order to teach dynamic psychiatry.

There was no statistically significant difference between the number of students whose neurosis worsened in either group.

13

STUDY OF EFFECTIVENESS OF GROUP PSYCHOTHERAPY IN THE TRAINING OF MEDICAL STUDENTS

RAMON GANZARAIN, M.D., HERNAN DAVANZO, M.D., ORNELLA FLORES, M.S.W., AND ESTER BURSTEIN DROBNY, PH.D., PSYCHIATRIC CLINIC, UNIVERSITY OF CHILE, SANTIAGO, CHILE

INTRODUCTION

Much has been said about improving techniques for teaching psychotherapy to medical students (Ebaugh and Rymer, 1942; Group for the Advancement of Psychiatry [GAP] Report, 1948). Ebaugh and Rymer (1942) observed that "students often exhibit antipathy to psychiatry . . . perhaps [because] they react in a highly personal way"

This chapter was first published in *International Journal of Group Psychotherapy* (1959), 9:475–487, and it is reprinted with permission.

toward its teaching which activates their own anxieties (p. 284–285).

The Group for the Advancement of Psychiatry (1948) emphasized that it is important in teaching psychiatry to medical students "to change the student's inner self and through this change to enable him to do better work with his patients." The need "not only to teach, but to treat certain students" was suggested by Ebaugh and Rymer (1942). Kohl (1951) reported that 25 percent of the students asked spontaneously for psychiatric help, several of them because of serious illnesses. Others (Strecker, Appel, Palmer, and Braceland, 1937) reported that 46.6 percent of them were neurotics. Ganzarain (1955) and Zambrano and his coworkers (1956) have observed the high frequency of psychiatric illnesses among medical students in Chile.[1]

Despite the recognition of the didactic and therapeutic needs of the medical student in the matter of psychiatry, very little has yet been written about how to meet these needs. Some papers on psychiatric education do not give sufficient information about it; others (Fey, 1955; Ganzarain, 1955; chapter 12; Hadden, 1956; Peltz, Steel, Hadden, 1955; Peltz, Steel, and Wright, 1957; Warkentin, 1954; Whitaker, 1954) feel that group psychotherapy could satisfy both of these needs. Some authors form psychotherapeutic groups constituted by the students themselves using the psychodynamic material produced by them with a double purpose: therapeutic and didactic.

We proved (see chapter 12), using a control group of students who attended "psychodynamic seminars" instead of group psychotherapy, that (1) the students judged

[1]This does not mean that they are "sicker" than the general population. We can reasonably assume that the rate of psychiatric illness is high also in the general community.

group psychotherapy as significantly better than psychodynamic seminars; (2) the experimental students (those who received group psychotherapy) answered significantly better than the controls when asked to quote an example of transference feelings they observed in themselves; and (3) thirteen experimental subjects improved in several neurotic symptoms as against three controls. These differences were all statistically significant.

In the discussion in the previous chapter, we pointed out the advisability of asking several questions about transference in future works evaluating group psychotherapy as a method of teaching dynamic psychiatry. We believed that "to be able to quote good examples of transference observed in oneself would reveal a deep understanding of this phenomenon." Therefore, we may expect that the better comprehension of transference obtained through group psychotherapy would manifest itself in a higher ability of the experimental students for answering other questions on the subject.

The purpose of the present chapter is to ascertain whether the results we obtained in 1954, as described in chapter 12, and published in 1958, persisted after two years. We wish, in addition, to find out if the better understanding of transference shown by the experimental subjects in 1954 in *one* question, would manifest itself in 1956 in a higher ability (higher, that is, than that of the control students) to answer a questionnaire with *numerous* questions about transference.

MATERIAL AND METHODS

The material was drawn from the sixty-seven medical students who finished their psychiatric training in 1954 in our clinic. In 1956 their ages varied from twenty-two to thirty-two years. There were twelve women and fifty-five men. We had divided them in 1954 into two groups matched for I.Q., neuroticism social contact, personality features, interest in becoming a psychiatrist, and for having received previous psychotherapy. During 1954 the experimental group, divided into five subgroups, had nineteen group psychotherapy sessions. The control group devoted the same number of hours to discuss cases psychodynamically studied. These cases were discussed regarding the psychotherapy techniques used with them. Reference to the relations existing between the material discussed and the psychological problems of the students was entirely avoided.

In our follow-up study in 1956 we administered to these students a questionnaire consisting of eighteen questions about transference. Sixteen of them had to be answered "true" or "false." We quote some of them: "Transference is unconscious"; "Transference is easily displaced from one person to another"; "It is easy to prove transference to the patient." We tried to have the sense of these questions point mainly to the students' actual experience of transference, rather than to its theoretical side. The two other questions asked the student to quote and explain examples of this phenomenon, observed by him, (1) in patients and (2) in himself. We also repeated a question asking for the student's opinion about group psychotherapy or "psychodynamic seminars." Each student was asked to write his opinion about the activity in which he participated. Finally we tried to find out whether the improvement of some neurotic symptoms observed in certain students by their classmates at the end of 1954 had persisted.

This questionnaire was administered collectively to the majority of the subjects in November 1956. However, some of them had to answer it individually, without any observer. We asked them, in the instructions, to answer it without consulting textbooks, notes, or other persons.

Ten of the students who had answered correctly in 1954 the question asking them to quote an example of transference observed in themselves,[2] in 1956, quoted examples insufficiently explained or left blank the space provided for it. Therefore we had to interview them. There were eight experimental students and two from the control group. We asked the two subjects who had explained their examples only briefly to write them again in more detail: One of them was in a hurry when he answered the first time, and because of his hurry he did it briefly. The other had a very personal example, which she did not wish to write about; but she was willing to explain it verbally. We asked the remaining eight students if they had left the space for this question blank out of ignorance or due to hurry. Two of them had been in a hurry.

In 1954 the observation of improvement of some neurotic symptoms by two or more classmates was the best method for evaluating therapeutic results. Twelve of sixteen students improved according to a battery of tests. The correlation coefficient between this partial criterion and the final one, obtained by the total of tests included, was 0.79. Therefore in 1956 we judged the persistence of improvement mainly through this criterion.

We also wanted to check the hypothetical therapeutic results in another way: the social-psychiatric interview of all the improved students, according to their classmates' opinions, made by a psychiatric social worker. It had the following objectives: (1) to find out about possible individ-

---

[2]The questionnaires including this question were answered anonymously in 1954. We were forced into a calligraphic study of them to identify each student's questionnaire. When this was achieved we were able to make comparisons between each student's answers in 1954 and 1956.

ual psychiatric treatment that would explain, totally or partially, the recorded improvement; (2) to get some information about the possible influence of life circumstances that though being especially favorable might have also contributed to their improvement (marriage, improvement of an unsatisfactory economic situation, and so on); (3) to find out about the evolution of the student's symptoms recorded in 1954, through the Maudsley, Bell, and Rorschach tests, his personal record, and the protocols of group psychotherapy; (4) to find out the influence of the psychiatric teachings and more specifically of group psychotherapy in those improvements, according to the student's opinion; and (5) to have the objective judgment of an experienced observer about the present mental state of the subject.

There were twenty-five students named as improved by two or more of their classmates. Nineteen were interviewed. The remaining six were out of town at this stage of our research (June, July 1957).

Each social-psychiatric interview was evaluated according to the following criterion: We considered the student improved if some neurotic symptom registered in 1954 had disappeared or had markedly diminished. We judged it by means of what the subject said and through his behavior during the interview. The social worker and one of the psychiatrists writing this paper discussed each interview.

RESULTS

Didactic Results

Two of the sixteen questions that had to be answered "true" or "false" were too difficult; in other words, the majority of both groups answered them incorrectly. Eight of the questions were too easy; that is to say, almost all the students answered them correctly. Five of the six remaining ones were answered correctly by more experimental students than those in the control group, but these differences were not statistically significant.

The question, "It is exceptional for the patient to treat the doctor as if he were a kind of omnipotent magician," was correctly answered by thirty-two experimental students and by twenty-two of the control group. This difference is statistically significant at the 0.5 level of probability (experimental chi square: 4,647; theoretical chi square: 3,84).

The answers to the question "quote and explain an example of transference observed in yourself," were qualified as "good," "fair," or "bad" according to the same criterion used in 1954: The repetition of attitudes or emotions of the past in the example quoted was scored 1 point. The explicit or implicit, but sufficiently clear, recognition of having experienced them as something unconsciously determined was also scored 1 point. An answer that got 2, 1, or 0 points was graded as "good," "fair," or "bad," respectively. We then validated this criterion as sufficiently objective (see chapter 12). The frequency distribution in each group in 1954 and 1956 is presented in Table 13.1.

These differences were statistically significant on both occasions. They indicate a systematic influence of group psychotherapy upon the understanding of transference.

The comparison between the numbers of "good," "fair," and "bad" answers in both tests reveals that there has not been any significant variation in the frequency distribution of each type of answer, although there were slight variations. A few more control students gave "good" answers in 1956, and in the experimental group there was a slight diminution of those answers. We also compared the answers of each student on both occasions. We thus confirmed the general impression given by Table 13.1.

TABLE 13.1.

Frequency Distribution of "Good," "Fair," and "Bad" Answers to the Question, "Quote and Explain an Example of Transference Observed in Yourself"

Group	Good		Fair		Bad	
	1954*	1956**	1954	1956	1954	1956
Experimental	23	20	2	5	10	10
Control	8	11	6	2	18	19

*The experimental chi square of this distribution is 8,61 at the 0.2 level with two degrees of freedom, and the theoretical chi square is 5,99.
**The experimental chi square of this distribution is 6,47 at the 0.1 level with one degree of freedom, and the theoretical chi square is 3,84.

The question about quoting an example of transference observed in patients was answered better by the experimental students. However, the differences were not significant.

The answers to the question, "impressions about group psychotherapy . . . or . . . psychodynamic seminars," were graded as "good," "fair," or "bad" (the same criterion was used as in 1954) respectively: (1) when the activity in question was approved without mentioning any defect; (2) when the student listed both positive and negative aspects of his activity; and (3) when, without mentioning any positive quality, the student criticized the defects of his activity. Table

13.2 presents the frequency distribution of each type of answer in 1954 and 1956.

TABLE 13.2.

Frequency Distribution of "Good," "Fair," and "Bad" Opinions about Group Psychotherapy and Psychodynamic Seminars

Activity	Good		Fair		Bad	
	1954	1956	1954	1956	1954	1956
Group psychotherapy	22	31	10	4	3	0
Psychodynamic seminars	1	7	12	12	19	13

The students' judgments were clearly in favor of group psychotherapy in both tests. The differences are significant, although it is not possible to treat them statistically because of the low frequencies (0 and 1) that appear in this table. Opinions about both activities tended to become better in 1956. Several students followed this general pattern of variation.

We quote now some of the opinions about group psychotherapy, expressed in 1956 by some students.

1. "The best part of the course, the one most useful for the student. He learns notions about psychotherapy and deepens his insight into human emotions—his own and others. Among other things it promotes better relations among the students."

2. "It contributed efficiently to demonstrate in practical terms, in ourselves, the psychodynamic features presented theoretically. I believe that in several cases (I have

observed it in myself) it served to clarify unconscious attitudes and to give us a wider and more complete idea about the influence of certain psychic processes in our behavior and also in the behavior of our patients."

3. "Excellent way of observing and studying problems of interpersonal relationships. It was a wonderful opportunity for getting closer to one another, the benefits of which can still be observed. I still consider it a personal experience of great value."

4. "Group psychotherapy constituted the most interesting work during the course. Together with promoting a better understanding of the psychodynamic mechanisms, it has been of great value in achieving a better knowledge of our own personalities and an understanding of people around us."

5. "One of the most interesting experiences of all my career. After more than two years, I would like to participate in it again."

6. "It undoubtedly brings personal benefits. It should be maintained and offered for as long as possible during the training course, so that better results may be obtained by the whole group. All the students should participate, and it should be introduced in the lower years of the course."

7. "It has been very useful, because it made it possible to approach the practical knowledge of several psychological phenomena which, if studied in textbooks or heard in class, are considered too technical or sometimes dry. Besides, it promoted self-knowledge by showing us several times characteristics entirely unsuspected in our own personalities."

8. "I believe it has important therapeutic possibilities and I can justify my opinion mainly through what I experienced in it, realizing how much you can discover of your own inner world. In teaching it seems to me an

equally good method on account of the ease with which psychodynamic phenomena appear and because of the usefulness of having general practitioners go through this experience."

We also graded each student's questionnaire with a global mark or "total score" according to how the eighteen questions about transference were answered. Each of the questions to be answered "true" or "false" got 1 point if correctly answered. The two asking to quote examples of the phenomenon got 2, 1, or 0 points if qualified as "good," "fair," or "bad," respectively, according to the criterion used in 1954 (see chapter 12).

Table 13.3 presents the frequency distribution of the total scores.[3]

The students trained with group psychotherapy answered the questionnaire about transference significantly better than the control group. This is new evidence of how group psychotherapy makes a better learning of transference possible than seminars in psychodynamics.

Therapeutic Results

Eighteen experimental students and seven control students had improved in 1956, according to the observation of improvements by two or more classmates. This difference is statistically significant at the 0.2 level of probability (experimental chi square: 6,13 and theoretical chi square: 3,84).

Ten students—eight experimental and two control—appear as improved with this criterion on both occasions. Curiously enough, ten experimental subjects and five from the control group named in 1956 as students in

---

[3]When we decided to present the results in this manner, we had misplaced one student's questionnaire and could not recover it.

TABLE 13.3.

Frequency Distribution of the Total Scores Obtained by Both Groups in the Questionnaire about Transference

	Frequencies	
Scores	Experimental Group	Control Group
18	2	1
17	1	0
16	1	0
15	6	3
14	7	4
13	5	5
12	4	3
11	3	9
10	3	3
9	0	1
8	1	2
7	1	0
0	0	1
Total:	34	32

Experimental t: 2,02 Theoretical t: 1,96

which improvements have "persisted" were not named as improved in 1954 by two or more classmates. On the other hand, among five experimental students considered as improved in 1954, four were named by only one classmate in 1956, and one was not named by anyone.

The social-psychiatric interview of nineteen to twenty-five students considered as improved by two or more classmates confirmed the classmates' impressions in fifteen cases (two control and thirteen experimental). The remaining four interviewed were not considered as improved. All of them belonged to the control group.

The influence of intercurrent factors in the fifteen students considered as improved by the social worker can be summarized as follows: Four of these subjects judged that their improvement could be attributed to other factors and not to group psychotherapy. Two, one control and one experimental, attributed it to individual psychological treatment, one (control) to the psychiatric knowledge that he had acquired, and one (experimental) thought that his improvement was due to the solution of his economic problems, which made it possible for him to get married.

Of the other eleven subjects, five said that group psychotherapy was the only determinant of their improvement, while six stated that it was the main factor. Two students of the latter group also received brief individual psychotherapy. The improvement of the remaining four subjects was favored by practical circumstances. However, some of these circumstances were a result of the students' own doing because of their group treatment. For example, one of them realized that his engagement to be married was of a neurotic nature and broke it off; another left and became independent from a frustrating home, after realizing that that was what he had unconsciously wanted.

On the basis of the aforementioned findings, we can conclude that group psychotherapy had a preponderant or exclusive influence in the causation of the improvements achieved by eleven subjects.

DISCUSSION

Through the results obtained, it appears that it would have been better if the questionnaire had included more than eighteen questions on transference. In addition, the fact that ten of them were too easy or too difficult shows that they were probably wrongly chosen.

The month in which we administered this questionnaire, November 1956, was not favorable because the students were devoting themselves to preparing for their examinations (end of year, graduation) and also writing their final theses. Because of this, we could not find all the students in their classes and had to deliver the questionnaires to them, asking them to answer them individually. The administration of the questionnaire, therefore, was not homogeneous.

The question asking them to quote an example of transference observed in patients was answered more correctly by the experimental students. However, the differences were not significant. We must point out that twenty subjects (eight experimental and twelve control) answered it by saying: "I have not had the opportunity to observe it." Several of them had a high score on the questionnaire. It is therefore possible that the lack of opportunity for a more personal contact with the patients they have seen as students prevented them from answering this question correctly.

We can only regret that the social-psychiatric interview could not be held with six students. Four who had been interviewed did not impress the social worker as improved. However, improvement was confirmed in fifteen of them. This would again prove that the criterion for judging improvement through the classmates' opinions is reliable, with only a small margin of error.

The fact that fifteen students (ten experimental and five control) considered improved in 1956 by two or more classmates were not so classified in 1954 could be explained in several ways. Almost all of them were named in 1954 by *only one* classmate. It is probable that this numerical difference has affected the results; in others this was clearly due to a mistake, as in the four control cases in which the social-psychiatric interview did not confirm any improvement.

For obvious reasons, we considered that the question, "It is an exception for the patient to treat the doctor as if he were a kind of omnipotent magician," should be answered "false" to be taken as correct. There were ten control students who did not answer correctly. This happened only with three experimental subjects. It is possible to interpret this result as due to the fact that the experimental students experienced in their relation with the conductor of their therapeutic group the dependency needs which caused them to idealize him—in some moment of their group's evolution—and to feel as if he were a kind of omnipotent figure. This may have made them comparatively more sensitive and capable of grasping the inner emotional reality of their patients in relation with the doctors than the control subjects.

The fact that the positive results of group psychotherapy persisted for at least two years after the ending of our 1954 experiment (see Tables 12.1 and 12.2) and proof that collective psychotherapy promotes a better understanding of transference than the parallel method used (see Table 12.3) are the positive findings of the present chapter. Together they show the value of group psychotherapy in the psychiatric training of medical students.[4]

In the future, we may make a new follow-up study

---

[4]We found statistically significant differences in spite of the fact that experimental and control students received information about transference in the remaining seven-and-half weekly hours devoted to the teaching of psychiatry. Actually during this period, all the students had lectures, bibliographic seminars, and clinical practice in which they learned about transference. Therefore, it seems that group psychotherapy actually promotes a better understanding of transference than do other methods of teaching it.

with these same subjects, using a higher number of more carefully prepared questions about transference, to ascertain the effect of their participation in group psychotherapy on their professional practice.

The present study proves again the usefulness of group psychotherapy in teaching dynamic psychiatry. Therefore, it seems advisable to devote some time to group psychotherapy during the study of medicine.

Conclusions

1. The experimental students again answered significantly better than the controls the question asking them to quote an example of transference observed in themselves. This result, observed in 1954, is still present after two years (see Table 13.1).

2. The students again judged group psychotherapy significantly better than seminars in psychodynamics (see Table 13.2), which is a classical method in teaching dynamic psychiatry. Several expressed gratitude to, understanding of, and knowledge acquired through collective psychotherapy.

3. The question, "it is an exception for the patient to treat the doctor as a kind of omnipotent magician," was answered significantly better by the students who received group psychotherapy.

4. The total scores obtained by the experimental students in the questionnaire dealing with transference were significantly better than those obtained by the control subjects. Therefore, the former students got a better comprehension of this important phenomenon (see Table 13.3), which is key to the doctor-patient relation.

5. Eighteen experimental subjects and seven control subjects with neurotic symptoms improved, according to the opinions of two or more classmates. These differences

are again statistically significant. Ten of these students (eight experimental and two control) were also observed as improved in 1954.

6. Nineteen of the twenty-five students thus considered as improved were interviewed by a psychiatric social worker. According to that interview, fifteen of them were improved in some neurotic symptoms. Group psychotherapy seems to have been the main or exclusive determinant of improvement in eleven of them.

7. All this indicates that group psychotherapy is a valuable element as part of the psychiatric training of medical students. Therefore, its extensive use in medical schools appears advisable.

14

HUMAN RELATIONS AND THE TEACHING-LEARNING PROCESS IN MEDICAL SCHOOL

RAMON GANZARAIN, M.D., GUILLERMO GIL, M.D.,
AND KETTY GRASS, M.S.W.

There is considerable interest in improving medical teaching by providing teachers with special training in education. The School of Medicine at the University of Chile has offered its faculty training of this nature. The courses are oriented toward strengthening the human relationship between teacher and student. Their immediate goal is to give the teachers an opportunity to assume the role of an actively learning student (Bennis, Schein, Berlew, and Steele, 1964; Bradford, Gibb, and Benne, 1964; chapter 12). Through this experience, it is hoped that the teachers will be more capable of stimulating their own students to adopt a pattern of active learning.

These courses have been called Laboratories in Human Relations and Medical Teaching.

This chapter was first published in *Journal of Medical Education*, (1966), 41:61–69, and it is reprinted with permission.

DESCRIPTION OF THE EXPERIMENT

The first Laboratory was scheduled for a two-week period during the 1962 winter vacation, to coincide with the slackening of teaching activities. It included six hours of work daily. Registration was limited because there were only two leaders for "training groups" (Bradford, Gibb, and Benne, 1964). The Dean personally extended an invitation to the professors of internal medicine and surgery to send delegates from their departments. It had been decided to give preference to instructors with five or ten years of teaching experience; however, the primary qualification was interest in the program. The twenty-six participants were divided into two groups in such a manner that no two delegates of any one department were in the same group.

Observers trained in evaluating group phenomena through experience with group therapy (Grass, 1960; Gil, 1962; Garcia, Grass, and Ganzarain, 1962) attended the sessions. They recorded nonverbal communication, made a summary of the discussion material, and commented to the leader on the evolution of the groups. These observations were recorded on magnetic tape.

The program included training (T) groups, discussions (D) groups, skill exercises, bipersonal interviews, and lectures (Table 14.1). In choosing lecture and discussion themes and in scheduling related activities, those planning and organizing the program took into account the phases of psychological evolution (Gil, 1962) through which a group passes when it follows an active learning method such as the T-group technique (Bradford, Gibb, and Benne, 1964).

There were thirteen T-group meetings; initially, two were held each day to allow more time for the participants to get acquainted, and later one meeting a day was scheduled.

TABLE 14.1.

Schedule for the Laboratory in Human Relations and Medical Teaching

First Week

	Monday	Tuesday	Wednesday	Thursday	Friday	Saturday
8:30	Introduction	Bipersonal Interviews				
9:00					Training	
9:30		Training	Training	Training	Groups	Training
10:00	Training	Groups	Groups	Groups		Groups
10:30	Groups					
11:00		Coffee Break			Discussion	Coffee Break
11:30		Lectures			Groups	Lectures
12:00						
12:30		Lunch				
1:00	Training	Training	Skill	Discussion	Skill	Discussion
1:30	Groups	Groups	Exercises	Groups	Exercises	Groups

Second Week

	Monday	Tuesday	Wednesday	Thursday	Friday	Saturday
8:30	Bipersonal	Lecture		Bipersonal	Interviews	
9:00	Interviews					
9:30			Training			
10:00	Training	Training	Groups	Skill	Training	Training
10:30	Groups	Groups	Coffee Break	Exercises	Groups	Groups
11:00	Coffee Break		Discussion	Coffee Break		
11:30	Lectures		Groups	Lectures		
12:00			Lunch			Forum
12:30						
1:00	Discussion	Discussion	Skill	Discussion	Discussion	
1:30	Groups	Groups	Exercises	Groups	Groups	

There were eight D-sessions. Groups were composed of the same members as the T-groups. Meetings began on the fourth day of the course after six T-group sessions had been held; they were scheduled at this point with the thought that emotional tensions would have diminished by that time and the members would have achieved a certain degree of familiarity conducive to exchange and discussion of ideas. The first of three skill exercises was held the same day.

The bipersonal interviews were planned to encourage mutual acquaintance and free communication among participants.

There were nine lectures; they constituted the only daily activity in which the delegates participated as a group. The general purpose was to create a common language and culture. After each lecture there was a discussion by all the delegates.

The organizers met daily outside the Laboratory to review the experiences of the day and to redefine, if necessary, partial objectives. Information on the progress of T-group was gathered to illustrate the concepts to be expounded in future lectures.

Training Groups

The T-groups are the essence of the program. They are the Laboratory for learning experiments. The objective of the groups is to provide each participant with a living experience in the process of learning and to demonstrate the influence of human relations on this process.

It was expected that the T-groups would help the participants to mature by encouraging greater integration and wider flexibility. Integration is defined as the synthesizing or resolving of the conflict of certain roles or concepts commonly perceived as essentially irreconcilable (adult versus child).

It is a human tendency for an individual to prefer to see himself in a "superior" or "good" role and to deny, or amputate, the parts of himself that might classify him as "inferior" or "bad." He often attributes negative aspects of his motivation or behavior to others. The integration promoted by T-groups involves an increasing capacity for putting oneself in the "other's" place. Teachers learn to be students; this identification with another, whose role is unfamiliar, requires flexibility.

Maturity makes possible the comprehension of conflicting roles and facilitates communication among the persons involved.

It was hoped that each group would reach group maturity, that is, democratic functioning; this requires that members have a common basis for understanding their tasks and that the contributions of each be integrated into the total group effort. Group performance of this kind is characterized by functional leadership, in which the leader is any person who best satisfies the needs of the group at a given moment, and by the exploration of the possible contributions of each component of the group.

The twenty-six delegates constituted two groups of thirteen members each. Each group had thirteen T-sessions, which lasted approximately one hour and forty-five minutes. Basic problems to be solved by each group included the following: initial confusion, authority, reciprocal acceptance, and separation. These problems are not necessarily successive phases with clearly defined boundaries, but rather problems that predominate at some point in the evolution of the group. Any individual in an active learning situation is generally confronted with these same four problems. The student is disconcerted when the teacher does not give him thorough directions as to what he should do. His fear of criticism by the teacher prevents him from fully assuming the responsibility of learning by himself, and he feels unsure, fearing that he is not capable of learning or of contributing effectively to the learning process of his companions. Finally, he feels uncertainty as to how to apply what he has learned, and this can easily lead him to underrate his own experiences. T-groups provide the opportunity to live the role of the student and to solve these crucial problems of his learning process. Thus the teachers' capacity to perceive the needs of the students improves.

Initial confusion

In both groups the members went through the experience of defining their objectives and methods. To decide the questions of what to do and how to do it, the groups had to explore their needs and set their goals. They were confused, and protested because the leader had not given them norms.

The initial disorientation was resolved when members understood the task that they were to carry out together— each was to contribute his ideas of the best teaching method as dictated by his own experience. At this point participants exhibited a defensive attitude. They seemed to fear that someone might blame them for the possible defects in the teaching in their departments; the someone would of course be the leader, whom they saw as the expert in education.

Authority

Participants expressed a growing concern over the lack of authority. The leader did not direct them. They did not know whether to protest the lack of active direction or to be grateful for the freedom and responsibility granted them.

The fear of the leader inhibited them, as it inhibits the students with their teachers (Ganzarain, 1960a). They were living the roles of students who must actively carry out a learning experience. They protested at not receiving more help, and wanted to force the leader to give it to them. They believed that they were incapable of carrying out their task well, and they feared that their contributions would not be accepted by the others.

When they recognized their own dissatisfaction it became easier for them to understand the needs of the students, and concern for satisfying those needs reappeared.

Reciprocal acceptance

Initially, each participant seemed to be seeking the approval of the rest. Later on they struggled in pairs or groups. They felt that the function of the leader was empty and wondered who would succeed him. Several tried. The rest manifested more or less opposition.

The groups went through an important experience: They overcame the fear of hurting each other, and arrived at reciprocal acceptance. Negative feelings, which form part of the interaction of all human groups, were discussed, and, in the course of this discussion, lost the disturbing nature they had had during the first sessions.

Separation

During the last days of the Laboratory, the delegates were preoccupied about ways to apply in their departments what they had learned, and they freely discussed how they would proceed.

It was emphasized that there is not just one good technique of teaching.

The problem of how to apply new knowledge was seen in the light of experiences in the T-group itself. In spite of the fact that each would be confronted with different circumstances, the delegates could avail themselves of the opportunity to compare their results in future meetings, which would be convened when necessary. For that purpose members elected a secretary. The separation also provoked a tendency to evaluate the Laboratory. Participants were encouraged to express their criticism of the Laboratory before leaving in order to counter such extreme reactions as "it is perfect" or "it is worthless."

A realistic attitude of dissatisfaction is also very important because it leaves a permanent interest in seeking better solutions to teaching problems. That result alone is worth all the efforts made.

Discussion Groups

Discussion groups are a way of utilizing dialogue among a relatively small number of persons to explore different points of view and new angles of a topic, and, in this way, to increase the capacity of the members to think for themselves, stimulating the development of their creative spontaneity and critical judgment.

A bibliography on pedagogy served to inform the members about educational subjects, which were later discussed.

Readings were distributed in such a way that delegates read about each subject only after they had already had a related experience in the Laboratory.

Through participation in these discussions the delegates developed their critical judgment and applied it to their personal teaching experiences; they envisioned relatively novel future projections of the ideas debated and acquired practice in the use of this educational technique.

After participating as students in the discussion series, the delegates criticized themselves for having entered the course seeking the magic wand of education. They now planned their future as teachers, stressing the importance of clearly setting the objectives of each activity and of doing so in collaboration with other members of the teaching team and in accordance with the needs of the students. Delegates criticized the system of evaluating students. They planned the future use of the descriptive mark instead of the numerical one in order to stimulate and orient the student's progress. Delegates decided that the teacher tends to feel unsure of himself when he leads a student discussion group; this makes it difficult for him to understand the student's defensive attitude, and the teacher loses his capacity to awaken in the students the desire to learn. Delegates realized how the anxiety of the teacher generally tends to make him more directive and informative than is desirable in discussion groups. They perceived that an essential factor is the exchange of ideas and experiences by the students, and that, if there is to be an exchange, the students must previously have read the bibliography assigned. But, at the same time, they observed difficulties in initially awakening interest in reading. They went through the process of seeing their own interest grow more or less rapidly, of feeling the stimulating effect of some questions, and of emulating other participants upon seeing them contribute valuable ideas.

In short, they found through experience that using discussion groups for teaching is not easy—that it does not always immediately work well. They perceived some of the difficulties in the application of this teaching technique and experienced possible solutions.

Skill Exercises

One of the goals of the Laboratory was to increase the ability of the delegates to comprehend group dynamics. Four exercises were planned so that they could observe their own way of participating in a group, as well as the methods used by others. Two exercises were role-playing drills and two were for comments upon the preceding discussion groups.

During the first drill, situations in which the members had to make decisions were dramatized. The comments were oriented toward an analysis of the performance of the role—dramatized by a delegate—of a director of a group that reaches decisions. This exercise was scheduled early in the program and served as an escape valve and a way of sounding out the emotions aroused in the T-groups.

In the other exercise, the dynamics of the discussion sessions were observed and commented upon. The first of these exercises was held after two discussion meetings and the second after delegates had had four more of these sessions. This made it possible to observe the evolution of the members' comprehension of this pedagogical technique.

In the last drill, the group dramatized a meeting of the Faculty of Medicine, held for the purpose of choosing persons to fill the roles of dean and secretary and of determining the requirements for professor, and the criteria by which candidates to this post should be evaluated. This was done at the end of the Laboratory so as to serve as a measure of cohesion and group integration and a way of ascertaining how well the delegates were able to apply what they had learned to a specific problem.

Bipersonal Interviews

Bipersonal interviews were informal, daily half-hour meetings during which each delegate had the opportunity of exchanging his impressions in rotation with the rest of his group companions. The purpose of the interviews was to promote communication, to encourage self-examination of attitudes, and to elicit comments upon the current learning experience.

Lectures

Lectures had the general objective of aiding the participants in the conceptual ordering of the experiences that they were having in the Laboratory and providing them with information related to these experiences, especially some fundamental concepts of the psychology of the learning process and of small groups. The lectures also provided an opportunity for communication between the organizers and the delegates. Time was always left at the end of each lecture for an exchange of impressions.

In planning the sequence and nature of the lecture themes, consideration was given to the needs of the delegates during their Laboratory experience, particularly in the training groups. The central problems were (1) orienting delegates to the Laboratory program and (2) integrating and consolidating each group, despite the personal emotions of its members. The initial lectures were designed to solve the first problem by providing participants with information and by outlining immediate and long-term goals. Another type of lecture dealt with the second problem by explaining the dynamics of small groups; the discussions that followed these lectures gave delegates the opportunity to conceptualize and air the individual emotions that threatened the cohesion of the group.

Delegates were also informed about educational investigations in medicine, including a Chilean experiment on a criterion of students' selection, to acquaint them with some work in this field and indirectly to awaken interest in doing pedagogical research, either apart from, or in connection with, possible future activities of the Laboratory.

Preliminary Evaluation

At this time it is only possible to make a qualitative evaluation of the success of the course.

The general impression of the course among the delegates and some faculty authorities has been favorable. The opportunities to talk about teaching problems have increased, as has the preoccupation with improving teaching methods.

In judging the effectiveness (see chapter 12) of the program, the basic question is: Have there been changes in the delegates? It is said that to learn is to change. If the participants in the Laboratory learned, their conduct as instructors should change; that is, modifications of some of their teaching attitudes should occur, particularly at the point of resolving the apparent student versus instructor conflict. Was this the case? The question can be answered affirmatively. Delegates went from "I" to the discovery of "you," developing a capacity for putting themselves in the place of the student. In some delegates the changes were very obvious.

Some declared that their families had noticed changes; they found them to be more sure and "human," more sensitive to the psychological reactions of others.

In several meetings held after the conclusion of the Laboratory, it was apparent by the action of the delegates that they had become agents of change in their departments, in addition to modifying their behavior as teachers.

ments, in addition to modifying their behavior as teachers. There were important differences among the various departments; first, in the teaching level that existed prior to the Laboratory; second, in the influence of the delegates in their departments; and third, in the differing degrees of receptivity to change. Each delegate therefore had to elaborate a strategy of specific change for his own situation. Following are some examples of the particular methods used by delegates.

Five had read a written report of their experience in the Laboratory at general meetings of their respective departments. This was not an effective technique in all cases since the written word does not always transmit to the reader exactly what is intended, and since the individual presenting the report runs the risk of appearing to be a critic and a "possessor of educational truth," an attitude that makes the atmosphere resistant to change. This actually happened in one department, and effective change consequently has become very difficult.

Six departments initiated teachers' meetings. One of the departments invites students to one of its four monthly meetings.

Several delegates have tried to improve their teaching techniques by giving more time to teaching activities, and all have recognized the need to promote closer relations between teacher and student, and to understand the requirements of the latter.

Eight delegates began to utilize discussion as a teaching technique. They verified that the first session may appear to be a failure but that afterwards a high degree of interest is developed. One delegate had used discussion groups before the Laboratory; but during the program, he came to understand that the essential factor is the multipersonal discussion among the students, not the bipersonal dia-

was perceived as essential. Several delegates have changed
their way of making demonstrations with patients, granting almost complete responsibility to their students.

In short, most delegates have increased their sensitivity
to the requirements of the student; hence their behavior
toward him has changed. Almost all have provoked a
greater preoccupation with teaching in their departments,
and some have achieved a notable increase in student
learning. Thus, the first steps toward the objectives of this
course are being achieved.

DISCUSSION

It would be extremely difficult to apply rigid scientific
techniques in an effort to evaluate a program of this
nature because of the multiplicity of variables present.
However, there is every indication that participants arrived at a greater consciousness of the needs of the student
directly as a result of their experience in the T-groups—
the experience of living the role of the student in a
democratic atmosphere. Thus, they were able to verify the
fact that the secret of obtaining vivid interest and a high
degree of student participation in the teaching process lies
in encouraging the student to assume the responsibility for
his own learning. Interest in learning is emotional in
nature, personal to each individual, and powerfully influenced by relations with companions in learning, whether
teachers or fellow students. Delegates learned that fear
and insecurity can extinguish genuine interest and that
therefore is not generally advisable to teach by using
threats or punishment. On the contrary, an atmosphere of
confidence and respect for individual differences, together with a sharing of responsibilities, quickens interest.

The delegates perceived that educational training is
not an apothecary's file of magic formulas, and that

gether with a sharing of responsibilities, quickens interest.

The delegates perceived that educational training is not an apothecary's file of magic formulas, and that different methods of teaching have their advantages and disadvantages. The effectiveness of pedagogical techniques depends greatly on the type of human relationship that is established with the student and on their being adapted to the objectives and requirements of the subject to be taught.

The change of teaching attitudes on the part of some delegates has been seen projected on their students, who are allowed to assume more responsibility for patients.

Some of the delegates have become part of the program's organizing team and have taken part in Laboratories, either by giving lectures, directing discussion groups, or carrying out educational investigations. However, conducting T-groups requires previous experience with groups. Therefore, new T-group leaders will need much more training than that received merely as a delegate to a Laboratory. It is indispensable that leaders have considerable experience in psychoanalytically oriented group psychotherapy, and it is highly recommended that before they assume the responsibility of leading a T-group, they take part in the planning and execution of a program or in the course for interns at the National Training Laboratories in Washington, D.C.

SUMMARY AND CONCLUSIONS

An educational training experience for medical faculty has been described.

Twenty-six teachers participated in the laboratory, which was scheduled six hours a day for fifteen days. The program included mainly training-group sessions, discussion meetings, and lectures.

2. The T-groups achieved their objectives of promoting in the participants a greater integration of the roles of student and teacher, and affording the opportunity to learn about education through a training process that culminates in the modification not only of ideas and didactic techniques, but of teaching attitudes and behavior as well.

3. D-groups fulfilled their objectives of exploring new points of view concerning the educational topics discussed.

4. Several delegates have changed their teaching behavior. It is of particular importance that they have come to understand how learning is considerably stimulated by granting greater participation and responsibility to the student.

5. Six departments initiated teachers' meetings.

Faculty administrators, the participants, and the organizers are unanimously agreed as to the advisability of repeating this course with other teachers.

ADDENDUM

Since July 1962, the authors have carried out seven courses such as that described in this chapter—six in Chile and one in Cali, Colombia.

Dr. Oliverio Tijerina (Tijerina, 1964), a neuropsychiatrist, was a delegate to the July 1963 Laboratory and afterwards carried out two courses in Monterrey, Mexico. Dr. Hernán Davanzo, professor of psychiatry in Ribeirao Preto, Brazil, and also a psychoanalyst and group therapist, collaborated in the planning and execution of the Laboratory held at the University of Chile School of Medicine in July 1964. Later on, he directed a similar laboratory in Belo Horizonte, Brazil, and in Caracas, Venezuela.

Medicine in July 1964. Later on, he directed a similar laboratory in Belo Horizonte, Brazil, and in Caracas, Venezuela.

The Pan American Health Organization (PAHO) has provided two of the authors with scholarships to study medical education. It has also sent foreign delegates to six of the courses that were held subsequent to the one described here. It engaged Dr. Edward M. Bridge of the University of Buffalo to serve as advisor for these courses and, later, to coordinate them from Washington as part of the PAHO program in medical education. Courses in Argentina, Peru, and Costa Rica are pending.

15

A PSYCHOANALYTIC STUDY OF SENSITIVITY TRAINING

RAMON GANZARAIN, M.D.

INTRODUCTION

I hope to clarify some issues, through a psychoanalytic study on the meaning and handling of anxiety, by trying to demonstrate how useful the object relations theory is to systematize concepts on group phenomena.

Among the many questions that sensitivity training nowadays raises are these:

1. Just what is sensitivity training?
2. How does one differentiate it from similar group experiences?
3. Does such training involve any risk of participants having an emotional breakdown?
4. Is sensitivity training "therapy for normals" or an educational experience?

This chapter was first published in *Interpersonal Development* (1974–1975), 5:60–70, and it is reprinted with permission.

Finally, should its primary task be to focus upon the individuals or upon the group?

Sensitivity training groups have been going by many names: encounter, T-groups, human awareness, human relations, human enrichment groups, synanon games, marathon groups, personal growth, sensory awareness, human potential groups, and so on. I prefer the term *training Group* (T-group), as the best known and the one that underlines the educational goals.

Originally sensitivity training was concerned with teaching participants to become better leaders, by broadening their understanding of group behavior and the process of change. The emphasis put on group behavior and change-agentry, not on the individual per se (except as further self-awareness) improved the use of one's own reactions in performing leadership functions.

The T-group method proved to be so flexible that it has adapted itself to many varied purposes, including teaching, therapy, organization development, community development, and social experiments. Such a vast field of activities cannot be clearly covered with just two words: *sensitivity training*. Consequently, there is a compelling need to redefine this term each time it is used. Its ultimate goals, their intermediate objectives, and how to accomplish the necessary tasks to achieve them are elements of each specific redefinition of sensitivity training.

For the practical purpose of following the explosive development of the "sensitivity training movement," a new professional society was organized called the International Association of Applied Social Scientists. They have subdivided the field according to several different goals into (1) personal growth groups; (2) organization development; (3) laboratory education (human relations); and (4) community development. This practical classification brings some clarification into the semantic confusion around sensitivity training.

ANXIETY AND SENSITIVITY TRAINING

If each person in a group is invited to write anonymously his or her three top personal secrets, all tend to come up with a startlingly similar inadequacy: "If others could really see me they would realize what a bluffer and how incompetent I am." The next most common secret is a sense of interpersonal alienation, the feeling that one cannot really care for or love another person. The third most frequent top secret is sexual, and often concerns homosexual inclinations.

These secrets can be "discovered" in any beginning T-group; they are written down by persons not labeled as psychiatric patients. Yet these concerns are qualitatively the same in many persons seeking professional help. They are dramatic expressions of the pervasive distribution of anxiety among human beings.

We can review, with a diagnostic attitude, the contents of these common human secrets. The conviction of basic inadequacy is typically depressive, though it may lead to a schizoid withdrawal—to hide one's self from others and thus prevent "discovery"—and it may also lead to a paranoid stance of assuming in everybody a certain contempt toward one's self. The sense of interpersonal alienation has the quality of despairing isolation within walls of narcissistic overinvolvement with oneself and mistrust of others. The sexual concern may lead to several reactions, quite frequently a paranoid, cautious, reserved one.

As Yalom (1970) wrote:

Loneliness, confusion, and alienation haunt T-groups and therapy groups alike. The great majority of individuals share a common malady, which is deeply embedded in the character of modern Western society. In much of America, the past two decades have

302   RAMON GANZARAIN

witnessed an inexorable decomposition of social institutions, which ordinarily provide for human intimacy;
the extended family living arrangement, the lifelong
marriage, the small, stable work group and home
community are often part of the nostalgic past. Yet the
human need for closeness persists and intimacy-
sponsoring endeavors like the sensitivity training
groups have multiplied at a near astronomical rate in
the past few years [p. 360].

The basic human need for closeness has triggered an
overproduction of myths around sensitivity training.
These myths have grown in the fertile soil of a certain
magic belief in the omnipotence of "group forces." Many
have come to expect *instant* intimacy at the touch of a
button, presumably harnessing those group forces, like a
television set utilizes electronic forces to provide us with
passive gratifications. Hundreds attend T-groups hoping
to get an emotional trip to happiness, to complete self-
realization, or a ticket to Social Utopia.

Furthermore, propaganda and salesmanship have also
contributed to distort the goals of sensitivity training. As a
result, professional ethical standards finally became necessary to regulate and prevent possible excesses.

In addition, magic belief in the omnipotence of group
forces has also stimulated intense fears of sensitivity training. Many declared enemies of T-groups see them as
"communist brainwashing," a series of "ego-shattering"
experiences or humiliating ways of "stripping naked a
poor fellow's psyche." Some criticism, however, correctly
points out the ambiguity of sensitivity training goals, or the
possible inadequate qualifications of a few self-proclaimed
trainers. But it would be unfortunate not to distinguish
between the great number of responsibly conducted sen-

sitivity training programs and a small number associated with certain excesses.

I would like to call attention to the grandiose, fantastic, psychoticlike nature of these magic beliefs in the omnipotence of group forces, whether they are feared as an awful evil or looked for as "manna from heaven."

Both our human anxiety about "How will I be seen by others?" as well as our defensive expectations of "What the group could do to us" have some psychoticlike characteristics.

I shall illustrate some aspects of this general concept with a vignette from my first T-group in Bethel, Maine, which happened to be composed of members from different countries. I represented Chile.

The trainer invited an observer to watch our group several sessions after the group had started. The visitor worked at the Italian embassy in Washington. He sat in the same room with the group, by himself, in a corner against the wall, while the group sat around a big central table. During the three sessions he attended, the visitor remained hidden most of the time behind a newspaper. He commented to me, outside the room, that he had singled me out "as a Latin." He criticized what he felt was the "ridiculous performance of the Americans" in that group. They were, according to him, "showing all their weaknesses" to the "mysteriously silent but contemptuous Oriental member." The Italian visitor said he would like to invite the Japanese psychologist to Rome so that he could get to know the "real, eternal values of Western civilization," completely misrepresented by the Americans in Bethel and "particularly in that stupid group."

I barely need to comment on his paranoidlike grandiosity, his contempt (projected onto the Japanese psychologist), and his suspiciousness. I should, however, remind myself that as a latecomer, outsider, and nonparticipant he

was placed in a very special position. Obviously, he must
have felt very lonely behind his newspaper. The whole
interaction had many typical structural characteristics of
intergroup phenomena, including the stirring up of paranoidlike reactions (which the visited group also had vis-
à-vis the intruder and his supposedly special relation with
the trainer). The visitor treated the group members as if
they were putting down his Western cultural values
through misrepresenting or despising them. This imagi-
nary attack apparently justified his counterattacks against
the Bethel cultural norms.

PSYCHOTIC ANXIETIES

The British School of Psychoanalysis made its basic
contributions to the development of the object relations
theory by studying the psychoticlike anxieties in children
and psychosis.

Let me clarify the meaning of the term *psychoticlike*. It
underlines similarities between functional psychosis and
certain specific anxieties regarding the styles of dealing
with the other persons (or "objects") and the prevailing
defense mechanisms mobilized to fight anxiety.

The British School of Psychoanalysis has described
"psychoticlike" anxieties that are part of the normal development of every human being. This school has underlined
how relatively easy it is to reexperience the psychoticlike
anxieties in everyday life. For instance, Heimann (1955),
in her article on paranoid defenses, reminds us of how
frequently we may have a feeling that everything goes
wrong with us on a certain day.

Object relations theory can be very helpful in conceptualizing group anxieties and defenses in a unified and
enriched perspective.

Bion (1959) wrote that the psychotic anxieties are the

basic core of group psychological life. His classical study of so-called group "basic assumptions" is a widely accepted description of group phenomena, used as defenses against the group's psychotic anxieties.

Bion (1959) compared briefly his own points of view on groups with those of Freud. He summed them up by saying: "Groups would, in Freud's view, approximate to neurotic patterns of behavior, whereas in my view they would approximate to the patterns of psychotic behavior. . . . The more disturbed the group the less it is likely to be understood on the basis of family patterns or neurotic behavior" (p. 181). He emphasized the use of some defensive mechanisms that are common to groups and psychosis, stating that the use of splitting and projective mechanisms through projective identifications are typical both of psychotic defenses and of group behavior.

Bion (1959) observed also that a feeling of depression is frequently present in groups, very much linked to the schizoid position, insofar as the group uses the paranoid-schizoid phenomena as a way of defending itself from experiencing depression, very much as some psychotic patients resort or regress to some paranoid or schizoid type of behavior as a way of defending themselves against the underlying depression.

Let me cite briefly another vignette from my first T-group. When that T-group was approaching its termination, Hemingway committed suicide on his sixty-second birthday. In a social gathering some members overheard our trainer comment that he himself was as old as Hemingway, that he did not feel like Hemingway did before killing himself, as if his current life was merely an empty routine. During one of the last sessions, the group members put the trainer on the spot, inviting him to talk about his personal reactions to Hemingway's suicide. He did tell us how deeply depressed he was when he heard the sad news. He evaluated his own life and compared it with that of Hemingway; he could not avoid thinking how old he was getting himself and how close he was to his own eventual death.

As termination was about to take place, the group began defending itself from experiencing depression about its current "aging" and impending "death." We projected our own depressive feelings on the trainer. In the meantime, the group experienced feelings that "we would never die." We experienced elation about the many assumed successes our group had achieved. The group members recognized many good omens about their future social enterprises. We certainly defended ourselves against the underlying depression!

SEPARATION AND DEFENSES AGAINST DEPRESSION

The participants usually experience the termination of the small T-group and the ending of the laboratory with depressive feelings, in spite of claims asserting its success. Moreover, such feelings can also be observed during the interruption of the activities in the middle of a laboratory, frequently coinciding with a weekend.

Those of us who have had the role of "counselors" (or psychiatric consultants) for the participants in Bethel have learned that the occasional psychotic breakdowns that occur tend to happen around the termination or the midlaboratory separation, and are frequently connected with guilt or other expressions of, or defenses against, depressive anxieties. Such people have feelings of irreparable loss of loved persons, who are perceived as hurt by their hostility.

Sometimes for some individuals the termination leads to idealizing the whole experience, building up a "lost paradise" syndrome, around what was left "back there in

Bethel." Idealization is a psychoticlike way of defending the whole experience from any hostility or aggressive connotations, transforming it into something extraordinarily good.

Maniclike terminations can also be observed, with "happiness" serving clearly as a defense. Such a feeling is connected with a strong belief in basic personal changes, which sometimes may be coupled with utopic grandiose expectations of changing the world. We may all remember in this connection the caricature conveyed in the American film *Bob and Carol, Ted and Alice* in which the problems of "reentry" of a couple, after a group experience, were presented in a humorous way.

Maniclike defenses of a blind belief in the omnipotence of love that would wipe out hate from the surface of the earth have the false quality of a pseudoreparation. But based upon denial, they fail to really solve the deeply rooted depressive anxieties. Sometimes these maniclike terminations fade away and in their place a delayed depressive reaction appears some days or weeks after.

HANDLING PSYCHOTIC ANXIETIES AND DEFENSES

Bethel culture alleviates individual and group psychotic anxieties according to Pages (1971), by offering participants satisfaction of a defensive nature, particularly protective love and the feeling of a mystical union with the other, the group. Love "is acquired cheaply through denying aggression and conflict" (Pages, 1971, p.268).

However, love can also be a torture when mixed with jealousy or envy. Love can as well be painful when facing the loss of the loved person. Love implies being concerned over the beloved's well-being, making such responsibility both lighter and enhanced.

Pages (1971) described how he had "to resist giving the

participants the satisfactions they demanded, particularly because the pressure on their part was so strong. Thus, I found myself playing the role of the psychoanalyst and adhering to the rules of abstinence" (p. 272). Overdemandingness is an expression of oral sadism. The participants may attempt to blackmail the trainer by displaying an escalation of guilt-provoking behavior, with the goal of forcing the trainer to give them more and more. We may remind ourselves that intense oral sadism has been linked by psychoanalysis to the psychogenesis of functional psychosis.

Believing in the omnipotence of the trainer can be understood as a group phenomenon with characteristics of a dependency basic assumption. The trainer is cast in the role of the idealized "good mother" as a way of pretending the fulfillment of dependent wishes. This pretense serves the defensive purpose of alleviating guilt—the depressive anxiety—about fantasied injuries inflicted on the trainer by the symbolic oral-sadistic attacks: The all-powerful trainer is assumed to escape uninjured from these excessive group demands to be able to go on giving incessantly.

The trainer, however, experiences such strong pressure upon him as an attack to force him to step out of his role, which is directly related to the assigned task of interpreting group phenomena. There is the possibility that the trainer may yield to the temptation of gratifying both the group's demands and his or her own narcissism by accepting to play an omnipotent role. However, if she or he sticks to interpreting group phenomena, such interventions will prove fruitful in terms of the learning experiences on group behavior that may become available for thoughtful reflection.

The sensitivity training technique, as frequently practiced in Bethel, tends to avoid exploring group psychotic anxieties, partly because it yields to the demands of the participants and builds what may seem very powerful defenses (Pages, 1971). Those defenses, however, are really brittle and very primitive, such as denial and idealization, with the staff members playing the role of "protective gods," while tolerating psychoticlike splitting and stimulating reactions against destructive devils "outside there."

The sensitivity training technique should really promote group interpretations of the psychoticlike anxieties. This approach reinforces reality judgment and increases the participant's learning about groups.

Sometimes the sensitivity training technique overstresses the individual approach, so much so that personal growth is fostered and studying the group life is entirely forgotten.

To me the distinction between personal growth and therapy seems still quite foggy. Personal growth through sensitivity training tends to promote expectations of fundamental individual changes, which to me appear quite unrealistic. Because, no matter how dramatic these personal changes, they tend to fade away with the passage of time. In my experience, lasting personality change happens slowly.

Sensitivity Training: Education or Therapy?

The NTL Institute for Applied Behavioral Science initiated the T-group and is currently offering programs in which this method is utilized. In the NTL program Announcement (1972) one can read: "In both means and goals, NTL Institute programs are educational and are not designed to cure or alleviate pathological, mental, or emotional conditions" (p. 5). This clarification is important to define for the prospective participants what they can really expect. Many come without ignoring such reality, but unaware of their unconscious motives of getting some professional psychological help.

Whatever their motivations, some participants do change. Such is the case of excessively "task oriented" people who are blind to the feeling or "maintenance" level of group functions. When such people participate in a T-group, some change their style of interacting with people, by learning to pay attention to feelings. Only a few, however, are able to keep for some time their newly acquired way of dealing with emotions. Most need a delayed "working through," or "recharging batteries," to reinforce their basic learning and to be able to keep in operation their changes in attitudes. Some may start psychotherapy later on to consolidate their modified style.

I have used T-groups for training faculty members of medical schools in the basic principles of the teaching-learning process (Ganzarain, 1966). T-groups have worked as an excellent method for studying the influence of emotions in learning.

I am currently in charge of the group dynamics program offered to psychiatric residents at the Menninger School of Psychiatry. Some students are both members of a small group in such a seminar as well as patients in a therapeutic group. These residents distinguished clearly between the learner's role and the role of patient. They helped the seminar to keep to its task of learning about group behavior as it happens, by focusing their attention mainly on group phenomena, while keeping the prevailing focus on individual difficulties or needs for their therapeutic group.

The differences in technique can be generalized by stating that T-groups do not constantly probe causes of motivations and reactions, while therapy groups delve into causes and deal with unconscious motivations. T-groups explore predominantly group phenomena while treatment groups examine mainly individual difficulties (although there are therapeutic "group-centered" interventions). While training groups are formed by "normal" people in the learner's role, therapeutic ones are composed of "patients" seeking help. The T-groups are short-term enterprises, and the therapy ones are generally long term. The T-group leader is frequently described as facilitator or catalyst of what goes on; for some writers the leader's role is closer to being a participant than an authority, although that is debatable. The group therapist sets himself apart in a special role as therapist; in a cohesive group, however, patients will learn and will be encouraged to act as therapists to each other.

From a theoretical point of view, distinguishing educational from therapeutic goals of sensitivity training may be relatively difficult in some areas such as personal growth programs, in which there is some overlapping between both types of goals. Therapy and education both aim at changing behavior. Both share the utilization of personal experiences as the basis for building up the changes desired, which leaves room for some confusion about the goals of personal growth sensitivity training. The ubiquity of human anxiety may make it both necessary and easier for some persons to further their psychological growth through an educational approach rather than looking directly for therapy.

To discuss exhaustively a parallel between education and therapy goes beyond the scope of this chapter. I shall, therefore, refrain from pursuing it. Before dropping the subject, however, I would like to underscore what, in my judgment, is the essential task of the training group: *to learn about the psychoticlike phenomena that unfold in the group.* The trainer should direct his or her efforts to make such learning possible. Keeping the attention focused on such a primary task, the trainer can better resist the strong pressures and overdemandingness of group members.

THE "NOW SHOCK"

We may speak of a "now shock," paraphrasing the title of the book on *Future Shock*.

The *now* contains all the anxious struggles of the individual in his efforts to become himself as well as a member of a group. It implies overcoming the depressive feeling of past failures and the paranoid one of extreme risks in the near future.

The *now* puts to test the human capacity to adapt ourselves to the ever-changing reality of everything flowing (to the "Panta Ree" of the Greeks). The *now* shocks us because it does away with our wish to establish permanent relations and values for guiding our behavior and threatens us with having to keep readapting our actions to constantly renewed expectations about us.

Sensitivity training helps to overcome the now shock, allowing people to stop running away from the *now*, and to realize how much we abuse ourselves by indulging in memory, running toward the past with our familiar, automatized behavior; or rush into desires, plunging into an illusory future which we can only minimally plan. Training methodology relies upon the current, immediate group behavior as the data for learning.

Many psychological theories have focused upon the now. It is a crossroad into which different schools have converged.

Although at first the analysis of the present was a tool or a means for the interpretation of the past in psychoanalysis, many analysts today regard the exploration of childhood events as a means toward understanding the current situation, mainly the most immediate one: the *now* in the interaction between the patient and the analyst.

"Memory is a dwelling on the unimportant to the exclusion of the important," Bion (1970) has written. Similarly, he stated: "Desire is an intrusion into the analyst's state of mind which . . . blinds him to the point at issue: that aspect of psychic reality that is currently presenting the unknown. . . . Memory and desire are 'illuminations' that destroy the value of the analyst's capacity for observation, as a leakage of light into a camera might destroy the value of the film being exposed" (p. 69).

"The growing emphasis on present-orientation in contemporary psychotherapy can be traced," wrote Naranjo (1970), to the impact of two other sources aside from psychoanalysis: encounter groups and the Eastern spiritual disciplines, with Zen in particular having contributed to the shaping of Gestalt therapy into its new form" (p. 52).

The term *encounter* was borrowed from the existential psychological approach, to enhance the rich potentialities of the now. A person's life may substantially change through the impact of meeting someone else. Every moment represents a challenge to fulfill the responsibility of making the right choices: those conducive to achieve authentic self-realization, without yielding to external cultural pressures to betray one's own, dramatically brief, destiny.

"Dwelling in the present is the cornerstone of some forms of meditation," commented Naranjo (1970). He quoted Nyaponika (1962) saying:

Right Mindfulness recovers for man the lost pearl of his freedom, snatching it from the jaws of the dragon Time. Right Mindfulness cuts man loose from the fetters of the past, which he foolishly tries even to reinforce by looking back to it too frequently, with eyes of longing, resentment or regret. Right Mindfulness stops man from chaining himself, through the imaginations of his fears and hopes, to anticipated events of the future. Thus, Right Mindfulness restores to man a freedom that is to be found only in the present [p. 54].

In Buddhism the now is not merely a spiritual exercise but the condition of the wise. . . . In a passage of the Pali Canon, Buddha first utters the prescription:
"Do not hark back to things that passed,
And for the future cherish no fond hopes:
The past was left behind by thee,
The future state has not yet come." [Naranjo, 1970, p. 67].

Sensitivity training has been enriched by all these schools of thought thanks to an intellectual openness to the most varied points of view. However, this gain was obtained at the high price of a conceptual confusion. Behind the semantic chaos there is a theoretical Tower of Babel in the sensitivity training field.

I believe that object (or if you prefer "personal") relations psychoanalytic theory offers a possible "universal language," capable of helping us to overcome the current chaos. Like English in the geographical world, object relations theory is at least partially spoken or understood beyond most ideological frontiers.

16

WORKSHOPS TO SHARPEN GROUP PSYCHOTHERAPISTS' SKILLS

RAMON GANZARAIN, M.D.

The participation in a brief psychotherapeutic group experience is a learning opportunity, open to qualified mental health professionals who wish to sharpen their skills as group psychotherapists. Several institutions run such workshops with diverse ideologies and valuable continuing education credits. They are scheduled over weekends and sometimes located in pleasant tourist resorts. The Kansas Group Psychotherapy Society, together with the Group Psychotherapy Service of the Menninger Foundation, has been offering such continuing education workshops since 1973. Lerner, Horwitz, and Burstein (1978) described the rationale, design, and organization of such workshops. For the last several years two seminars were available in Topeka, Kansas, in the fall and spring, and one was held in Aspen, Colorado, during the summer. Undergoing the experience of being a patient in a group, the workshop's participants increase their empathy for their own clients' situation in their groups. Battegay (1983) added that "colleagues who have passed through an [analysis] make acquaintances with different sides of their personality than those seen in the dyadic psychotherapeutic situation. For example [they] recognize narcissistic disturbances" (p. 209). A model of object relations group psychotherapy is practiced to help the participants understand better some basic concepts such as regression, transference, splitting, projective identification, and technical principles such as abstinence, the timing of interpretations, and so on. "The backbone of the approach is the demonstration of technique within a brief, but intense group psychotherapeutic experience. Learning is furthered by a few didactic groups" (Lerner, Horwitz, and Burstein, 1978, p. 465), where concepts and strategic techniques are discussed.

It is difficult to describe in general the participants in these workshops. However, a few frequent characteristics are the following. (1) Their ambivalence toward the psychoanalytic approach. They bring a curiosity to learn about it, mixed with fears and doubts about its value or effectiveness; they wish to learn from the faculty but at the same time they resent their knowledge and expertise and sometimes relish giving faculty a hard time. (2) The mental health professionals often are so involved in helping their patients that they tend to forget their own personal needs and the tensions generated by their work and develop a sense of loneliness and emotional deprivation because they usually fail to take good care of their own emotional needs. (3) They are also somehow anxious about losing prestige among their colleagues and therefore display an increased sensitivity about confidential issues they can bring up only under protected circumstances. (4) The participants also wish to alternate between learning and having a good time in their extracurricular hours, either visiting the Menninger Foundation campus in Topeka or enjoying the tourist resort's social activities. Some attempt to have a good time, as they would when attending a convention away from home, and enjoy the release from normal work responsibilities. (5) Many come determined to work on specific emotional conflicts or issues in their lives while others tend to have a "wait-and-see" attitude, expecting someone else to take risks while they see how effective the psychotherapy offered can be. But rather than talking in general, this chapter will focus on specific learning situations shared by mental health professionals during these brief group psychotherapeutic experiences. Because of reasons of confidentiality, I have disguised the participants' identities without altering, however, the essence of their emotional learning.

I shall first attempt to describe in general terms the evolution of these workshop groups and later on describe two different experiences which I have labeled (1) existential "angst" and (2) The Tower of Babel. I shall afterwards review briefly the problem of casualties.

Initially these groups deal with the therapist as an authority figure (Bennis and Shepard, 1956). A member may address direct questions to the therapist regarding either some practical information (i.e., where to have dinner) or a statement of a personal emotional need; if not answered satisfactorily, frustration creeps in, leading sometimes to irritation and escalating anger or to a mixture of sadness and hostility. For instance, a participant responded with tears of anger when no one in the group paid attention to his personal request; when the therapist called the group's and his attention to these exchanges, he shared that being isolated and not taken care of was the story of his life. He was the son of alcoholic parents who divorced. He grew up all by himself, being himself the only emotional resource available to him. He also became an alcoholic, while working in the post office. After being helped by Alcoholics Anonymous, he developed an interest in helping people and got his social work degree, specializing later in mental health. He experienced in the group a mixture of frustration, loneliness, sadness, and anger, casting the therapist as uncaring, unavailable, and insensitive. He epitomized some of the feelings frequently expressed during these first group meetings. Participants feel mistrust and turn away from the therapist. Withdrawal and lack of trust do have a schizoparanoidlike flavor. If anger prevails, there may be then a tendency to fight the therapist's authority and to unseat authority, while participants help each other and rely on their collective resources. Often mental health professional adapt themselves to conflicting relations with their self-centered mothers by developing since their childhood a false self, like Roth's (1982) "Type 3" of borderline personality disorder individuals, who have "an exquisite sensitivity to understand someone else's unconscious but a complete intolerance to explore one's own mind" (p.17). Likewise, Miller (1981) described her "prisoners of childhood" syndrome, typical of those who need to please mother by becoming her caretaker. Participants gradually realize they themselves avoid or deny their own personal needs in their deeply ingrained attitude to please by forgetting about themselves and instead taking care of somebody else's needs. Getting acquainted with these internal narcissistic obstacles to gratification may sometimes clear the way to begin exploration of other styles of dealing with their needs (Battegay, 1983).

The relationships with peers prevail during the next stage: Competing with each other, jockeying for power, fearing the peer's attacks alternate with attempts to "come together" and to develop a group cohesiveness, a camaraderie, and efforts to work together.

Soon after, the group will end and depression sets in regarding the loss of these new relationships with therapist and participants, triggering a replay of previous depressive experiences when significant objects were lost.

The above description contains everything but does not say anything specific. Hence, there is a need to add some flesh to this skeleton. The participants' responses to these workshops' time framework deserves some attention. The fact that the whole experience is "so brief" and "will soon be over" is used as a resistance attempting to terminate the experience before it begins. It is therefore important to address this specific resistance to help the participants realize how they are denying themselves the use of the really available time all together with a therapist in their group; pretending that the twenty scheduled hours had already gone is a concrete, defensive distortion of reality. The therapist, on the other hand, should keep in mind that time goes faster in these workshop groups than in the usual ones, so that when an opportunity comes up to explore an issue, one should take it up, since it may never come back again during the limited time available. Naturally, this sense of immediacy should be concordant with the criteria for appropriate "timing" to intervene respecting the participants' defenses. In other words, one does not have to interpret all the deep unconscious meanings of all material that comes up, but the brief duration of the experience reminds us of the need to intervene somehow faster than usual.

Since meaningful psychotherapeutic exchanges happen in the context of detailed interactions, I must present clinical material to convey how the object relations group psychotherapy approach is applied in these workshops to sharpen the group psychotherapists' skills.

EXISTENTIAL ANGST*

During the summer of 1984 the group I treated in Aspen, Colorado, started with statements about the therapists' loneliness because they themselves deny their emotional needs and learn to use a "plastic shield" to hide from people, particularly from those who can read their minds. Although lonely, these mental health professionals wanted to protect themselves from the "x-ray" glances of their colleagues in the group. Some, particularly John, stated their dependency and anger at me for not going out of my way to help them. John said then that he had a disseminated cancer: Metastases of an old malignancy had recently spread. He had decided to participate in the workshop and wished to be understood and supported but not treated with "condescending sympathy." Only a few persons in John's life knew then about his recent complications. Since he planned to go on with his private practice, he did not want referrals to stop coming his way and consequently decided not to let his colleagues know about his probable impending death. He planned to work for as long as he could.

Amy responded by sharing her guilt because of ambivalence vis-à-vis her husband's fatal chronic disease. He had been dying for years, and Amy often caught herself thinking, "Why don't you die soon?!" Afterwards, she felt guilty for hating him. She also depended extremely upon her husband. For instance, she did not drive and he had to take her places, in spite of his restrained mobility. Elizabeth then told about her depression and suicidal plans, stating that she will not fail as mother did on five occasions. She would plan it, not leaving any chance to fail. Her depression deepened after her husband stated frankly

---

* As stated earlier, the participants' identities are disguised.

that he did not love her any more. George defended himself by bringing intellectualized views of the group-mates' problems and also by inviting them to become a "feelie, touchy California-type of group with all of us getting naked into a Jacuzzi." Three other members claimed to be just "babes in the wood," simply beginners who would rather take a back seat and watch the "experts" interact.

There was a poster of General Custer behind the armchair I occupied during this group meeting. It was really ugly, but served a therapeutic purpose when Dora expressed her anger at "General Custer"—while pointing at me—because of my alleged emotional unavailability; soon afterwards Dora tried to please me by sitting close to me. All these exchanges were commented as a "sexist revolution" whereby General Custer—male power—was deposed, while Lucile was promoted to "big mother." All loved the "advent of matriarchy," particularly John who felt up to now deprived in his needs to be nurtured by a good mother. The group briefly relished having found a good mother among them. However, when Lucile felt the burden of responsibility to respond to John's emotional needs, she started feeling insecure; she had doubts about herself as a mother. She had, for instance, a difficult relationship with her daughter who often accused her of being a "smothering mother." Lucile agreed with her daughter. She could really be a smothering mother! Lucile explained that she was a victim of her mother's demand-ingness and was pushed into taking care of mother and forgetting about herself; in the process she had lost her own self. Lucile came across as a "prisoner of childhood," out of Alice Miller's book. She had been a child sacrificed to the narcissistic emotional needs of her mother and trained to fulfill somebody else's emotional needs while losing her own self. Gretel shared, with anxiety and guilt, that she was a sexually abused child, by her nanny, but she stated also her own responsibility: Perhaps she was a "bad girl" who might have initiated the seduction. Gretel grew up during World War II while her father was in the service and she was taught to be a good girl so that he would return from the war; however, Gretel was "really mean," and feared to cause her father's demise as a consequence of her misbehavior. She connected those guilty feelings with her self-reproaches, after her husband's death, while she accused herself of not taking good care of him. The group ended the third session, with Dora and Rose saying they would like to go out with a male groupmate. However, no one responded. Upon returning to the next session, George said that he was "basically an oedipal man" who would like to have a harem and hated the trend the group was taking into becoming a "protoplasmatic, pre-oedipal, let's share everything with everyone" group, so he wanted to openly state his rivalry and competition with the other men in the group, and let everybody know that he had "made a pass" at Lucile, the "group's mother." He was angry at her for rejecting him. She had turned down his invitation to go on a raft trip. Lucile rushed to say she was utterly surprised by George's invitation, that she had had no previous indication of George's intentions.

The next session started with John telling us that he had a wonderful time on a raft trip with Rose—the younger, most attractive female member—George came late and stated that he was late and was planning not to attend the last session, the following day, because he came to Aspen "to have fun and not to go to a mortuary." Rose quickly agreed saying, "Yeah, it's already all over now!" Amy shared her excitement after having been propositioned by a man while having some beers; she had been drinking and for her it was something out of the ordinary to be again propositioned; she said, the "animal side of myself was very pleased."

Hypomanic group defenses were then rampant and had blossomed during the time available for extracurricular activities. Most members were claiming as their primary goal to "have fun"; others were stating that the whole experience was already over. But John reminded the group that the whole experience was yet unfinished; he illustrated his point by reminding Dora, Rose, and George that they had not shared their emotional conflicts with the group. Dora responded by telling us her conflicts in dating: how she had a longstanding relationship with a man who was an alcohol and drug addict, very much like her father, but a passionate lover. Dora was also dating a professional man, who was seriously interested in her, with whom she had an asexual relationship. Dora struggled to terminate with her lover and had temporarily succeeded in doing so, but when her father died she felt lonely and resumed the relationship with her lover. She was confused, not knowing what to do with her life. She knew that she should end with her lover but did not feel attracted to her other suitor, in spite of his serious interest in her. She had consulted an individual psychotherapist and had felt misunderstood by him, not helped at all.

I felt the group was rushing into a premature termination and in a conflict between intense depressive potentials and denial of guilt by running away, rushing to getting excited with fun experiences, thus also avoiding any sadness. I decided then to legitimize the healthy aspects of hypomanic defenses, which allow human beings to modulate the amount of sadness and pain they can take—at a given time. Consequently, I said: "With all the many heavy things you are going through in your lives, it is no wonder that you need time for fun and laughter; but life is not only a time for fun; there is also a time to cry, a time to be sad. It doesn't have to be either/or. We should pay attention to both aspects of life—laughter and sorrow." Gretel remembered then how guilty she felt because of "being mean," and thus making her father's return from war magically impossible.

The final therapeutic meeting was preceded by three important events. All the participants attended a "fishbowl" whereby they watched a public staff meeting conducted. I had shared there a dream dramatizing my anxiety before starting a workshop, and I was criticized by competing staff members, who presented a "better" dream. Gretel and others had witnessed a helicopter rescue of mountain climbers who were found dead; it was a dramatic interaction with death! Finally, John experienced a sudden loss of control of his muscles while playing tennis; he was overtaken with fear but had recovered, thinking this was only an anxious reaction to the group's termination. He was able to finish his tennis game.

My reporting a dream, stimulated the group members to report their dreams. Witnessing mouth-to-mouth resuscitation that failed to reanimate persons who were already dead brought up memories of being at the bedside of dying relatives. John's attempts to go on with his normal life, knowing his health was deteriorating, dramatized the entire group's effort "to keep going."

George reported a dream representing his confusion about where he was. He was searching for "Route 27," preoccupied with some "fag" who appeared interested in him. He associated "27" to the number of persons attending the "fishbowl" where I had reported my dream. He liked me more there and experienced some "homosexual anxiety." Elizabeth reported a wish-fulfillment dream: She saw her beautiful new house, made of fine materials and wonderful in every way. The house represented her as she wanted to appear now, wonderful. Lucile also reported a

dream: While attending a meeting she had lost her characteristic white personal car from a parking place; but
someone in the dream gave her a beautiful new red car.
She associated to having lost her "old self," built to please
mother, wishing to develop another self, whereby she
could be legitimately concerned with her own needs.
Gretel was overtaken by her intense reactions upon seeing
the dead mountain climbers. She had vivid memories of
feeling mean vis-à-vis her dying mother, seriously ill for a
long time, as well as feeling unresponsive vis-à-vis her
sibling's sudden death. Somehow she dramatized the tendency of the group members to feel guilty in dealing with
John's fears about death or with the group's upcoming
death. Amy stated her confusion, like George, not wanting
to make a fool of herself by believing everything would be
rosy and wonderful upon returning home to her chroni-
cally ill husband; it was not clear how she would behave
back home.

Dora dramatized the group's emotional conflicts about
termination with a dream in which she saw an incom-
pletely skinned cat who had difficulties in dying. She had
a gun and was ready to shoot the cat to put an end to his
suffering. It was not clear who had skinned the cat. Dora
associated to her wish to get rid of her depressed lover and
to a vision of her father returning from a psychiatric
hospitalization, but not fully recovered from depression,
seated in an armchair half drunk, naked, and pointing a
gun to his head. Dora was watching him from a distance,
feeling like "coaching" him "to go ahead and shoot" to put
an end to his miserable life.

Paradoxically all these heavily depressed topics did not
prevent the group from sharing Elizabeth's childlike plan
to become like the new house in her dream or Lucile's wish
to have her brand new self, or Amy's temptation to have a
sexual escapade before going back to her sick husband.

There was also admiration and loving care for John's struggles to go on with his life "as usual" in his northwestern state. Everyone struggled to keep their enjoyment with life while aware of being doomed to die, a dramatic metaphor of human beings' essential "existential angst!"

They had dealt with the healthy side of manic defenses and intertwined them with some working through of depressive anxieties, identifying themselves with a lost loved object, experiencing guilt for damaging loved persons, being seductive or abusive, or sometimes like a "smothering" mother, but yet also wanting to help the loved objects (i.e., the skinned cat); trying to do some clumsy yet vigorous reparation efforts to find their peace of mind, caring for others, and also attempting to take better care of themselves.

The participants started "behind a shield," hiding their alleged worthlessness or meanness. Soon they discussed depressive anxieties: suicidal plans, low self-esteem, struggles with lethal disease, guilt over wishes to get rid of an invalid spouse, and so on. Manic defenses were called upon to soothe such pain when a member said then: "Let's have fun!" Later on, a defensive regression made members look for a "good mother" within the group, upon whom to depend for emotional nurturance and support. But some members resisted such regressive trends proclaiming instead their mature, oedipal needs. Narcissistic self-doubts appeared then: "Am I a smothering mother?" or "I can be mean, abusive, seductive, and exploitative with those who need me, and I can use them to gratify my narcissistic/perverse wishes, so can I still really care for my patients?" Thus, the participants discussed an important risk in psychotherapy: An identification with a narcissistic mother can be activated in the treater's mind, during the therapeutic relationship, so that the treater gets the vital emotional gratifications by helping people but in a self-centered way, rather than in a patient-centered approach.

To explore these problems among nonjudgmental peers was a most valuable learning opportunity. The group could repeatedly observe how feelings of isolation and depressive despair triggered the defensive search for fun, sometimes even for questionable excitement. Manic defenses function to temporarily protect from mental pain caused by guilt, shame, dependency, or hostility. Manic defenses can be understood as powerful emergency resources to cope with acute depressive struggles with the human existential "angst." After all, if one is to keep going with life, in spite of death's inevitability, one has to value certain pleasant persons, relationships, or activities that give apparent meaning to our brief existence.

However, the consolation offered by manic defenses is only illusory and transient, since such defenses are based upon denial and omnipotence. Their healthy, helpful effects last only briefly, until denial and omnipotence are dismissed as big lies to one's self. When such a "moment of truth" arrives, only real concern for, and slow but effective reparation of, the damaged loved objects can solve the depressive anxieties, by putting one's self, through identification, in the loved object's painful situation. As Unamuno, the Spanish existentialist philosopher, wrote (1951): "To love is to feel compassion . . . and if pleasure makes bodies one, sorrow brings souls together" (p. 851). Dora's dream about "finishing" her dying pet's suffering dramatized her identification with her damaged objects (her father's and her lover's agony), including, in the here-and-now, John's and the group's current struggles to die with "as little pain as possible." Her dream represented both the nonomnipotent, limited effectiveness of human love and the comforting consolation that compassion-reparation can offer.

THE TOWER OF BABEL

The Ninth International Congress of Group Psychotherapy was held in Zagreb during August 1986. It was preceded by the first International Institute of Group Psychotherapists, and I was one of the treaters. We worked for fourteen hours in the outpatient group psychotherapy rooms of a Zagreb psychiatric outpatient clinic. The group was formed by five men and six women who spoke eight different languages: English, French, Spanish, Italian, Serbo-Croatian, Japanese, Dutch, Danish, and Swedish (the last three were not used during the group meetings). The official language was English, actually "bad" English, as demonstrated by the fact that the only member who came from the United Kingdom was often not understood by the rest of us!

The group was initially planned for ten members but the Tower of Babel started when I decided to accept a latecomer, member number eleven, a talkative, attractive, middle-aged Italian woman who did not speak English.

There was yet another relatively misplaced member, a Japanese woman, young and attractive, who spoke only a little English and had arrived to participate in an experiential group on psychodrama, which was not available as it turned out. She was sent instead to my group. She needed a dictionary and shyly avoided bringing one. However, the group soon allowed, or rather ordered, her to bring her dictionary.

The immediate countertransference response I had was that of visiting the Tower of Babel, with six languages to use, but with Italian prevailing, since the latecomer monopolized the group's time. I decided to stick to my role as a therapist, and to forget the narcissistic temptation to "show off" my knowledge of four languages. The struggle was difficult, since I have often been in Italy, love that country, and speak the language, but I said to myself: "Be a therapist, not a translator!" I expected the group resources would be mobilized. Sure enough, a Swiss member sat beside the Italian woman and translated her back and forth, with the "supervision" of a Dutch member. The group was initially going along with this overidentification with the "lonely," "isolated," foreign latecomer. When her Swiss guardian angel was asked why she had volunteered to be a translator, pushing her own participation aside, she explained she was an adopted child given away by her poor biological parents, so she could easily identify herself with lonely persons. Her Dutch "supervisor" had been excluded from his parents' secrets by their constant use of foreign languages to conceal topics of conversation from their children, which stimulated him to learn several "mysterious" languages, attempting to be "included" in his parents' "intimate secrets." Representatives of different languages sat together: Two French-speaking women offered support to each other; a Dane and a Swede sat together; and the two Yugoslav psychiatrists did likewise. The Italian member went too far in monopolizing; for instance, commenting on some interesting, exotic experiences like doing group psychotherapy in Vietnamese in Ho Chi Min (formerly Saigon) City; but her reports did not engage the group's attention. The Italian member finally alienated her Swiss translator, who started "forgetting" to translate or made blatant mistakes that the Dutchman only occasionally corrected. I interpreted that the translators were tired and betraying her. I quoted, in Italian, "*traduttore-traditore*" or translator-traitor. Our Italian member realized then that she was not always welcome by her groupmates. I invited a female Yugoslavian psychiatrist to put into words her unequivocal nonverbal messages of irritation against the monopolizer. She said that the monopolizer was like her Italian mother, who was also overtalkative. She said she knows fluent Italian but did not want to help because of her irritation, often felt regarding her mother's self-centeredness.

The monopolizer shared then her conflicts between her ideal of self-sufficiency and her need to depend. Her right arm was broken and in a cast for months, until recently; she needed then the learn to ask for help. She claimed that accepting the translation was quite an achievement, a proof of her having learned to accept help. She then started "building bridges" with other members. For instance, she role reversed the situation with the Yugoslavian female, letting her know that although she was an Italian citizen she was born in Yugoslavia, spoke fluent Serbo-Croatian, and was very happy to be "back home." The following session she brought a newspaper with a headline stating in Serbo-Croatian "Freedom To Be Weak!" She succeeded also in bringing out a silent Yugoslavian male group member, when she sang for him a Serbian song of nostalgia for the lost hometown. She associated his situation to her own, being away from home. She told him that she also tended to become distant when feeling "treated as an alien or out of place." They joined their voices singing a Serbian melody. The male Yugoslavian colleague elaborated about what it meant to be brought up in the Serbian culture and adapting himself, later on, to the Serbo-Croatian world.

She also tried to invite the Swedish member to say more about himself, by praising him as a "romantic fellow" who came to Zagreb accompanying his girlfriend. The Swiss lady compared me then to her real, biological father, who was "dark-eyed, cold, and distant," but had a sense of humor, which allowed her to have good times with him, mainly singing together. She compared, by contrast, her adoptive father with the young Swedish blue-eyed member, whom she liked a lot. She made jokes about herself, describing herself as a good Swiss cow "offering milk to the world," thus making fun of her need to mother everyone.

The Dutchman tried to incite the Danish member to speak up about his frustrations. Since in Denmark they follow "Foulkes's group analysis," the Danish colleague was confused because I was not working with Foulkes's matrix. Consequently, he could not understand what was going on in the group. The Dutchman also volunteered to translate from French when the French ladies made some comments, but he was soon provoked by one of them into a quarrel—which they carried on in French reaching a peak of irritation with each other. The other French-speaking lady was actually from Mexico, but kept her Spanish hidden from the rest, and only spoke it with me during breaks. The Dutchman was pleased that his boss—the institute's organizer—had put him in my group. He had often struggled, both as a patient and as a therapist, with the hostile use of hopelessness and helplessness. When the group became depressed, he shared his dramatic struggles with past moments of intense depression he then utilized to express his anger at the world.

The Yugoslavian colleagues expressed jokingly their curiosity and relative mistrust of me. For instance, the female Yugoslavian colleague asked me: "Are you Russian? Are you Gagarin's cousin?" She said she had difficulties putting together my being originally from Chile (a country known to her by President Allende and the Nobel laureate poet Neruda) but living in the United States and practicing at the Menninger Foundation in Topeka. I was a puzzle for her, a riddle. She seemed to epitomize our confused views at the Tower of Babel.

After all, confusion is often experienced as a punishment for curiosity, for the wish to know, to explore something new and different. That was the case in the biblical myth of the Tower of Babel where wanting to reach Heaven, to enjoy the knowledge of "another world," was punished by God with the confusion of tongues and the impossibility to communicate.

From an object relations theory viewpoint, confusional states occur when the efficiency of defensive splitting fails to separate "good" from "bad" objects or internal states and they consequently become indistinguishable from each other. The participants at the Zagreb International Institute were actually wishing to find out, to know about "another world" different from theirs, in terms of theoretical concepts and psychotherapy practices. They were extremely curious about my background and experience and they succeeded in finding out something about me. But some felt they should also be punished with confusion. However, they were actually less confused than they appeared to be. For instance, they clearly learned: (1) how deceiving verbal communications can be (i.e., *"traduttore-traditore,"*) or how words are often used to hide real meanings; (2) nonverbal communications were fruitful, direct, and effective, although often apparently ignored in groups; such was the case with the Yugoslavian lady's bodily movements of irritation against the Italian late-comer or the friendly, joyful smile of the Japanese participant presenting herself as a butterfly of friendship; (3) the magic power of music and songs to communicate meaningfully; and (4) how curiosity stimulates acquiring new knowledge, but may generate intense anxiety, related unconsciously to "primary scene" fantasies.

CASUALTIES

The possibility of casualties among participants haunts the faculty members during these workshops. One cannot directly screen or select the "shaky" ones. However, there are some indirect ways such as advising the participants to consult with their psychotherapists before coming to these group seminars or contacting supervisors. But these indirect screening procedures are not a warranty that there will be no casualty among participants.

In my twenty-five years of experience as therapist and/or director of such events, I can only remember three casualties from among some 750 participants in workshops I taught. The first one happened in Santiago, Chile, when I was training faculty members of the local medical school in human relations T-groups. One of the participants in my group started to develop some thought process disorders. Her groupmates correctly diagnosed that whenever she spoke "a conceptual fog came down on the group," without anybody really understanding what she meant. She was lucky that her stomach also responded to stress: She had a mild gastric hemorrhage. The gastroenterologist advised her to rest in bed, without further stressful participation in the group. Some groupmates went to visit her. She recovered after resting and avoiding further emotional tension.

At Menninger, we had, between 1978 and 1987 two casualties among our workshop participants. A woman left her first workshop frustrated, but registered in the next two. When she came back, she secretly plotted among her groupmates a "palace revolt" against their male group psychotherapist. With her paranoid-political skills, she managed shrewdly to convince her groupmates that they should revolt against his tyranny. No one dared to challenge her secret paranoid plotting or to bring her pathologic behavior out into the open during group meetings. Instead, they went along with her plot to oust the "tyrant." When the "moment of truth" came up, she had secretly left town, leaving her coconspirators to handle the upcoming revolution. A silent, slowly developed subclinical paranoid reaction had taken place, fooling both her group therapist and groupmates—all skilled clinicians!—who went along with her quasi-delusional system, but without bringing it up in the group.

A few years later, in a group I treated, one of the participants had also a paranoid reaction. He was single and lived with his aging mother. His purpose in taking care of her was to prove to her "what real love means," since he did not get enough love from her. He was now "getting back" at her, showing her what really good care meant. However, living with his mother was very difficult and painful, since his mother was senile and had lost her mental faculties. Hence, groupmates advised him to place her in a nursing home. But he responded with utter indignation since he had planned to prove to his mother what "real love" means, he was not ready to send her now to a nursing home. He would have felt defeated! From then on, he felt misunderstood and provoked the group-mates to treat him as a "scapegoat." Hence, he complained of being "abused" and remembered his favorite childhood game: putting himself in a barrel, rolled or thrown down-hill by the neighborhood kids who kicked, hit, or threw stones against it. This game was a caricature of his mas-ochistic style through life! He felt particularly abused by a couple of female participants whom he singled out as the ones allegedly planning to "do him in." Upon the work-shop's final session he still quarreled with these two "bad girls" and with the therapist, complaining all three had abused him. As with his mother, he had devoted his life to proving himself "better than thou." He also illustrated his characteristic pattern reporting that as a psychologist on an inpatient psychiatric unit, he used his evenings and weekends to treat the patients there, as they "really should be treated," extending his personal friendship, offering them what they really wanted, but without any interaction or discussion with nurses, physicians, or social workers on the team. For the patients, he became the "most popular" professional on the team. But the psychiatrist, the administration, and other mental health professionals turned against him. They did not approve of his being "better than them," he said, without realizing his blatant hostility against colleagues.

Percentagewise the probability risk of casualties is quite low. But since careful previous screening of participants is not feasible, the staff members' fear of casualties often haunts the first meetings of these workshops. However, it is reassuring to realize that "casualties" are not "products of the group experience," but chronic, ill-adjusted, severe personality disorders marginally adapted to their lives. Workshop therapists should be aware of (1) the relatively low incidence of casualties and (2) that when a possible breakdown is beginning, it is better "to prevent than to cure." Hence, early interventions, even removing the potential casualty from the group sessions, may be considered. It is not always easy, however, to detect such early developments, since they may happen secretly, beyond the faculty members' awareness.

DISCUSSION

The proposal of a brief psychoanalytic therapeutic experience is a contradiction in terms, insofar as analytic work is predicated upon working through, which requires the passage of time. It is consequently clearer to say that these workshops offer a sample of a psychoanalytic group therapy experience, comparable to a first vaccination shot to be followed by other shots later on. After attending these workshops, several participants may start personal psychotherapy. On the learning side, many analytic concepts are understood from personal experience such as transference, projective identification, splitting, neutrality, or defenses/resistances. Many learn how to work with the unconscious meanings of dreams. These are first-hand personal experience with basic analytic concepts and methods that participants treasure and welcome.

The possible confusion between group relations conferences (or group dynamic seminars) and group psychotherapy deserves a few lines. Both have in common that they take place in a small group, led by an "expert," promoting interchanges among groupmates as a powerful resource to learn. However, their primary tasks distinguish these activities: Learning about the small groups' behavior and dynamics is the primary task of "group relations conferences" or "group dynamic seminars"; these have an *educational goal*. Helping people to understand themselves with their personality difficulties and unsatisfactory interpersonal exchanges, with the purpose of ameliorating difficulties in their mental functioning, is the primary task of group psychotherapy workshops; they had a *therapeutic purpose*.

Matters of confidentiality can also be a source of anxiety. Some ways to reduce tension in this area are not to include coworkers, relatives, or close friends in the same group, so that each participant can benefit from the mixture of anxiety and freedom to be among strangers to talk about him- or herself, without concerns regarding possible reverberations "back home." Offering these workshops outside the participants' usual working area puts them in a more relaxed frame of mind, like going on vacation, thus inviting participants to explore usually avoided personal issues.

The content of didactic meetings can also be briefly discussed. Usually workshops cosponsored by the Kansas Group Psychotherapy Society focus on object relations theory concepts used in the analytic group psychotherapy modality practiced at our Group Psychotherapy Service.

As a rule, the didactic meetings are not as significant as the therapeutic sessions. The participants have some curiosity to raise questions and problems to learn more, combined with a relatively low motivation. We often use, as a supplement in these teaching sessions, edited videotapes carefully selected, which provide an opportunity to see some faculty members actually doing therapy with another group, and to observe some typical group situations, resembling those experienced by the workshop groups. The parallel between events observed in the tapes and those happening during the workshop enhances their learning.

The participants are asked to fill out evaluation forms at the end of these workshops. They consistently value what they have learned. Often they send other staff members of their psychiatric institutions to attend the next workshops. Hence, we have been able to keep them going for fifteen years, initially four a year, currently three. The volume has fluctuated, following the state of the country's economy, from a maximum of sixty participants in Aspen in 1978, to a minimum of twenty. In May 1987, we had thirty-five registrations and had to turn down five other applicants. Some participants repeat the experience, sometimes more than once. After some time, some colleagues contact the faculty to ask for supervision or a consultation regarding clinical problems. Some invite faculty members to present our experiences to their state group psychotherapy societies. During February, at the 1986 AGPA Annual Conference held in Washington, DC, eighty persons registered for a one-day didactic special institute, followed by two days of experiential participation in a psychotherapy group treated by a member of our faculty. All of the above speaks for itself, that the participants value what they learn during these workshops.

AFTERWORD

There are many different theories explaining and guiding the practice of psychotherapy. In spite of their conceptual differences, all claim similar percentages of improved cases, as their clinical outcome. What all these theories have in common is their "shared focus on clinical interactions" as Wallerstein (1988) wrote regarding the "many psychoanalyses" (p. 19). What initially distinguished one theory from the next was a particular ideological focus highlighting some aspects of the complex, multifactorial pathogenesis of functional mental illnesses, or particular mechanisms of psychotherapeutic change. Later on, each psychotherapeutic modality gradually developed exclusive "territorial claims" and "trade-mark" labels. For instance, some talk about "group analytic," "interactional," or "psychodynamic" psychotherapies, to name a few. This book now attempts to coin another label: "Object Relations Group Psychotherapy."

I propose this approach because it makes specific contributions that are conceptually unique and clinically useful. I described here my group experiences over thirty-five years; some support my belief better than others. I should here add a few lines about my own ideological evolution during this period, to underline what object relations theory adds to my understanding of groups and psychotherapy. When we used group psychotherapy for the psychiatric training of medical students (see chapters 12 and 13), we were not yet sufficiently acquainted with Bion's work with groups. We were instead influenced by Foulkes's 1948 book about the practice of group psychotherapy. I later became better informed about Bion's incipient theoretical formulations, and realized that only Bion—following Melanie Klein's observations and concepts—concerned himself with the psychotic parts of the personality and the early anxieties reactivated in groups, remobilizing primitive defense mechanisms. I think that learning about groups or working psychotherapeutically with them should include dealing with those anxieties, with such defenses and with the psychotic style of thinking characteristic of groups.

All of our theories of psychotherapy are, however, only approximations to the truth about how the human mind works. As Wallerstein (1988) wrote: "When we look beyond [the clinical interactions] to the realm of the "past unconscious" or "general theory" we posit our metaphors or various explanatory symbolisms" (p. 19). He ellaborates here on Wurmser's (1977) viewpoint which he quotes as follows: "Metaphors, understood as symbols, are the language of science we possess, unless we resort to mathematical symbols" (p. 483). When I stated that object relations theory is "my dream" (see chapter 1), I meant that it constitutes both my ideal goal and my very tentative attempt to formulate a few metaphors to symbolize and generalize my observations.

Theories are also relative regarding their relationship to actual observation. While observation as opposed to theory is the basis of science, it is also important to acknowledge how theories guide our observations, often limiting them and occasionally distorting them by making us look with tinted glasses at the observable facts.

Theories are simply conglomerates of hypotheses,

which are both useful and disposable. Object relations theory is useful as a coherent group of ideas that provides systematic explanations of some mental and group phenomena; but it is only a clinical theory that has guided my thinking and practice of group psychotherapy. Object relations theory can also be "disposed of." When a better, clearer theory arises explaining more mental phenomena, or developing universal, quasi-mathematical symbols to understand the human mind, I shall wake up from "my dream." Meanwhile, I am enjoying it, as I love my old, comfortable shoes, ready to change them if I find a better pair! However, like all great adventures, theory making is more of a promise than an actual achievement; hence the questions and the search should go on forever.

REFERENCES

Abse, W. D. (1974), *Clinical Notes on Group Analytic Psychotherapy.* Charlottesville: University Press of Virginia.

Ajar, E. (1979), *King Solomon's Anxiety (L'Angoisse de Roi Solomon).* Paris: Mercure de France.

Alonso, A. (1984), T-groups: An essential model in the training of group therapists. *Groups*, 8(2):45–50.

American Psychiatric Association (1980), *Diagnostic and Statistical Manual of Mental Disorders* (DSM-III), 3rd ed. Washington, DC: American Psychiatric Press.

Anthony, J. (1971), Comparison between individual and group psychotherapy. In: *Comprehensive Group Psychotherapy*, ed. H. I. Kaplan & B. J. Sadock. Baltimore: Williams & Wilkins, pp. 104–117.

Anzieu, D. (1966), Psychoanalytic study of real groups. *Les Temps Modernes*, 242:56–73.

Austrup, C., & Noreik, K. (1966), *Functional Psychoses: Diagnostic and Prognostic Models.* Springfield, IL: Charles C Thomas.

Bacal, H. (1985), Object relations in the group from the perspective of self-psychology. *Internat. J. Group Psychother.*, 35:483–501.

Bales, M. (1950), *Interaction Process Analysis.* Cambridge, MA: Addison-Wesley.

Balint, M. (1949), Changing therapeutic aims and techniques in psychoanalysis. In: *Primary Love and Psychoanalytic Technique.* London: Hogarth Press, 1952.

Bar-Levav, R. (1977), The treatment of preverbal hunger and rage in a group. *Internat. J. Group Psychother.*, 27:457–469.

Barsky, A. J., & Klerman, G. L. (1983), Overview: Hypochondriasis, bodily complaints and somatic styles. *Amer. J. Psychiat.*, 140(3):273–283.

Battegay, R. (1983), The value of analytic self-experience groups in the training of psychotherapists. *Internat. J. Group Psychother.*, 33(2):199–213.

Bennis, W., Schein, E., Berlew, D., & Steele, eds. (1964), *Interpersonal Dynamics. Essays and Readings on Human Interaction.* Homewood, IL: Dorsey.

————Shepard, H. (1956), A theory of group developments. *Hum. Rel.*, 9(4):415–437.

Bergler, L. E. (1949), *The Basic Neurosis, Oral Regression and Psychic Masochism.* New York: Grune & Stratton.

Berman, L. (1953), Group psychotherapeutic technique for training in clinical psychology. *Amer. J. Orthopsychiat.*, 23:322.

Berne, E. (1966), *Principles of Group Treatment.* New York: Oxford University Press.

Bion, W. R. (1948–1951), Experiences in groups I–VII. *Hum. Rel.*, 1–4.

————(1952), Group dynamics: A review. *Internat. J. Psycho-Anal.*, 33:235–247.

————(1959), Experiences in groups. In: *Group Dynamics: A Review.* London: Tavistock, pp. 141–191.

————(1961), *Experiences in Groups.* London: Tavistock.

————(1962), A theory of thinking. *Internat. J. Psycho- Anal.*, 40:306.

————(1964), *Attention and Interpretation.* New York: Basic Books.

————(1967), *Second Thoughts.* London: Heinemann.

————(1970), *Attention and Interpretation*, 2nd ed. New York: Basic Books.

Blay Neto, B. (1986), The invisible group. *Internat. J. Group Psychother.*, 36:297–303.

Bleger, J. (1967), *Symbiosis and Ambiguity (Simbiosis y Ambiguedad).* Buenos Aires: Paidos.

Bloch, G. R., & Bloch, N. H. (1976), Analytic group psychotherapy of post-traumatic psychoses. *Internat. J. Group Psychother.*, 26(1):49–57.

Boatman, B., Borkan, E. L., & Schetky, D. H. (1981), Treatment of child victims of incest. *Amer. J. Fam. Ther.*, 9:43–51.

Borriello, J. F. (1973), Patients with acting out character disorders. *Amer. J. Psychother.*, 27(1):4–14.

————(1979), Group psychotherapy with acting out patients: Specific problems and techniques. *Amer. J. Psychother.*, 33(4):521–530.

Bowers, W., Gauron, E., & Mines, R. (1984), Training of group psychotherapists—An evaluation procedure. *Small Group Behav.*, 15(1):125–137.

Bradford, L., Gibb, J., & Benne, K. (1964), *T-Group Theory and Laboratory Method.* New York: John Wiley.

Brodsky, B. (1967), Working through: Its widening scope and some aspects of its metapsychology. *Psychoanal. Quart.*, 36:485–497.

Corwin, D. (1983), Family treatment of father-daughter incest. In: *Therapeutic Intervention in Father-Daughter Incest.* American Psychiatric Audio Review: Symposium of the 1982 American Psychiatric

Association Annual Meeting. Washington, DC: American Psychiatric Press.

Durkin, H. (1964), *The Group in Depth*. New York: International Universities Press.

Dworak-Peck (1987), Future of mental health delivery systems. *InfoMedix*, T-122-1.

Ebaugh, F. G., & Rymer, C. A. (1942), *Psychiatry in Medical Education*. New York: Commonwealth Fund.

Ebersole, G., Leiderman, P., & Yalom, I. (1969), Training the nonprofessional group therapist. *J. Nerv. & Ment. Dis.*, 149:385.

Eisold, K. (1985), Bion's contributions to group analysis. *Amer. J. Psychoanal.*, 45(4):327–340.

Ekstein, R. (1965), Working through and termination in analysis. *J. Amer. Psychoanal. Assn.*, 13:57–78.

Epstein, L. (1979), Countertransference with borderline patients. In: *Countertransference*. New York: Jason Aronson, pp. 375–405.

Ezriel, H. (1950), A psychoanalytic approach to group treatment. *Brit. J. Med. Psychol.*, 23:59–74.

———(1952), Notes on psychoanalytic group psychotherapy: II—Interpretation and research. *Psychiatry*, 15:119–126.

Fairbairn, W. R. D. (1952), *Psychoanalytic Studies of the Personality*. London: Tavistock.

———(1954), *An Object-Relations Theory of the Personality*. New York: Basic Books.

Fey, W. (1955), Two psychiatries: Problems in teaching them. *J. Med. Ed.*, 30:97.

Finell, J. S. (1985), Narcissistic problems in analysts. *Internat. J. Psycho-Anal.*, 66:433–445.

Foulkes, S. H. (1948), *Introduction to Group-Analytic Psychotherapy*. London: Heinemann.

———(1964), *Therapeutic Group Analysis*. New York: International Universities Press.

———(1975), *Group Analytic Psychotherapy: Method and Principles*. London: Gordon & Breach.

———Anthony, E. J. (1957), *Group Psychotherapy: The Psychoanalytic Approach*. Harmondsworth, UK: Penguin.

Fowler, C., Burns, S., & Roehl, J. E. (1983), Counseling the incest offender. *Internat. J. Fam. Ther.*, 5:92–97.

Frank, J. D., Margolin, J., Nash, H., Stone, A., Varon, E., & Ascher, E. (1952), Two behavior patterns in therapeutic groups and their apparent motivation. *Hum. Rel.*, 5:289–317.

Freud, A. (1968), Acting out. *Internat. J. Psycho-Anal.*, 49:165–170.

Freud, S. (1905), Three Essays on the Theory of Sexuality. *Standard Edition*, 7:125–245. London: Hogarth Press, 1953.

———(1912), To Sandor Ferenczi, March 18, 1912. In: *The Life and*

Work of Sigmund Freud, Vol. 2: *Years of Maturity: 1901–1919*, ed. E. Jones. New York: Basic Books, 1955, pp. 453–454.

———(1914a), On narcissism: An introduction. *Standard Edition*, 14:73–102. London: Hogarth Press, 1957.

———(1914b), Remembering, repeating, and working through. *Standard Edition*, 12:147–156. London: Hogarth Press, 1958.

———(1921), *Group Psychology and the Analysis of the Ego*. London: Hogarth Press, 1948.

———(1931), Female sexuality. *Standard Edition*, 21:225–243. London: Hogarth Press, 1957.

Fried, E. (1961), Techniques of psychotherapy going beyond insight. *Internat. J. Group Psychother.*, 11:297–304.

Fuentes, C. (1986), *The Old Gringo*. New York: Harper & Row.

Ganzarain, R. (1951), Primeras impresiones sobre psicoterapia de grupo después de un año de experiencia. *Rev. de Psiquiatría y Disciplinas Conexas*, 16:56.

———(1955), La psicoterapia de grupo en la formación psiquiátrica del médico general. *J. Clín. Viña del Mar.*, 9:3.

———(1960a), El autoritarismo en la universidad y su influencia en el aprendizaje de la psicoterapía. Paper presented at the Second Latin American Congress of Group Psychotherapy, Santiago, Chile.

———(1960b), Research in group psychotherapy (Die Forschungarbeit in der Gruppentherapie). *Psyche*, 14:524–537.

———(1966), Human relations and the teaching-learning process in medical school. *J. Med. Ed.*, 4:61–69.

———(1972), Object relations psychoanalytic theory. A contribution to a symposium at the AGPA 29th Annual Conference, New York.

———(1974), A psychoanalytic study of sensitivity training. *Interpers. Devel.*, 5:60–70.

———Buchele, B. (1988), *Fugitives of Incest*. Madison, CT: International Universities Press.

———Davanzo, H. (unpublished), Un método para evaluar la mejoría y la evolución espontánea de la neurosis mediante el test de Rorschach.

Garcia, A., Grass, K., & Ganzarain, R. (1962), *Sobre la Relación Conductor-Observador en Grupos Terapeuticos*. Argentina: University of Chile.

Garland, C. (1982), Taking the non-problem seriously. *Group Anal.*, 15:4–14.

Gelinas, D. J. (1983), The persisting negative effects of incest. *Psychiatry*, 46:213–232.

Gibbard, G. S., & Hartman, J. (1973), The significance of Utopian fantasies in small groups. *Internat. J. Group Psychother.*, 23:125–147.

Gil, G. (1962), Evolucion de los grupos terapeuticos. Paper presented at the Third Latin American Congress of Group Psychotherapy, Rio de Janeiro, Brazil.

Glatzer, H. T. (1969), Working through in analytic group psychotherapy. *Internat. J. Group Psychother.*, 29:292–306.

Goulding, R. (1972), New directions in transactional analysis: Creating an environment for redecision and change. In: *Progress in Group and Family Therapy*, ed. C. J. Sager & H. S. Kaplan. New York: Brunner/Mazel, pp. 105–134.

Grass, K. (1960), Algunos problemas emocionales en la relacion conductor-observador en un grupo terapeutico. Paper presented at the Second Latin American Congress of Group Psychotherapy, Santiago, Chile.

Greenacre, P. (1972), Crowds and crisis, psychoanalytic considerations. *The Psychoanalytic Study of the Child*, 27:136–154. New York: Quadrangle.

Greenberg, J., & Mitchell, S. (1983), *Object Relations in Psychoanalytic Theory*. Cambridge, MA: Harvard University Press.

Greenson, R. R. (1965), The problems of working through. In: *Drives, Affects, Behavior*, Vol. 2, ed. M. Schur. New York: International Universities Press, pp. 277–314.

Grinberg, L. (1968), On acting-out and its role in the psychoanalytic process. *Internat. J. Psycho-Anal.*, 49:171–178.

———Sor, D., & Tabak de Bianchedi, E. (1975), *Introduction to the Work of Bion*. Perthshire, UK: Clunie.

Grotjahn, M. (1972), Learning from dropout patients. *Internat. J. Group Psychother.*, 22:287–305.

Grotstein, J. S. (1983), The dual tract theorem: Dual consciousness and its importance for the understanding of metaphor, complementarity and paradox. Paper presented at the Topeka Psychoanalytic Society, March.

Group for the Advancement of Psychiatry (1948), Report on medical education, No. 3.

Guntrip, H. (1967), Discussion of H. Segal's paper "Melanie Klein's Technique." *Psychoanal. Forum*, 2:212–227.

———(1971), *Psychoanalytic Theory, Therapy, and the Self*. London: Hogarth Press.

Gustafson, J. P., & Cooper, L. (1979), Collaboration in small groups: Theory and technique for the study of small group processes. *Hum. Rel.*, 31:155–171.

Hadden, S. (1947), The utilization of a therapy group in teaching psychotherapy. *Amer. J. Psychiat.*, 103:644.

———(1956), Training. In: *The Fields of Group Psychotherapy*, ed. S. R. Slavson. New York: International Universities Press.

Hansen, E. B. (1968), Hypochondriacal paranoia (Die hypochondrische Paranoia). *Acta Psychiat. Scand. Suppl.*, 203:33–37.

Hartmann, H. (1965), *Essays on Ego Psychology: Selected Problems in Psychoanalytic Theory.* New York: International Universities Press.

Hearst, L. (1981), The emergence of the mother in the group. *Group Anal.*, 14:25–32.

Heimann, P. (1952), Certain functions of introjection and projection in early infancy. In: *Developments in Psychoanalysis*, ed. M. Klein. London: Hogarth Press.

———(1955), A combination of defense mechanisms in paranoid states. In: *New Directions in Psychoanalysis*, ed. M. Klein, P. Heimann, & K. Money-Kyrle. London: Tavistock.

Herman, J., & Schatzow, E. (1983), In: *Therapeutic Intervention in Father-Daughter Incest.* American Psychiatric Audio Review: Symposium of the 1982 American Psychiatric Association Annual Meeting. Washington, DC: American Psychiatric Press.

Horwitz, L. (1983), Projective identification in dyads and groups. *Internat. J. Group Psychother.*, 33(3):259–279.

Jacobson, E. (1971), Depersonalization. In: *Depression.* New York: International Universities Press.

Jung, C. G. (1946), Psychology of transference. In: *The Collected Works of C. G. Jung,* Vol. 16. London: Routledge & Kegan Paul, 1959, pp. 163–321.

Kellner, R. (1985), Functional somatic symptoms and hypochondriasis: A survey of empirical studies. *Arch. Gen. Psychiat.*, 42:821–833.

———Abbott, P., Pathak, D., Winslow, W., & Umland, B. (1983), Hypochondriacal beliefs and attitudes in family practice and psychiatric patients. *Internat. J. Psychiat. in Med.*, 13:127–139.

Kernberg, O. F. (1968), The treatment of patients with borderline personality organization. *Internat. J. Psycho-Anal.*, 49:600–619.

———(1974), Further contributions to the treatment of narcissistic personalities. *Internat. J. Psycho-Anal.*, 55:215–240.

Klein, M. (1952), Notes on some schizoid mechanisms. In: *Developments in Psychoanalysis.* London: Hogarth Press, chapter 9.

———(1957), *Envy and Gratitude.* New York: Basic Books.

———(1961), *Narrative of a Child Analysis.* New York: Basic Books.

Kohl, R. N. (1951), The psychiatrist as an adviser and therapist for medical students. *Amer. J. Psychiat.*, 108:198.

Kohut, H. (1968), The psychoanalytic treatment of narcissistic personality disorders. *The Psychoanalytic Study of the Child*, 23:86–113. New York: International Universities Press.

———(1971), *The Analysis of the Self.* New York: International Universities Press.

———(1977), *The Restoration of the Self.* New York: International Universities Press.

————(1979), The two analyses of Mr. Z. *Internat. J. Psycho-Anal.*, 60:3–27.

Ladee, G. A. (1966), *Hypochondriacal Syndromes*. New York: American Elsevier.

Langs, R. (1974), *Therapeutic Interaction*, Vol. 2. New York: Jason Aronson.

Laplanche, J., & Pontalis, J. B. (1973), *The Language of Psychoanalysis*. New York: W. W. Norton.

Lerner, H., Horwitz, L., & Burstein, E. (1978), Teaching psychoanalytic group psychotherapy: A combined experiential-didactic workshop. *Internat. J. Group Psychother.*, 28:453–466.

Levy, S. (1984), *Principles of Interpretation*. New York: Jason Aronson.

Lewin, K. (1952), *Field Theory in Social Science*. London: Tavistock.

Main, T. F. (1957), The ailment. *Brit. J. Med. Psychol.*, 30:129–145.

Malan, D., Balfour, F. H. G., Hood, V. G., & Shooter, A. (1976), Group psychotherapy: A long-term follow-up study. *Arch. Gen. Psychiat.*, 33:1303–1315.

Mally, M. A., & Ogston, W. D. (1964), Treatment of the "untreatables." *Internat. J. Group Psychother.*, 14:369–374.

Marmor, J. (1972), Sexual acting-out in psychotherapy. *Amer. J. Psychoanal.*, 32(1):3–8.

Masson, J. (1982), *The Assault on Truth: Freud's Suppression of the Seduction Theory*. New York: Farrar, Straus, & Giroux.

Meissner, W. (1982), Psychotherapy of the paranoid patient. In: *Technical Factors in the Treatment of the Severely Disturbed Patient*, ed. P. L. Giovacchini & L. B. Boyer. New York: Jason Aronson, pp. 349–384.

Meltzer, D. (1978), *The Kleinian Development*. Perthshire, UK: Clunie.

Menninger, K. A. (1963), *The Vital Balance*. New York: Viking.

Miller, A. (1981), *Prisoners of Childhood*. New York: Basic Books.

Miller, J. (1971), Living systems: The group. *Behav. Sci.*, 16:302–398.

————(1975), General systems theory. In: *Comprehensive Textbook of Psychiatry*, Vol. 2, ed. W. Freeman, H. I. Kaplan, & B. J. Sadock. New York: Williams & Wilkins, pp. 77–78.

Modlin, H. C. (1955), An evaluation of the learning process in a psychiatric residency program. *Bull. Menn. Clin.*, 19:139.

Money-Kyrle, K. (1950), Varieties of group formation. In: *Psychoanalysis and the Social Sciences*, ed. G. Roheim. New York: International Universities Press.

Moreno, J. L. (1951), *Sociometry, Experimental Method and the Science of Society*. Beacon, NY: Beacon House.

Naranjo, C. (1970), Present-centeredness: Technique, prescription and ideal. In: *Fagan and Shepherd Gestalt Therapy Now*. Palo Alto, CA: Science of Behavior Books.

Nemiah, J. C. (1985), Hypochondriasis (hypochondriacal neurosis). In:

Comprehensive Textbook of Psychiatry, 4th ed., ed. W. Freeman, H. I. Kaplan, & B. J. Sadock. Baltimore: Williams & Wilkins, pp. 937–942.

Neruda, P. (1966), *The Heights of Macchu Picchu*, trans. N. Tarn. New York: Farrar, Straus, & Giroux.

Novey, S. (1962), The principles of working through in psychoanalysis. *J. Amer. Psychoanal. Assn.*, 10:658–676.

NTL Institute for Applied Behavioral Science (1972), Program Announcement.

Nyaponika, T. (1962), *The Heart of Buddhist Meditation*. London: Rider.

Ogden, T. H. (1979), On projective identification. *Internat. J. Psycho-Anal.*, 60:357–373.

Ormont, L. R. (1969), Acting in and the therapeutic contract in group psychoanalysis. *Internat. J. Group Psychother.*, 19(4):420–432.

O'Shaughnessy, E. (1983), Words and working through. *Internat. J. Psycho-Anal.*, 64:281–289.

Pages, M. (1971), Bethel culture, 1969. Impressions of an immigrant. *J. Appl. Behav. Sci.*, 7:267.

Parloff, M. (1968), Analytic group psychotherapy. In: *Modern Psychoanalysis*, ed. J. Marmor. New York: Basic Books, pp. 492–531.

Peltz, W., Steel, E., Hadden, S., Schwab, M., & Nichols, F. (1955), A group method of teaching psychiatry to medical students. *Internat. J. Group Psychother.*, 5:270.

——— ———Wright, S. (1957), Group experiences with medical students as a method of teaching psychiatry. *Amer. J. Orthopsychiat.*, 27:145.

Perry, S., Frances, A., & Clarkin, J. (1985), *A DSM-III Casebook of Differential Therapeutics: A Clinical Guide to Treatment Selection*. New York: Brunner/Mazel, pp. 227–233.

Pines, M., ed. (1985), *Bion and Group Psychotherapy*. London: Routledge & Kegan Paul.

Pinney, E., Wells, S., & Fisher, B. (1978), Group psychotherapy training in psychiatry residency programs—A national survey. *Amer. J. Psychiat.*, 135:1505–1509.

Poggi, R., & Ganzarain, R. (1983), Countertransference hate. *Bull. Menn. Clin.*, 47:15–35.

Prochaska, I., & Norcross, G. (1983), Contemporary psychotherapists: A national survey of characteristics, practices, orientations, and attitudes. *Psychother.: Theory, Res., & Prac.*, 20:161–173.

Racker, H. (1960), *Studies about Psychoanalytic Technique (Estudios Sobre Tecnica Psicoanalitica)*. Buenos Aires: Paidos.

Redl, F. (1963), Psychoanalysis and group psychotherapy: A developmental point of view. *Amer. J. Orthopsychiat.*, 33:135–147.

Retterstol, N. (1968), Paranoid psychoses with hypochondriac delusions as the main delusion: A personal follow-up investigation. *Acta Psychiat. Scand.*, 44:334–353.

Rey, J. L. (1961), Complaint and envy (Queja y envidia). *Rev. Uruguaya de Psicoanal.*, 4:55– 85.

Richards, A. D. (1981), Self theory, conflict theory, and the problem of hypochondriasis. *The Psychoanalytic Study of the Child*, 36:319–337. New Haven, CT: Yale University Press.

Rioch, M. (1970), The work of W. Bion on groups. *Psychiatry*, 33:55–66.

Rosenfeld, H. (1979), Transference psychoses in the borderline patient. In: *Advances in Psychotherapy of the Borderline Patient*, ed. J. LeBoit & A. Capponi. New York: Jason Aronson, pp. 485–510.

Roth, B. (1982), Six types of borderline and narcissistic patients: An initial typology. *Internat. J. Group Psychother.*, 32(1):9–27.

Rush, S. (1982), Discussion. *Internat. J. Group Psychother.*, 32:49–56.

Rutan, J. S., & Stone, W. N. (1984), *Psychodynamic Group Psychotherapy*. Lexington, MA: Collamore/D. C. Heath.

Sandler, J., & Sandler, A. M. (1984), The past unconscious, the present unconscious and the interpretation of transference. *Psychoanal. Inq.*, 4:367–399.

Scheidlinger, S. (1964), Identification, the sense of belonging and of identity in small groups. *Internat. J. Group Psychother.*, 14:291–306.

———(1974), On the concept of the mother-group. *Internat. J. Group Psychother.*, 24:417–428.

———(1982), *Focus on Group Psychotherapy: Clinical Essays*. New York: International Universities Press.

Schermer, V. L. (1985), Beyond Bion: The basic assumption states revisited. In: *Bion and Group Psychotherapy*, ed. M. Pines. London: Routledge & Kegan Paul, pp. 139–150.

Schindler, W. (1981), Commentary on Hearst's (1981) paper. *Group Anal.*, 14:132–133.

Searles, H. F. (1973), Concerning therapeutic symbiosis. (Transactions of the Topeka Psychoanalytic Society.) *Bull. Menn. Clin.*, 37(3):295–300.

Segal, H. (1964), *Introduction to the work of Melanie Klein*. London: Hogarth Press.

———(1967), Melanie Klein's technique. *Psychoanal. Forum*, 2:198–211.

Semrad, E., & Arsenian, J. (1951), The use of group processes in group dynamics. *Amer. J. Psychiat.*, 108:358.

Sifneos, P. E. (1972), *Short-Term Psychotherapy and Emotional Crisis*. Cambridge, MA: Harvard University Press.

Skynner, R. (1976), *One Flesh: Separate Persons*. London: Constable.

Slater, P. (1966), *Microcosm*. New York: John Wiley.

Slavson, S. R. (1950), *Analytic Group Psychotherapy with Children, Adolescents, and Adults*. New York: Columbia University Press.

————(1964), *A Textbook in Analytic Group Psychotherapy*. New York: International Universities Press.

Spanjaard, J. (1959), Transference neurosis and psychoanalytic group psychotherapy. *Internat. J. Group Psychother.*, 9:31–42.

Stenback, A., & Rimon, R. (1964), Hypochondria and paranoia. *Acta Psychiat. Scand.*, 40:379–385.

Stone, W., & Gustafson, J. (1982), Technique in group psychotherapy of narcissistic and borderline patients. *Internat. J. Group Psychother.*, 32:29–47.

Strecker, E. A., Appel, E. E., Palmer, H. D., & Braceland, F. J. (1937), Psychiatric studies in medical education. Manifestations of emotional immaturity in senior medical students. *Amer. J. Psychiat.*, 93:1197.

Sullivan, H. S. (1953), *The Interpersonal Theory of Psychiatry*. New York: W. W. Norton.

Sutherland, J. D. (1952), Notes on psychoanalytic group therapy. II-Therapy and training. *Psychiatry*, 15:111.

————(1985), Bion revisited: Group dynamics and group psychotherapy. In: *Bion and Group Psychotherapy*, ed. M. Pines. London: Routledge & Kegan Paul, pp. 47–86.

Tijerina, O. (1964), Un laboratorio de relaciones humanas. El segundo curso de pedagogia medica. *Rev. Med. de Chile*, 92:227–231.

Trist, E. (1985), Working with Bion in the 1940s: The group decade. In: *Bion and Group Psychotherapy*, ed. M. Pines. London: Routledge & Kegan Paul, pp. 1–46.

Unamuno, M. (1951), On the tragic sentiment of life (Del sentimiento tragico de la vida). In: *Essays (Ensayos)*. Madrid: Aguilar, p. 851.

von Bertalanffy, L. (1966), General systems theory and psychiatry. In: *American Handbook of Psychiatry*, ed. S. Arieti. New York: Basic Books, pp. 705–717.

————(1968), *General Systems Theory, Foundations, Development, Applications*. New York: Braziller.

Votos, S. A., & Glenn, J. (1953), Group techniques in overcoming medical students' resistance to learning psychiatry. *Internat. J. Group Psychother.*, 3:293.

Wallerstein, R. (1988), One psychoanalysis or many? *Internat. J. Psycho-Anal.*, 69:5–21.

Warkentin, J. (1954), An experience in teaching group psychotherapy. Paper presented at the APA Division Symposium.

Whitaker, C. A. (1954), An experiment in the use of a limited objective in psychiatric teaching. Unpublished manuscript.

Whitaker, D., & Liebermann, M. A. (1964), *Psychotherapy through the Group Process*. New York: Atherton.

Whiteley, J. S., & Gordon, J. (1979), *Group Approaches in Psychiatry*. London: Routledge & Kegan Paul.

Winnicott, D. W. (1965), *The Maturational Processes and the Facilitating Environment*. New York: International Universities Press.

Wurmser, L. (1977), A defense of the use of metaphor in analytic theory formulation. *Psychoanal. Quart.*, 46:466–498.

Yalom, I. (1970). *The Theory and Practice of Group Psychotherapy*. New York: Basic Books.

——(1975), *The Theory and Practice of Group Psychotherapy*. New York: International Universities Press.

——(1985), *Inpatient Group Psychotherapy*. New York: Basic Books.

Zambrano, V., Oyarzún, F., Viel, B., & Keller, M. (1956), Relaciones entre nivel intelectual, grado de neuroticismo, biotipo y estado económico-social con el rendimiento en los estudios en primer año de medicina de 1954. Unpublished doctoral dissertation, University of Chile.

Name Index

355

SUBJECT INDEX